Reflections of a POLITICAL ECONOMIST

Reflections of a POLITICAL ECONOMIST

Selected Articles on Government Policies and Political Processes

WILLIAM A. NISKANEN

CATO INSTITUTE
WASHINGTON, D.C.

Library of Congress Cataloging-in-Publication Data

Niskanen, William A., 1933–
Reflections of a political economist : selected articles on government policies and political processes / William A. Niskanen.
p. cm.
Includes bibliographical references and index.
ISBN 978-1-933995-20-5 (alk. paper)
1. United States—Economic policy—2001– 2. United States—Economic conditions—2001– I. Title.

HC106.83.N57 2008
330.973--dc22 2008029684

Cover design by Jon Meyers.

Printed in the United States of America.

CATO INSTITUTE
1000 Massachusetts Ave., N.W.
Washington, D.C. 20001
www.cato.org

Contents

Part II: Public Choice

Part III: Book Reviews

Introduction: On Maturing as a Political Economist

This book is a selection from the articles, reviews, and speeches that I have written beginning in 1997. One prior article, on "Oil, War, and the Economy" (here titled "Oil Is Not Worth a War") was presented at a Cato Institute conference eight days before the start of the Gulf War in 1991 and is included because of its relevance to the substantial continued U.S. military presence in the Middle East. The other selections are reproduced in chronological order and reflect what I thought about these topics at the time. In some cases I have added a prescript or a postscript to put the article in context, but I have not revised or updated the selections even though my views and the data on some of these topics may have changed somewhat over time.

I have been privileged to serve as the chairman of the Cato Institute since April 1985, following four years as a member and acting chairman of the Council of Economic Advisers under President Reagan. My Cato position involves a variety of responsibilities and is the longest that I have served in any position. And I am now 75 years old. So the selection of papers in this book probably represents the focus, diversity, and quality of anything I might write in the future.

The past 10 years have been a very productive period, both for Cato and for me. Cato has developed into one of the nation's most effective policy institutes and has maintained a consistent commitment to the principles of individual liberty, free markets, limited government, and peace—principles that have led us to be increasingly critical of the policies of the Bush administration and congressional Republicans. The sad prospect is that these same principles will probably lead us to be increasingly critical of the coming Democratic administration and congressional majority. Cato's major new activity has been to broaden the reach of our message to the world. In addition to our long-standing Spanish-language website, for example, Cato now has websites in Arabic, Russian, Chinese, Portuguese, Kurdish, Persian, and French—making it possible to bring both the classical and modern literature of liberty to a broader audience.

In addition to the articles from which those in this book are selected, I also wrote or edited several books during this period:

- *Autocratic, Democratic, and Optimal Government*, published in 2004, develops and applies models of the fiscal and economic effects of the major alternative forms of government and of variations of the characteristics of democratic government. Chapter 16 of this book summarizes my early analysis of this topic.

  For two years, I studied the lessons for public policy from the collapse of Enron and several other large corporations early in this decade. This led to the following two edited books:
- *Corporate Aftershock: The Public Policy Lessons from the Collapse of Enron and Other Major Corporations*, published in 2003, was co-edited with Christopher Culp.
- *After Enron: Lessons for Public Policy*, published in 2005, for which I was both a contributor and the editor. Chapter 12 of this book is an effective summary of these lessons.

Much of my time during the past two years has been reading and discussion in preparation to write a book on restoring a constitutional federalism in the structure of American government. For the moment, I have suspended this effort, primarily because of my increasing pessimism about this prospect. Someday, hopefully in a more optimistic mood, I expect to return to this task.

Other professional activities during this period include serving on the editorial boards of the *Cato Journal*, *Regulation*, and *Public Choice* and serving as president of the Public Choice Society. My professional honors include receiving the Aaron B. Wildavsky Award for Lifetime Scholarly Achievement in the Field of Public Budgeting and Finance in 2001, a University of Chicago Alumni Association Lifetime Professional Achievement Citation in 2005, and an honorary doctorate from the University of Economics in Prague in 2008.

As always, I am grateful to my Cato colleagues for being friendly critics and to the many Cato sponsors for their trust and support. I am especially grateful to my research assistant Jason Kuznicki for helping me organize this book and to my administrative assistant Allison Griffin for helping me keep peace with my computer.

Part I

Policy Analysis

1. Oil Is Not Worth a War

Oil, jobs, and the American way of life, according to the administration, are only part of what is at stake in the Middle East. My primary task is to analyze the economic effects of alternative outcomes of the Persian Gulf confrontation. That should permit all of us to focus better on the more relevant, but necessarily more nebulous, interests at stake.

The first important lesson is that the Iraqi invasion of Kuwait did not, by itself, cause the recent spike in the price of oil. The invasion, however deplorable, neither reduced the world supply of oil nor increased the world demand for oil. The recent spike in the price of oil was a consequence of the U.S. response to the Iraqi invasion, specifically the effects of the U.S.-organized embargo on oil exports from Iraq and Kuwait and the temporary increase in inventories in anticipation of a possible war. The embargo, which reduced the world supply of oil by nearly 4 million barrels a day, should have been expected to increase the price of oil to about $36 a barrel in the short run and about $21 a barrel in the long run, both relative to the price of about $18 a barrel before the Iraqi invasion. The peak price of about $41 a barrel was clearly due to the combination of the embargo and temporary inventory building in anticipation of a possible war. The unusual spread between the spot and the future prices of oil has been consistent with this perspective.

The second lesson is that the economic effects of a reduced oil supply from any region depend on a nation's net exports or imports of oil but not on the source of the imports. Specifically, the cost to the United States of an increase in oil prices is a consequence of oil imports being nearly half of U.S. consumption, even though we

This article was presented at a Cato conference on January 8, 1991, eight days before the Gulf War and was first published in *America Entangled: The Persian Gulf Crisis and its Consequences*, ed. Ted Galen Carpenter (Washington: Cato Institute, 1991). My thanks to the Cato Institute for its permission to republish this article.

import relatively little from the Gulf nations. As a rule of thumb, an increase in the annual average price of oil of $10 a barrel now increases the costs to U.S. consumers by about 1 percent of the gross national product and reduces real GNP by about one-half of 1 percent. Similarly, for other nations, the effect of an oil price increase on consumers is proportional to consumption, and the effect on real GNP is proportional to net exports or imports. The U.S.-organized embargo of oil exports from Iraq and Kuwait has increased the costs to consumers around the world, increased the returns to producers of oil and other sources of energy in all nations, sharply reduced the real GNP of Iraq and Kuwait, somewhat reduced the real GNP of the United States and the other oil-importing nations, and increased the real GNP of the oil-exporting nations—most substantially the gulf nations we are now defending—by about twice the net cost to the United States.

The third lesson is that an unchallenged threat of an Iraqi invasion of Saudi Arabia would probably have reduced the near-term price of oil. Such a threat would have reduced the security of Saudi property rights in oil, relative to Saudi-owned assets in other nations, and would probably have increased Saudi oil production and exports. The Iraqis may or may not have planned a subsequent invasion of Saudi Arabia, but their invasion of Kuwait clearly increased the credibility of that threat. The irony of the U.S. response to the Iraqi invasion is that it foreclosed the short-term economic benefits from the increased credibility of an invasion of Saudi Arabia.

The fourth lesson, based on the calculations by David Henderson, is that Iraqi control of all the oil production in the Gulf, except that of Iran, would probably have only a small effect on the price of oil. As of July 1990, Iraq and Kuwait produced about 7 percent of the world oil supply (outside the communist countries). Iraqi control, either by occupation or intimidation, of the oil production of Saudi Arabia and the several Gulf emirates would increase their share of current production to nearly 20 percent. The U.S. Department of Justice approves mergers of that magnitude every year. The price of oil that would maximize net revenues to Iraq, given that limited degree of monopoly power, is probably around $25 a barrel—higher than the price in July but lower than the current spot price. Such estimates are necessarily subject to some error, but there is no basis for an estimate that Iraq could maintain an oil price higher than $30 a barrel.

In summary, if we consider only the economics of oil, the costs of the U.S. response to the Iraqi invasion are higher than any potential benefits from deterring any further Iraqi aggression. Oil is clearly not worth a war.

Let's now turn to the economic effects of war. In the short run, wars have been good for the American economy. One might hope that this is not why the business community has been extraordinarily quiet about the gulf confrontation. My own estimate is that real U.S. GNP increased about 1.4 times the increase in real defense spending during the Korean and Vietnam wars. The major offsetting condition in a Gulf war would be the probable increase in the price of oil caused by damage to oil loading and transportation facilities. Some representative calculations indicate the relative magnitudes of those two effects. An intense short war that increased U.S. defense spending this year by $50 billion would increase U.S. GNP by around $70 billion. A war that increased average annual oil prices by $10 a barrel (much higher for a brief period) would reduce U.S. GNP by nearly $30 billion. The net effect of the two conditions would be an increase in GNP of about $40 billion. You can make your own estimate from other war scenarios that involve different combinations of the two conditions, but there does not appear to be a plausible scenario that would have adverse short-term net economic effects on the United States. Such effects do not justify a war, but they are not an argument against a war that is important on other grounds.

The long-term economic effects of a war, however, are clearly adverse. That is why the financial markets, which pull forward or capitalize expected future effects, are so spooked by the prospect of war. Wars generally increase taxes, regulation, inflation, and the economic powers of the government. Although total government spending does not appear to be subject to any "ratchet effect" of the spending for war, many of the emergency powers authorized during a war tend to stay in place. For example, Richard Nixon's authority to impose price and wage controls in 1971 was based on emergency powers authorized in 1917. Those of us who are especially concerned about the long-term growth of the government have a special reason to be cautious about wars. In the current case, the major midterm cost of a Gulf war would be the continued delay of any peace dividend from our victory in the Cold War.

So far, my comments are rather standard economics, and those economists who disagree with me are probably wrong. My colleagues, however, are likely to overlook two economic dimensions of the Gulf confrontation. Iraqi control of most of the Gulf oil would not much increase the monopoly price of oil, but it would substantially increase Iraq's power to raise the price of oil if it chose to reduce production below the rate that maximizes its net revenues. An Iraqi government with important objectives other than maximizing wealth would thus have a larger potential to harm the oil-importing nations. A second dimension that my colleagues may overlook is that we are not indifferent to the distribution of wealth in the Middle East. If another emirate, for example, had invaded Kuwait, few Americans would have noticed and fewer cared. The record of the Iraqi government, however, makes us concerned about how it might use additional wealth; that would be the case even if the United States consumed none of the resource Iraq controlled or if we were a net exporter of that resource.

In summary, the important economic dimensions of the Gulf confrontation are not its economic effects on us but on the capability of an aggressive nation to pursue policies that threaten its neighbors. President Bush has acknowledged that the Gulf confrontation "is not about oil. It's about naked aggression." That is at least a relevant rationale. The important issue is whether that rationale is sufficient to merit a war.

On that issue, my views may differ from those of many of my economic colleagues. The United States has not responded and cannot respond to every episode of "naked aggression," so some other criteria must be brought to bear to identify those aggressions to which we should respond. In this case, however, the characteristics of both the aggressor and its victim do not meet the traditional criteria for a U.S. military response. True, Iraq is an aggressive nation and its leader is a vicious tyrant, but that was also the case when the U.S. government supported Iraq with naval forces in 1987 and loans in 1988, and it does not distinguish Iraq from some of our strange new allies. More important, Iraq did not harm the United States, is not a threat to us, does not have the potential to be a significant threat, and is not an agent of a larger nation, specifically the Soviet Union or China, that has been a threat. Kuwait and Saudi Arabia are feudal monarchies, more than 6,000 miles distant, with which the United States has no security agreement or significant cultural ties. The timing of the Gulf confrontation is also bad.

Our foreign policy attention should be focused on the dramatic developments in Eastern Europe and the Soviet Union, rather than on a sideshow in the Middle East. In summary, the Gulf confrontation does not meet the traditional criteria of responding to a direct attack on or a threat to the United States or of stopping the spread of communism, fulfilling our security agreements, defending democracy, or securing our backyard. President Bush is correct to define his foreign policy vision as "a new world order," but one wonders what it has to do with the shared concerns of the American people.

For the United States, a war against Iraq this winter would be the wrong war in the wrong place at the wrong time. Our government would make a tragic mistake in initiating that war.

Postscript

This warning, of course, was not sufficient to deter President George H. W. Bush from initiating the Gulf War, and the issues addressed by this article did not go away. Somewhat to my surprise, President George W. Bush never used an oil security rationale for the Iraq War, although this was broadly believed to be his primary objective. In Alan Greenspan's autobiography, for example, Greenspan states that

> I am saddened that it is politically inconvenient to acknowledge what everyone knows: the Iraq war is largely about oil. . . . Until industrial economies disengage themselves from, as President George W. Bush put, "our addiction to oil," the stability of the industrial economies and hence the global economy will remain at risk.

Greenspan may be correct about the internal rationale for the Iraq War, but it makes no more sense than the several public rationales that were offered by the administration.

2. R&D and Economic Growth: Cautionary Thoughts

> American history clearly demonstrates the importance of American leadership in science and technology to the future of our Nation. Investments in science and technology drive economic growth, generate new knowledge, create new jobs, build new industries, ensure sustained national security, and improve our quality of life.
>
> President Bill Clinton, Budget Supplement, FY1997

I wonder to which American history President Clinton was referring. The United States had become the richest nation in the world long before there was significant "American leadership in science and technology." Most federal programs to promote science and technology, except in defense and agriculture, were initiated after World War II. In the subsequent years, U.S. economic growth has been among the lowest of the major nations. The historical and cross-national record reveals a strong relation between real expenditures for research and development (R&D) and the level of national output—but little relation with the rate of economic growth. This record is more consistent with a hypothesis that R&D is an income-elastic consumption good, something that rich people and rich nations do, rather than an investment that will increase future economic growth.

Maybe something has changed in recent years. Clinton's proposed budget for fiscal year 1997 goes on to state:

This article was presented at an American Enterprise Institute conference on February 6, 1997, and was first published in *Science for the 21st Century: The Bush Report Revisited*, ed. Claude E. Barfield (Washington: American Enterprise Institute, 1997). My thanks to the American Enterprise Institute for its permission to republish this article.

> The post–Cold War era is one of intense global economic competition. Our country also faces new national security challenges, including threats from environmental degradation, emerging infectious diseases, the proliferation of nuclear and biological weapons, and regional conflicts. *Thus* [my emphasis], the Federal Government has an indispensable role to play in investing in S&T [science and technology]—a role critical to the country's economy, national security, environment, health, and other social needs. This is especially the case when the risk is too great for individual companies to make the needed investment, or when the public benefit is large, but the private benefit is small. Our Nation also must support a balanced mix of S&T investments (i.e., basic research, applied research, and technology development) since the steps involved in technological innovation are so profoundly interwoven.

Now they tell us. But it does raise the question of how the United States survived and prospered for so many years without all this government help.

The above quotation, with a few changes for time and place, could have been written by Francis Bacon. In his 1605 book *The Advancement of Learning*, Bacon almost invented the idea of progress as cumulative learning based on the inductive method, and he was a strong promoter of government support of undirected basic research. This book had a strong appeal to the small community of scientists and philosophers who were just beginning to break their Aristotelian chains. Or it could have been written by Vannevar Bush, the electrical engineer who was the entrepreneur and architect of post–World War II U.S. science policy. In *Science: The Endless Frontier*, Bush proposed a program for postwar scientific research based on federal support of scientists "working on subjects of their own choice." This book had a strong appeal to the large community of scientists who had been involved in defense research and worried about what they would do next. The Bacon-Bush perspective is now so broadly shared that the Clinton budget statement proceeds from a short list of national challenges to a proposed $73 billion R&D program without pausing to make an argument why the federal government has "an indispensable role" to meet these challenges.

In the 50 years or so since the Bush Report, science policy in the United States has been on what is variously called "the linear model" or "Bacon's chain."[1] The implicit argument seems to be as follows:

- *government financing* is necessary to provide the adequate level of
- *basic research*, which is necessary to provide the scientific foundation for
- *advanced technology*, which accounts for a large part of
- *economic growth.*

This chain of reasoning may be correct, but it should not go unchallenged. A lot of money and the productivity of science and technology are at stake.

The objective of this chapter is to evaluate the strength of Bacon's chain, first by examining each of the three critical links and then by examining the aggregate relation between federal R&D spending and U.S. productivity growth.

Bacon's Chain

As an economist, I am more comfortable evaluating Bacon's chain in the reverse direction, first examining the dependence of economic growth on technology.

Economic Growth and Technology

A number of leading economists, including several Nobel laureates, have made their reputations by estimating that technology accounts for about 50 percent of economic growth and more than 80 percent of productivity growth. These estimates are now used casually, including in Clinton's FY1997 budget, as support for government science and technology programs. The larger community, however, may not recognize that "technology" is one of economists' two favorite code words for what they do not understand. (The other favorite is "tastes.") All these estimates of the effects of technology are residuals, estimates of the percentage of economic growth that economists cannot explain by the measured increase in conventional inputs. Any underestimate of the increase in the quantity or quality of labor or capital, for example, increases the magnitude of the residual, attributed without any direct evidence to an increase in technology.

Similarly, any condition that improves the allocation of resources, such as economies of scale or a reduction in the distortive effects of taxes, tariffs, regulation, and litigation, is also attributed to an increase in technology. Over some periods, of course, some of the unmeasured inputs or conditions may have deteriorated, in which case the unexplained residual called technology is smaller. In any case, this residual is a measure of what we do not understand about economic growth, not a direct measure of the effects of technology.

In a recent article, "The Discovery of the Residual," Zvi Griliches notes that

> All of the pioneers of this subject were quite clear about the tenuousness of such calculations and that it may be misleading to identify the results as "pure" measures of technical progress.

And he concludes that

> such calculations should be interpreted, primarily, as an "indication of where we need to concentrate our attention." At this point, the gauntlet has been thrown: even though it had been named "efficiency," "technical change," or most accurately a "measure of our ignorance," much of observed economic growth remained unexplained.

In summary, technology has surely made an important contribution to economic growth; we should not deny the evidence of our common sense perceptions, even if economists have not produced any direct evidence of the magnitude of this effect. Increases in technology may be either more important or less important to economic growth than the most careful estimates by the economists. The point is: we just don't know, and we will make better public policy by acknowledging this uncertainty than by assuming knowledge that does not exist.

Technology and Science

The middle link in Bacon's chain is the dependence of technology on science. Until about 100 years ago, the evidence on this issue was clear and negative: almost all major technological improvements were made by farmers and artisans with little or no scientific training or contact with the scientific community. Surely, however, modern technology must be more dependent on scientific progress. As it turns out, there is now a much more complex exchange between academic science and industrial technology.

But the basic story has not changed very much: only a small share of major improvements in technology appears to be dependent on recent academic research, but a substantial part of academic science appears to be a response to the technical challenges of industry.

The Department of Defense has provided the largest government support of science and technology for many years and was the first to sponsor a careful study of the dependence of technology on basic research. Project Hindsight organized 13 teams of scientists and engineers to identify the key research events that contributed to 20 weapon systems. The final report, published in 1969, identified 700 research events that contributed to these weapon systems, but only two such events came from basic research. Major advances in technology appear to be more dependent on technical innovations than on basic science.

About the same time, the IIT Research Institute prepared a study for the National Science Foundation on the key research events that contributed to five major civilian technologies. This study concluded that "nonmission" research made a major contribution to each of these technologies and that most of this research was conducted at colleges and universities. The most important of these research events, however, occurred 20 to 30 years prior to the technological innovation.

Later studies are more consistent with the Project Hindsight conclusion about the origin of the key research events, and they reinforce the finding by the IIT Research Institute about the long lags between the key events and the technological innovation.

A study by J. Langrish and colleagues (1972) examined the origin of 84 major technical innovations in British industry, concluding that "although scientific discoveries occasionally lead to new technology, this is rare." A study by Gellman Associates for the National Science Foundation (1976) found that about 10 percent of technological innovations were attributable to recent academic research. The most comprehensive of these later studies is by Edwin Mansfield (1991). Mansfield surveyed 76 firms in 7 manufacturing industries to determine the share of the firms' new products and processes that could not have been developed without academic research conducted within the prior 15 years. He concluded that "about 11 percent of new products and 9 percent of new processes could not have been developed, without substantial delay, in the absence of recent academic research." Moreover, Mansfield found that those products and processes that were dependent on academic research accounted for only 3 percent of sales and 1 percent of the industry savings attributable to technological innovation.

Most of these studies, however, may have underestimated the effective lag between research and technological innovation. In a related study, James Adams (1990) developed an annual series of the "stock of knowledge" available to 18 manufacturing industries and then estimated the effect on productivity growth by industry of the stock of knowledge specific to that industry and to other industries. Adams finds that productivity growth is strongly dependent on both types of knowledge, but with very long lags—about 20 years for the stock of knowledge specific to that industry, and about 30 years for the knowledge coming from other industries.

For a more complete understanding, it is also important to recognize the substantial contribution of technology to science. Industry provides a significant part of the funding for academic research, along with the improved instrumentation necessary for some types of research. More important, perhaps, many academic scientists choose their research topics based on the technical challenges identified from their consulting to industry, a finding documented by both Project Hindsight and Edwin Mansfield (1995).

In the short term, in summary, most technological innovation is based on other advances in technology, with little contribution from recent advances in basic research. The long-term contribution of basic research is substantially higher, but with lags of 20 to 30 years. And basic research, in turn, is quite dependent on both industrial support and recent technological innovations and challenges.

Science and Government Support

The third link in Bacon's chain, finally, is the dependence of basic research on government support. From Francis Bacon to Thomas Jefferson to Richard Nelson to Kenneth Arrow, the argument for government support of science has been roughly the same: the benefits of knowledge, but not the costs, are a function of the number of people to whom it is made available. Therefore, the government ought to finance basic research and make it available to others without charge. The contribution of contemporary economists to this argument is not much more than a mathematical gloss and the term "public good." Interestingly, none of these eminent supporters of the inductive method provided any empirical support for this argument, treating it as self-evident. The traditional example of a public good, of course, was the lighthouse, until Ronald Coase pointed out that many lighthouses had been built and maintained without any government support.

In fact, there has long been substantial private finance of basic research, and private finance was the largest source of support until the 1950s. Some of this support is direct grants for academic science by individuals, corporations, and foundations. A substantial amount of in-company research is motivated by the potential for profitable patents—the only type of federal policy for civilian science, incidentally, that is authorized by the Constitution. An increasing amount of private research expenditures is motivated by the substantial first-mover advantage, even when the research cannot be patented. And many company scientists are hired to ensure that the company is informed early about important relevant research conducted elsewhere. For these reasons, private firms have a substantial incentive to support basic research. A study of 16 major oil and chemical firms by Edwin Mansfield (1980) found that the productivity growth by firm was dependent on its investment in basic science. A more comprehensive study of 911 firms by Zvi Griliches (1986) found that a firm's profits were dependent on its investment in basic science.

Basic science is clearly not a pure public good; there was and would be a substantial amount of basic science in the absence of any government support. A number of important questions, however, remain to be addressed. Private incentives to support basic science, even though substantial, are probably insufficient; but it is not self-evident that government support is desirable. Our political processes respond to different information and incentives. If the government funds much the same type of activities as do private firms, the government funds may reduce private support. If the government funds different types of basic research, there is less reason to expect the research to contribute to technological innovation. And the increase in taxes necessary to finance the government support will have some negative effect on economic growth.

Some information is available on these several possible effects. First, the rapid growth of real federal outlays for R&D does not appear to have reduced the continued growth of real private expenditures for R&D or for basic science.[2] Second, most federal R&D

outlays are for defense and space technology, activities that are less likely to displace private expenditures. The growth of real federal outlays for R&D, thus, has clearly added to total U.S. expenditures for R&D, but most of the benefits of the additional expenditures may be specific to the value of the improvements in defense and space technology. The several major federal programs to fund civilian technology, such as the supersonic transport and synthetic fuels, proved to be expensive failures. Third, there is little other than anecdotal evidence on which to base an estimate of the effects of the additional support for basic science, either in terms of technological innovation or economic growth. And fourth, total federal outlays for R&D were never more than 2.2 percent of GDP (in FY1964) and are now only 0.9 percent of GDP, so the negative effect of the taxes necessary to finance these outlays is quite small.

All this leaves us about where we started. Each of the links in Bacon's chain is plausible but empirically weak. Neither the theory nor the available evidence provides a satisfactory guide to federal science policy.

Productivity Growth and Real Federal R&D Outlays

A different approach may be more useful. Maybe Bacon's chain is stronger than its weakest link. Only a direct test of the relationship between productivity growth and real federal R&D outlays would provide evidence of this effect. Since a comprehensive federal science policy, however, has a history of only 50 years, such tests may provide little information if the effective lags in this relation, as estimated by some studies, are 20 to 30 years in length.

Let's start with what we know. For the past 50 years, the politicrats of American science have been very effective in using Bacon's chain to raid the Treasury. Total real federal outlays for R&D are now at about 10 times the level they were when the National Science Foundation was established in 1950. As illustrated by Figure 2.1, however, the pattern of real outlays differs substantially among the major types of programs. Real outlays for defense, civilian, and space R&D programs each increased rapidly until the mid-1960s. Since that time, real outlays for defense R&D declined until the Carter-Reagan defense buildup, real outlays for civilian R&D have increased at a steady slow rate, and real outlays for space programs declined sharply after the peak spending for the Apollo mission.

Figure 2.1
REAL FEDERAL R&D OUTLAYS, FY1950–FY1995
(BILLIONS OF 1987 DOLLARS)

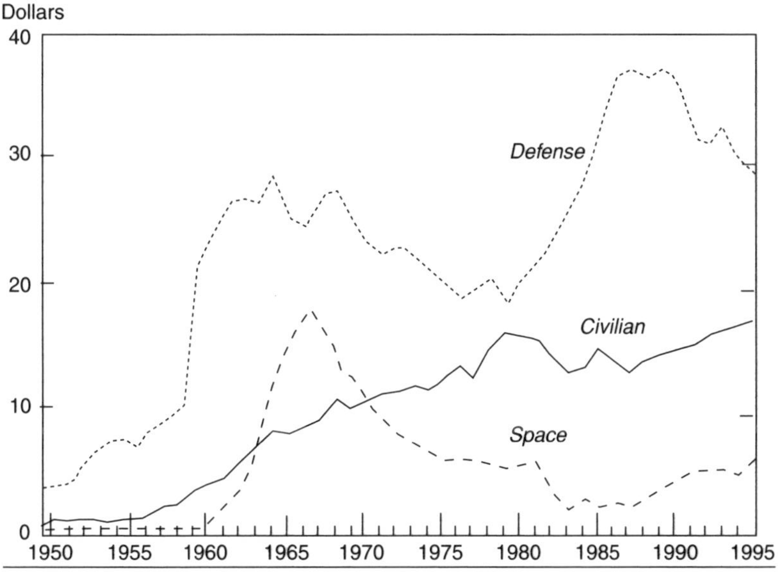

SOURCE: Historical Tables, *Budget of the United States for Fiscal Year 1997.*

Next, let's examine the relation between productivity growth and real federal R&D outlays, as illustrated by Figure 2.2. The average productivity growth rate is the five-year, moving-average percentage change in business-sector output per hour (centered on the middle year). The dashed line indicates the total real federal R&D outlays per civilian employee. These two series present a similar pattern: both series increased sharply until the mid-1960s, then declined substantially until 1980, and since then have increased slightly. Changes in productivity growth, however, appear to lead changes in real R&D outlays. This suggests that the short-term relation of these series may better reflect the demand for R&D than a contribution to productivity growth.

Maybe regression analysis would help sort this out. I have estimated the effects on the annual productivity growth rate of different aggregations of real federal R&D outlays per civilian employee for the years 1956 through 1995. The several regressions also control

Figure 2.2
PRODUCTIVITY GROWTH AND REAL FEDERAL R&D OUTLAYS, 1956–1993
(1987 DOLLARS PER U.S. CIVILIAN EMPLOYEE)

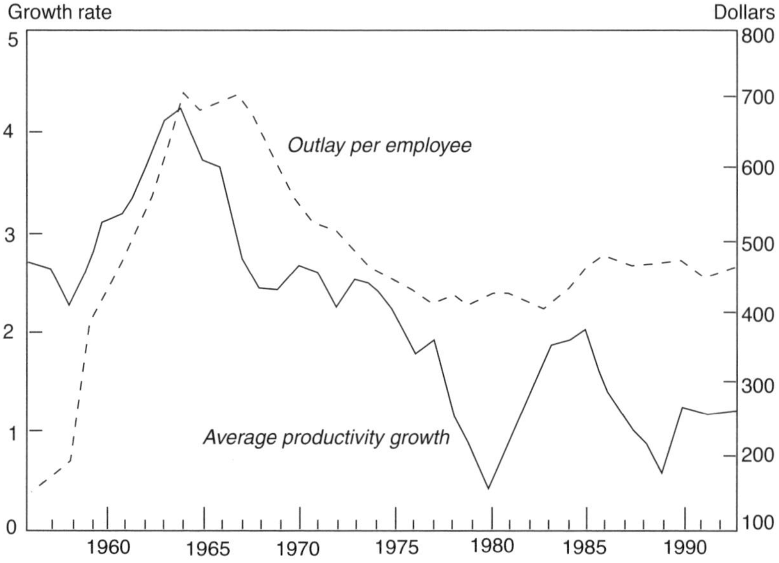

SOURCE: Author's calculations based upon the Historical Tables, *Budget of the United States for Fiscal Year 1997*; and *Economic Report of the President, 1996.*

for the business cycle and for other major conditions that affect the productivity growth rate. The primary result of these regressions is that a $100 increase in real (1987) federal R&D outlays per employee (which would increase current federal outlays by about $17 billion) might increase the annual productivity growth rate by about one-quarter of a percentage point within five years. All the near-term effects of R&D outlays on productivity growth, however, appear to be specific to defense R&D. Civilian and space R&D outlays appear to have no effect on near-term productivity growth, either independently or in combination with other types of R&D spending. The long-term effects on productivity growth may be higher but cannot be estimated from this sample. See the annex for more detail on these regressions.

In summary, we still do not have a very good estimate of the effect of federal R&D spending on productivity growth. And what effect we can see appears to be in defense R&D, not civilian R&D.

Some Reflections on U.S. Science Policy

A cautionary note: my concluding comments may be as disjointed as current U.S. science policy.

More accurate estimates of the effects of government science programs would help to inform science policy, but an understanding of the comparative advantage of different institutions is more important. Private organizations almost surely have better information and incentives to support the type of R&D that most contributes to economic growth, but their incentives are probably not sufficient to induce the optimal level of R&D.[3] A market imperfection, however, does not imply that government can improve this outcome. Government-sponsored science programs may increase the total level of R&D expenditures, but the allocation of the incremental expenditure is unduly influenced by vocal user and supplier interests. These institutional conditions and the cumulative evidence summarized in this chapter lead me to question whether the government should directly finance basic research. The government's interest in improved technology for defense or some other constitutional role is probably best served by purchasing the technology, rather than prejudging the basic research that is most likely to contribute to the improved technology. Suppliers of the new technology have better information and incentives to select the most valuable research and the places where it should be performed.

For the same reasons, science policy would probably make a larger contribution to economic growth by merely augmenting private R&D expenditures, leaving the allocation decisions entirely to private organizations. The federal tax code may be a sufficient instrument for this purpose. The current code permits firms to expense the cost of research and experimentation (R&E). The tax credit for incremental R&E expenditures and grants to universities, however, expired in 1995, in favor of higher spending for civilian R&D projects selected by the government. My reasoning leads me to conclude that these recent changes in federal science policy will reduce economic growth, however valuable they may be according to other criteria. The case for government support of civilian R&D is that the return to the economy is higher than the return to a firm, not that the government has better information on what R&D has the highest return.

The most effective instrument to support civilian technology, thus, is likely to be a tax credit for private R&E expenditures. This tax credit, however, should probably differ from the recently expired incremental tax credit in two dimensions:

- The credit should apply to the total R&E expenditures by a firm, not merely to the increment above some base period. (The incremental credit favored firms with increasing R&E expenditures relative to other firms with the same level of expenditures.)
- The credit should be refundable to avoid a bias against start-up firms with no near-term tax liability.

Similarly, the most effective instrument to support basic research in universities is likely to be a matching grant to funds raised from private sources. University-based scientists, thus, would make their case to private firms and foundations rather than to some government-appointed peer-review committee, shifting the decisions on the location of these grants from the professional communities that supply basic research to private organizations that demand the research.

These considerations bear on the processes for allocating govnment support for R&D and do not directly bear on the level of this support. For defense and other programs for which government is the final purchaser, the level of R&D would continue to be determined by the government's demand for improved technology based on considerations beyond those addressed in this chapter. The proposed shift to tax credits and matching grants as the primary instruments to support civilian R&D, in contrast, would make the level of government support endogenous to the private demands for such search. The outcome of these proposed changes in the public instruments to support R&D may be either a higher or a lower total level of support; I do not know or much care. My concern is to make government support of science and technology something more than a raid on the Treasury.

Annex

The following regression has been estimated for different categories' real federal R&D outlays:

Table 2.1

EFFECT OF ADDITIONAL $100 PER EMPLOYEE OF REAL R&D OUTLAYS ON THE ANNUAL PRODUCTIVITY GROWTH RATE

(1987 DOLLARS)

	Regression				
	A	B	C	D	E
Total	.26 (.10)				
Defense		.51 (.26)	.52 (.18)		
Civilian		−.54 (1.61)		1.04 (.52)	
Space		.36 (.72)			.48 (.27)
R^2	.563	.550	.572	.530	.521

SOURCE: Author.

$$P = C + bU_{-1} + \Sigma c_i X_i + \Sigma d_j\, PDL(R_j) + u, \text{ where}$$

P = percent change in business sector productivity,

U_{-1} = civilian unemployment rate in the prior year,

X_i = other major contributors to productivity growth, and

$PDL(R_j)$ = polynomial distributive lag on the real (1987) federal outlays per civilian employee in the prior five fiscal years for R&D category j.

(Where necessary, an autoregressive term is also added to adjust for serial correlation of the residuals.) The sample for these estimates is for the years 1956 through 1995.

Table 2.1 presents estimates of the effects of five different aggregations of real federal R&D outlays (the d_j coefficients), the standard errors of these coefficients (in parentheses), and the R^2 for each regression. A $100 increase in real (1987) R&D outlays per employee would increase current federal outlays by about $17 billion. Regression A suggests that an increase of total real R&D outlays by $100 per employee would increase annual productivity growth by about one-quarter of a percentage point. *All the near-term effect of R&D*

outlays on productivity growth, however, appears to be specific to defense R&D.

Regressions B and C suggest that an increase of real defense R&D outlays by $100 per employee would increase annual productivity growth by about one-half a percentage point. Regressions B and D indicate no significant near-term effect of civilian R&D on productivity growth, possibly because about half of civilian R&D funds are now spent for health research. Regressions B and E indicate no significant near-term effect of space R&D on productivity growth. Again, the effect of civilian and space R&D on productivity growth may have much longer lags, but such long-term effects cannot be estimated from these data.

References

Adams, James. (1990) "Fundamental Stocks of Knowledge and Productivity Growth." *Journal of Political Economy* 98 (August): 673–702.

Bacon, Francis. (1605) *The Advancement of Learning.*

Budget of the United States Government: Supplement, Fiscal Year 1997. (1996) Washington, D.C.: U.S. Government Printing Office.

Bush, Vannevar. (1945) *Science: The Endless Frontier.* Washington, D.C.: U.S. Government Printing Office; all citations refer to the 1990 reprint of the report issued by the National Science Foundation.

Griliches, Zvi. (1986) "Productivity, R&D and Basic Research at the Firm Level in the 1970s." *American Economic Review* 76: 14–54.

______. (1996) "The Discovery of the Residual: A Historical Note." *Journal of Economic Literature* 34 (September): 1324–30.

Kealey, Terence. (1996) *The Economic Laws of Scientific Research.* New York: St. Martin's Press.

Langrish, J. et al. (1972) *Wealth from Knowledge: A Study of Innovation in Industry.* New York: Macmillan and Wiley.

Mansfield, Edwin. (1991) "Academic Research and Industrial Innovation." *Research Policy* 20 (February): 1–12.

______. (1995) "Academic Research Underlying Industrial Innovations: Sources, Characteristics, and Financing." *Review of Economics and Statistics* 77 (February): 55–65.

Mowery, D. D., and Nathan Rosenberg. (1989) *Technology and the Pursuit of Economic Growth.* Cambridge: Cambridge University Press.

National Science Foundation. (1968) "Technology in Retrospect and Critical Events in Science." Report prepared by IIT Research Institute. NSF C535, December.

Office of the Director, Defense Research and Engineering. (1969) *Project Hindsight.* Washington, D.C.

______. (1976) "Indicators of International Trends in Technological and Innovation." Report prepared by Gellman Associates. Washington, D.C.

Stephan, Paula. (1996) "The Economics of Science." *Journal of Economic Literature* 34 (September): 1199–1235.

Notes

1. This phrase is from Kealey (1996), although it may have been used by an earlier author. In any case, Kealey (1996) and Stephan (1996) are the primary sources of information and inspiration for this chapter.

2. Kealey (1996, 159–60), based on data from Mowery and Rosenberg (1989).

3. Advocates of government support of science often assert that there is another major market imperfection that private firms will not finance activities with a payoff as long as 20 to 30 years. The magnitude of this problem, however, is a function of the tax wedge between the pretax and posttax return on capital.

Governments do not have a comparative advantage because they can borrow at a lower rate; the opportunity cost of government borrowing is the pretax rate of return on the private investment displaced. Moreover, governments are often the most myopic institutions in society, given the limited political payoff of conditions beyond the next election. Clinton's argument for government support "when the risk is too great for individual companies to make the needed investment" is an example of this fallacy.

3. Too Much, Too Soon: Is a Global Warming Treaty a Rush to Judgment?

President Clinton has endorsed a global warming treaty, the details of which are expected to be resolved at a December conference in Kyoto. For this treaty to merit our support, the proponents should be asked to demonstrate the accuracy of all of the following statements:

1. A continued increase in the emission of greenhouse gasses (primarily carbon dioxide [CO_2]) will increase the average global temperature.
2. An increase in average temperature will generate more costs than benefits.
3. Emissions controls are the most efficient means to prevent an increase in global temperature.
4. Early measures to control emissions are superior to later measures, whether to control emissions or adapt to a temperature increase.
5. Emissions controls can be effectively monitored and enforced.
6. Governments of the treaty countries will approve the necessary control measures.
7. Controlling emissions in the rich countries is desirable even if emissions in the poor countries are not controlled for several decades.

The case for any one of these statements is surprisingly weak.

The case for a global warming treaty, which depends on the accuracy of all of these statements, is shockingly weak. Let me count the ways. . .

This article was first published in *Jobs and Capital* 6 (Fall 1997): 14–19. My thanks to the Milken Institute for its permission to republish this article.

How Good Is the Science of Global Warming?

The continued debate in the scientific community about global warming is based on only a few hard facts: The concentration of CO_2 in the atmosphere is about 25 percent higher than in preindustrial times. The average (measured) global temperature has increased about 0.5° Celsius since the 1880s. And the increased concentration of CO_2 may have contributed to the increase in temperature. One might hope for a more solid scientific foundation for a major international treaty. According to a 16 May 1997 article in *Science* magazine, however, ". . . many climate experts caution that it is not at all clear that human activities have begun to warm the planet—or how bad greenhouse warming will be when it arrives."

The substantial remaining scientific issues about global warming will have to be sorted out within the scientific community, preferably by scientific standards rather than by a politically forged consensus. Sooner or later, however, scientists should be asked to explain some conditions that puzzle informed and intelligent people in the broader community:

The increase of 0.5°C in the average (measured) global temperature seems very small relative to the variance of natural conditions and possible measurement errors. Natural water vapor constitutes about 98 percent of global warming gasses, so a small variation in water vapor or the reflectivity of the atmosphere would overwhelm the effect of a change in CO_2. For this economist, it also seems implausible that average global temperatures were measured very accurately in the past century.

The relative timing of the increase in average global temperature and CO_2 emissions also seems inconsistent with an anthropogenic interpretation of the temperature increase. Most of the temperature increase occurred by 1940, but most of the CO_2 emissions have been in the subsequent years.

Although the 1980s was an unusually warm decade, neither the satellite nor the weather balloon measures of the temperature in the lower atmosphere show any net warming over the past 18 years.

Scientists may yet demonstrate that a continued increase in CO_2 emissions will increase the average temperature, but such evidence is not yet sufficient to support measures that would impose substantial economic costs.

Should We Fear Some Moderate Warming?

Suppose the scientists are correct that a continued increase in CO_2 emissions will increase the average global temperature by one to several degrees Celsius by the end of the next century. Should that be a basis for concern? In the stilted language of economists, are the incremental costs likely to be higher than the incremental benefits? Again, this issue is not clear, and the answer may differ substantially among people in different parts of the world.

In part, the answer is dependent on whether the increase in average temperature increases or reduces the variance of temperature over time and region. On this issue, the science is relatively clear. Most of the warming is expected to be at night, in the winter, and in the high northern latitudes. This suggests that heating costs will be reduced by more than the increase in cooling costs. The increase in arable land in Canada and Siberia is likely to be substantially higher than the reduction in arable land due to more arid conditions in some regions or flooding in other regions. And a reduction in the temperature variance by region is also likely to reduce the frequency of severe storms.

On one issue, the science is also quite clear: An increase in the concentration of CO_2 in the atmosphere increases the growth of many plants, including most food crops. This effect, plus the net increase in arable land, is likely to reduce the relative price of food and fiber in most regions of the world, as has been the case during the whole period of small net warming to date.

Substantial costs and many scare stories have been attributed to the effect of global warming on the sea level. An increase in the sea level would lead to substantial flooding in such regions as Bangladesh, the Maldive Islands, Florida, and Louisiana. Any increase in the average sea level, however, would be at a very slow rate, allowing plenty of time for people to move or to build protective barriers. Moreover, the effect of global warming on the sea level is not yet clear, as it depends on the relative effects of warming and of increased snow on the polar ice masses.

On net, it is not yet clear whether some moderate warming should be a cause for concern. The balance of conditions suggests that moderate warming may generate net benefits to people in the temperate regions and net costs to people in the tropics. As now envisioned, however, the major costs of the measures presumed necessary to avoid global warming would be borne by people in the rich countries in the temperate regions. In that case, a global warming treaty should be considered an instrument of foreign aid and should be evaluated on that basis.

Are Emissions Controls the Most Efficient Instrument?

So far, the proponents of a global warming treaty have assumed, without apparent analysis or evidence, that emissions controls are the most efficient, maybe the only effective, means to avoid an increase in the average global temperature. That may prove to be correct, but it has yet to be demonstrated. There are two alternative types of measures that may be sufficient to offset the effects of increased emissions:

1. Spreading trace quantities of iron in the oceans and reforestation would each increase the absorption of CO_2 from the atmosphere. The first measure would also have the beneficial side effect of increasing the yield of ocean fisheries. And much of the current deforestation in the tropics is uneconomic on other grounds.
2. Spreading fine particulates in the upper atmosphere would increase the albedo (reflectivity) of the atmosphere, offsetting the warming effect of any given concentration of greenhouse gasses, but this measure may also have some adverse side effects.

For any given warming effect of CO_2 emissions, it is important to know the most efficient means to counter this effect. Preliminary estimates suggest a very high payoff to "salting" both the oceans and the stratosphere but, as far as I know, no thorough analysis of the relative efficiency of the alternative means to avoid global warming has been undertaken. Since the potential cost of emissions control may be very high, it is especially important to evaluate the potential alternatives, with care to recognize both the direct and indirect effects, before making a commitment to control emissions.

What's the Hurry?

The case for a commitment to early control of greenhouse gas emissions, in turn, should be based on a demonstration that the expected rate of return on these measures is higher than on alternative private and public investments. Since the potential benefits of emission control lag the costs of the control measures by decades, this is a very demanding test. The average real return on private investment in the United states (including taxes) is about 9 percent. The average rate of return on research and development and on education and public health in the poor countries may be over 20 percent. At a 9 percent rate, control measures that cost $1 billion this year must generate benefits of about $74 billion 50 years from now to meet this test. At a 20 percent rate, such control measures must generate benefits of about $9,100 billion 50 years from now to meet this test. The most optimistic estimates of the benefits of emissions control fail to meet this test. If our objective is to improve our own economic well being, we are much better advised to increase expenditures for research and development and for private investment in the United States. If our objective is to help the people in the poor countries, we are much better advised to help them finance their education and public health, even if most of the potential benefits of emissions controls would later accrue to people in these countries.

Moreover, there is another important payoff to deferring a commitment to emissions controls: we should know a lot more about this issue in the next 10 to 20 years. Klaus Hasselmann, a leading climate modeler at the Max Planck Institute for Meteorology in Hamburg, acknowledges that "The signal is not so much above the noise that you can convince skeptics. It will take another decade or so to work up out of the noise." More refined climate models will be complemented by a near doubling of the important sample of satellite measures of the global temperature. In the meantime, someone should also have made more precise estimates of the costs of emissions controls, the costs and effectiveness of alternative means to avoid global warming, and whether the net effects of some warming are likely to be adverse or benign.

Such considerations led William Nordhaus, maybe the wisest economist to write about the global warming issue, to endorse ". . . three modest steps to slow global warming while avoiding precipitous and ill-designed actions that may later be regretted":

- Improve our knowledge—about the magnitude, causes, and consequences of global warming;
- Develop technology—that would reduce the greenhouse emissions per unit of output, sequester carbon emissions, and offset emissions by increasing the reflectivity of the atmosphere; and

- Promote "no-regret" policies—that are most likely to be worthwhile on other grounds.

Since 1990, when Nordhaus endorsed this approach, no substantial information has developed that would make the case for more comprehensive and costly measures such as a carbon tax or emission permits.

Can Emission Controls Be Monitored and Enforced?

The problems of implementing and enforcing emission controls have received almost no attention. First, CO_2 emissions cannot be directly measured by source. The estimates of CO_2 emissions by country are based on the known emissions per unit of fuel by type and records of the amount of fuel used by type. The emissions estimates, thus, are accurate only if the reports of the amount of fuel used by type are accurate. A government participating in an international emissions control agreement, however, has an incentive to understate or misstate the amount of fuel used by type in order to reduce the relative price of fuel used in that country. There is no obvious way for other governments to directly monitor the amount of fuels burned by type in another country.

A second type of problem would probably arise, primarily in the poor countries. A carbon tax or effective controls on the use of coal, oil, and natural gas would probably increase the use of wood as a fuel. This would create two problems: the burning of wood creates a high amount of CO_2 emissions per BTU, and the deforestation would reduce the amount of CO_2 sequestered from the atmosphere.

There is less likely to be an internal black market for fuels than would be the case with other products subject to a high tax. Coal, oil, and natural gas are distributed through restricted channels and, even with such a tax, would have a relatively low value per unit of volume compared to such products as cigarettes and CFCs. Governments probably have the ability, if maybe not the incentive, to enforce such a tax without a substantial evasion problem.

The final problem concerns the methods of enforcing the emission controls by country. What would other governments do if the estimated emissions from one country are higher than allowed by the international agreement? There has been some vague talk about using trade sanctions to enforce such an agreement without much evidence that the implications of using such sanctions have been considered. Trade sanctions against one country also harm the economies of those countries that had traded with the target country, and these derivative costs will differ substantially among the other countries. This is likely to lead to a relatively ineffective and highly arbitrary enforcement of the sanctions, because the other countries face quite different costs of enforcing the sanctions. During the Cold War, for example, the United States and allied governments were quite effective in enforcing the restrictions on the export of military technology, because they faced a formidable common adversary. Since then, however, the different interests of individual governments have led to quite different policies about the export of military technology.

In summary, thus, it is still far from clear that an international agreement on emissions controls can be monitored and enforced.

Would Governments Approve Effective Control Measures?

The record to date does not provide a basis to expect the major governments to approve effective measures to control CO_2 emissions. The U.S. record is most important, because no international agreement would be effective without effective U.S. action. For many years the U.S. government, almost alone among the rich countries, has resisted an increase in the gasoline tax to a level higher than necessary to finance highway expenditures. In 1993 President Clinton's proposal for a general BTU tax was not approved by a Congress controlled by his own party. Most important, in July 1997 the U.S. Senate approved a resolution by a vote of 95 to 0 opposing any global warming treaty that exempts the poor countries from emissions controls or that would seriously harm the U.S. economy.

The types of measures that could provide effective control of CO_2 emissions include the following:

1. a tax on fossil fuels in proportion to the CO_2 emissions per unit.
2. emissions permits that are tradable and are initially auctioned by the government.
3. emission permits that are tradable and are initially distributed to current users, and
4. specific regulations on allowable technology, fuel use, and so on.

Any of the first three measures would also be the most efficient means to achieve effective emissions control.

The first step toward understanding the politics of this issue is to recognize the magnitude of the potential changes. A tax of about \$100 per ton of CO_2 emissions would be necessary to eventually reduce annual emissions by 40 percent relative to the projected baseline path, roughly the amount necessary to meet the target proposed by the European Union to reduce emissions to 15 percent below the 1990 level by 2010. This would increase the mine-mouth price of coal by nearly 300 percent, the wellhead price of natural gas by nearly 100 percent, and the wellhead price of oil by nearly 75 percent. Such taxes would yield revenues to the U.S. government of over \$200 billion a year. Nor is this the likely limit; a carbon tax of over \$300 per ton would be necessary to reduce emissions to an annual rate consistent with stabilizing the concentration of CO_2 in the atmosphere. Taxes of this magnitude would substantially change the composition of the U.S. economy and reduce economic growth, costs that would be amplified by the interaction with the current structure of U.S. taxes. Congress deserves much more accurate answers to the questions addressed above before it commits us to start down this path.

A number of leading economists, including William Nordhaus and Dale Jorgenson, have made an effective case that the net cost of emission controls could be much reduced by using the revenues from such taxes (or from auctioned permits that would reduce emissions by the same expected amount) to reduce the more misallocative provisions of our current tax code, especially the high marginal tax rates on the income from capital. They are correct to make this point, but this is primarily a case for tax reform—not to finance this reform by large tax increases on fossil fuels.

The choice between a carbon tax and a system of auctioned emissions permits involves only a minor political issue: A carbon tax leaves some uncertainty about the magnitude of the emissions effects, whereas permits focus the remaining uncertainty on the relative price effects. There is a much more important political issue in the choice between either a carbon tax or auctioned emissions permits and a system of permits that are "grandfathered" to current fuel users. The first two measures would each involve a massive wealth transfer from the suppliers and consumers of fossil fuels to those who would benefit from an increase in government spending or a reduction in taxes. These measures would create two political effects that would be minimized by choosing a system of grandfathered permits: Opposition by the suppliers and consumers of fossil fuels may defeat or defer the appropriate measures to control CO_2 emissions, and the expected revenue from these measures may bias the government's decision on the level of tax rates or permits. On the other hand, a system of grandfathered permits would not generate revenues that could be used to finance a major tax reform, but it is probably unrealistic to expect government to use the revenues in this way rather than to compensate some of the losers from the emissions control measures or to reward other favored constituencies.

Whatever the merits of the case for controlling CO_2 emissions, there are no good arguments for using regulatory measures for this purpose. Such measures are grossly inefficient, often arbitrary, and are likely to be insufficient to achieve the desired emissions reduction. The Environmental Protection Agency, however, has apparently considered a variety of regulatory options to reduce CO_2 emissions, some of which EPA may have the authority to implement without new legislation. A regulatory approach to this issue should be dismissed out of hand. The case for a global warming treaty is weak enough without burdening it with the least efficient of the alternative control measures.

In summary, the politics of global warming suggests that governments are unlikely to choose the appropriate type and level of control measures.

Should the Poor Countries Be Exempt?

Since the Berlin Mandate of 1995, the continued negotiations toward a global warming treaty have proposed commitments by the governments of the rich countries to reduce the emissions of greenhouse gasses—exempting the poor countries from a similar commitment, at least for the next few decades. This suggests that the negotiators are more concerned about some symbolic treaty than about reducing the prospect of global warming. For an exemption of the poor countries would create at least two problems: About half of the global CO_2 emissions are expected to come from the now-poor countries by the year 2020; the exemption of these countries would substantially dilute and delay any net reduction in carbon emissions. And the exemption of the now-poor countries would increase the costs to the rich countries of meeting their emission targets, by reducing their comparative advantage in the world market. The U.S. Senate was correct to oppose any global warming treaty that exempts the poor countries. Either global warming is a serious concern or it is not. There is a good case to defer consideration of a global warming treaty until our knowledge base is substantially greater. There is no case for exempting any country with substantial carbon emissions, either now or in the future.

It is also important to recognize the implications for the world economy if the governments of the poor countries agree to limit carbon emissions and emission permits are tradable among countries. In that case, the rich countries are likely to be net buyers of the emissions permits, in effect paying the poor countries a bounty not to industrialize. Another effect is that the exchange rate of the poor countries is likely to increase, making it more difficult to export goods and services other than emissions permits. The combination of a global commitment to reduce carbon emissions and a global system of tradable permits is surely the most efficient means to achieve any specific emissions target, but some of the probable side effects are not very pretty.

Conclusion

Scientists have been correct to alert political officials about the possibility that a continued increase in the atmospheric concentration of CO_2 may increase average global temperatures. My judgment, however, is that many political officials have over-reacted to this warning, and that many scientists have themselves been swept up in this momentum. As suggested by William Nordhaus, there are some near-term actions that are likely to be valuable—continue to improve the information base, somewhat reorient technological priorities, and implement a few "no-regret" policies. There are too many scientific, economic, and political issues yet to be resolved, however, to support an early international commitment to control the emission of greenhouse gasses. A global warming treaty in the next decade or so would be a rush to judgment.

Postscript

With my characteristic optimism, my 1997 paper on global warming remarked that "We should know a lot more about this issue in the next 10 to 20 years." Unfortunately, there has been a rush to judgment on this issue without a significant increase in the information on which to base this judgment.

The cumulative increase in average world temperatures since the 1880s is now estimated to be 0.80°C, but there is no clear relation between the level of carbon dioxide in the atmosphere and the average level of global temperatures. Much of the estimate increase in temperature was before 1940, prior to any substantial accumulation of carbon dioxide in the atmosphere. There is still no explanation of the significant cooling from 1940 to 1975, despite a substantial increase in atmospheric carbon dioxide; the climate alarmists of the 1970s were predicting a new ice age. The historical record does not yet provide sufficient evidence that the increase in atmospheric carbon dioxide is the primary cause of the increase in average world temperatures.

There has been a rush to judgment, unfortunately, that abatement of carbon dioxide emissions is the optimal strategy to reduce the prospect of a continued increase in average world temperatures. For an abatement strategy to be optimal, however, the following conditions must apply:

- An increase in atmospheric carbon dioxide is the primary cause of the increase in global temperatures,
- An international treaty to reduce carbon dioxide emissions must include the governments of all nations that are major emitters, regardless of their level of economic development,
- A violation of the terms of such a treaty can be identified and would (somehow) be enforced, and
- An abatement strategy is more efficient than any alternative strategy.

There has not been sufficient attention, however, to two other strategies:

1. Geoengineering approaches to reduce the amount of sunlight reaching the earth would not be dependent on knowing the primary cause of the temperature increase, would require an international agreement only on cost sharing, and may be more efficient than an abatement strategy.
2. An adaptation strategy would also not be dependent on knowing the cause of the temperature increase, would allow every family, firm, and government to choose an adaptation option

> that best serves its own interests, would not require an international agreement to be effective, and may be more efficient that either an abatement or geoengineering strategy.

Some organizations and governments now appear likely to endorse an abatement strategy, largely for symbolic reasons, a strategy that will prove to be both costly and ineffective. My judgment is that most of the world will implicitly endorse an adaptation strategy for the next decade or so, at least until the nature and magnitude of the prospective temperature increase and the most efficient form of any collective response is much clearer than is now the case. Until there is much better and broader understanding of this issue, a rush to judgment on the optimal response to the increase in global temperatures is the greater danger.

4. Next Steps toward Health Policy Reform

President Clinton's Health Security Act is dead—the consequence of a misunderstanding of the popular concerns, a misdiagnosis of the major problems, the arrogance of the technocrats, and Clinton's own tendency to overreach his mandate. Unfortunately, many of its supporters have not learned the real lessons of the debacle, while many opponents of the Clinton plan still do not fully understand what is wrong with the U.S. health care system and what is needed to correct it.

Before Congress reconsiders health policy, all those concerned should reflect on the following questions:

- What are the major problems of our health care system?
- What are the major causes of these problems?
- What principles should guide the selection among the competing health policy reform proposals? And,
- What are the necessary and appropriate changes in health policy that only the federal government can make?

All of us—inside and outside Congress—should reflect on these questions *before* we jump back into the process of proposing or legislating specific health policy reforms.

The Problems

Most of the health reform plans considered to date focused on reducing the number of the uninsured with little attention to or with inappropriate means to control costs. The number or percent of

---

This article was presented at the University of Michigan Forum on Health Policy on November 18, 1994, and was first published in *Health Policy: Understanding Our Choices from National Reform to Market Forces*, ed. Marilynn M. Rosenthal and Max Heirich (Boulder, CO: Westview Press, 1998). My thanks to the Westview Press for its permission to republish this article.

people who do not have health insurance, however, is not, by itself, a problem. We did not have a health care crisis in 1940 when few people had health insurance. We do not now have a crisis when few people have insurance against earthquakes, floods, and asteroids. Contrary to the Clintons' rhetoric, the employers that do not provide health insurance and their employees are *not* free riders; for the same labor skills, employers in a competitive labor market pay higher wages for the uninsured and employees pay higher taxes. Universal health insurance coverage is not necessary to control health care costs; broader insurance coverage, in contrast, would almost surely increase costs.

Those without health insurance present two quite different, rather small problems.

1. Some of the uninsured do not receive some types of medical care that the rest of us, if necessary, would be willing to help finance. Those who are both uninsured and uninsurable, however, are only about 1 percent of the population under age 65 and could be folded into existing high-risk insurance pools for an annual subsidy of less than $1 billion. Most of the uninsured are a quite healthy lot or will be again within a few months.
2. The uninsured, in fact, receive a substantial amount of medical care, for some of which the providers are not compensated. And the distribution of the costs of this uncompensated care is quite arbitrary. Again, this is a surprisingly small problem. As of 1991, the net amount of uncompensated care to the uninsured was around $20 billion, far less than the amount by which providers are undercompensated by Medicare and Medicaid. To the extent that these costs are shifted to private insured patients, most of the cost shifting is due to undercompensation by the public insurance plans, not the uncompensated care to the uninsured.

The primary problem of our health care system is the continuing rapid increase in the relative price and real expenditures for medical care. Over the years since 1965, the relative price of medical care has increased at a 2.5 percent annual rate, and real expenditures per capita have increased at a 5.2 percent annual rate. Payments for health insurance are now the most rapidly growing component of both private payrolls and government budgets. The rapid increase in health insurance premiums is the primary reason for the increase in the percent uninsured.

Some recent news stories have conveyed the perception that the relative inflation in medical prices and expenditures has eased. These stories are misleading. Despite substantial efforts by private firms and insurance companies to control costs, these trends have continued. The relative price of medical care increased 2.8 percent in 1993, and real expenditures per capita increased 5.4 percent in 1991—both *higher* than the average increase since 1965. And despite the increasing undercompensation of providers by Medicare and Medicaid, real federal expenditures for health programs increased 7 percent in fiscal 1993. The unsustainable increase in the relative price and expenditures for medical care has continued, but was progressively ignored as the debate on health reform developed. There are some who opposed any major reform on the basis that the major problems of our health care system are being resolved. They were correct to oppose the major reforms considered this year, but they were wrong in concluding that a major change in federal health policies can be long deferred.

The Causes

Most of the proposed health reforms seem based on a premise that broader health insurance would solve most of the problems of our health care system. Most of these problems, however, are a *consequence* of *too much* of the *wrong type* of health insurance. Too much because employer-provided health insurance is not included in taxable income. The wrong type because there is no similar exclusion for individual health insurance. The wrong type because the tax and regulatory preferences for the Blues displaced the older form of commercial indemnity policies with policies providing cost-based reimbursement. At present, patients pay about 5 cents on the dollar for insured hospital services and about 20 cents on the dollar for insured physicians' services. The unusual form of health insurance has nearly eliminated any incentive for either the patient or the provider to control costs.

- One consequence of this condition is that insured patients spend too much on medical care; we have the highest quality medical care in the world but, at the margin, it costs more than it is worth.

- Another consequence is that the rate of inflation in medical care prices and expenditures, both over time and across types of treatment, is strongly related to the percent of costs covered by private or public insurance.
- The preference for employer-provided insurance, in turn, restricts the opportunity to choose your own coverage and risk pool or to maintain your policy when self-employed, not employed, or changing jobs.

Most of the proposed health reforms, however, would broaden employer-provided health insurance and try to offset the problems of cost control, portability, and so on, by price controls and other regulations. Again, the unusual form of American health insurance is the cause, not the solution, to most of the problems of the American system of health care.

The Principles

A valuable next step would be to reflect on the principles that should guide the choices among the proposed health reforms. Without claiming any unique ethical insight, let me suggest four principles to guide these choices and the major policy implications of each of these principles.

1. Government policy should not bias the choice of means by which health care is *financed*.

In other words, to the extent possible, government policy should be neutral with respect to whether any specific method of treatment is financed by employer-provided insurance, individual insurance, or by direct patient payment. The implications of this principle are clear: No monopoly purchasing cooperatives. No federal standard benefit package. No state mandates on insurance coverage. The tax exclusion for employer-provided insurance should be either eliminated or broadened to include both individual policies and medical savings accounts.

2. Government policy should not bias the choice of means by which health care is *provided*.

Again, to the extent possible, government policy should be neutral with respect to the choice of provider, method of treatment, and form of organization. And again, the implications are clear: No subsidies or restrictions by type of provider. No "any willing provider" restriction. No bias for or against home care, physician care, hospital care, HMOs, PPOs, fee-for-service, and so on.

3. Any government subsidies for either health insurance or health care should be on the budget, transparent, and subject to periodic review and approval.

This principle, of course, rejects the three other major pieces of the Clinton plan: employer mandates, community rating, and price controls. Each of these measures is an effective tax on some group to pay for health insurance or health care to others and differs from explicit taxes only in that the coerced transfer does not go through the federal treasury.

We already make massive subsidies, of course, to provide health insurance to the aged, the poor, veterans, and so on. Our political system may, and possibly should, subsidize insurance or care for some others. The point of this principle is that the government is likely to make a much better decision on this issue, both initially and over time, and the distribution of the burden of these subsidies will be much less arbitrary, if these subsidies are on the budget than if they are buried in mandates and regulations. The political test of whether broader subsidies for health insurance or health care is desirable is whether Congress is willing to reduce other spending or increase explicit taxes to pay for these subsidies. That may be the primary reason, of course, why most of the proposed new subsidies are not on the budget.

4. The focus of federal health reform should be on those policies that *only* the federal government can change.

This principle, of course, rules out any comprehensive reform plan that includes measures that could be changed by state and local governments or private organizations. Federal health reform should focus on changes in federal health programs, the federal tax code, on federal regulations, and, maybe, nothing else. There may be some health policies that the state governments could change for which a single national policy may be better, but I doubt it. I am especially unconvinced, for example, that the federal government should establish a single national policy on insurance regulation or medical malpractice. As with crime, the other major domestic policy issue of 1994, it is especially important to *decentralize* the policy choices on issues for which a uniform policy may not be best for all jurisdictions, because of regional differences in preferences or conditions, or when there is considerable uncertainty about what is the best policy. The guiding spirit of a wise federal health reform plan is humility, not hubris.

The Policies

At this stage, we should declare a 90-day moratorium on promoting specific health reform proposals, and I will follow my own advice. Let me conclude, however, with some suggestions about the types of federal policy changes that should be considered.

1. The most important broad reform would be to change the federal tax treatment of health insurance. Two quite different changes should be considered:
   a. Eliminate the exclusion of employer-provided health insurance from taxable income, combined with a revenue-neutral reduction in the payroll tax rate. This would be sufficient to eliminate the tax bias against both individual insurance and against direct patient payment. This policy would reduce health insurance coverage but increase wages and employment.
   b. Replace the exclusion of employer-provided health insurance with a revenue-neutral tax credit. Broaden the credit to individual policies (to eliminate the current bias against individual policies) and to medical savings accounts (to eliminate the bias against direct payment). This policy may or may not reduce health insurance coverage and would require some other change in spending or taxes to offset the revenue loss of the broader tax credit.
2. Changes in the benefit structure of the major federal health insurance programs should also be considered. Three changes merit special attention:
   a. Income-test the deductible for both Medicare and Medicaid, maybe at 7.5 percent of adjusted gross income (the same rate as in the current federal tax code). This would gradually reduce the benefits of both programs as a function of the recipient's income.
   b. Eliminate the prohibition on balance billing on medical services reimbursed by Medicare. This would transform the Medicare reimbursement rates from price controls into lump

sum payments, increasing the incentive of providers to serve Medicare patients and the incentive of patients to choose low price providers.

c. Allow the state governments almost complete flexibility in designing the Medicaid benefit structure, eliminating most of the federal mandates as well as the restrictions on the use of federal funds from AFDC, food stamps, and other welfare programs. The case for decentralizing the decisions on these policies is powerful, primarily because of the uncertainty about the most effective combination of those measures in any jurisdiction.

3. Finally, most of the political demands for broader health insurance seem to be based on a concern about those who are both uninsured and uninsurable. We are a rich and generous nation, and we should help these people. In fact, state governments have already designed an effective if mis-designed policy to provide health insurance coverage to this group. At present, 28 states have created high-risk insurance pools for those who have been denied coverage based on some severe preexisting condition. The premium on such high-risk pool insurance is typically set up to 50 percent higher than for comparable coverage to the healthy people, and the states provide small subsidies to make these pools financially viable. The premium caps are set moderately high, and they have been quite effective both to encourage those affected to find other coverage and to limit the level of the subsidy. A hard-liner would say that state governments can solve this problem without any federal policy, and they are correct. A political realist might conclude that we would be fortunate to limit the demands for new health insurance subsidies to provide coverage to this group.

I will leave you to surmise what may be my own personal preferences among the several types of federal health policies that should be considered.

5. The Economic Basis for Military Capability

On occasion, I agree to write a paper to discover what I think about some issue. This is one of those occasions. And I ought to have something to say about the economic basis of military capability. I am an economist with 40 years of professional experience, the first 13 years of which were as a defense analyst. For all that, I am much less confident about my judgment of this issue than as a young defense analyst. A part of what shaped my present perspective were some key events that happened in the meantime. Five of the eight nations that developed nuclear weapons, for example, had a GNP that was a small fraction of the U.S. GNP. A much poorer Soviet Union developed the first satellites and some technologically impressive weapons systems. And U.S. military forces, to be blunt, lost the war in Vietnam to the forces of a nation with a GNP that was a tiny fraction of the U.S. GNP. There is a reasonable basis for concluding that the U.S. economic capability to fund a substantial military buildup in the 1980s contributed to the collapse of the Soviet Union, but in this case there are more plausible hypotheses than facts. Maybe my present uncertainty about this issue is a consequence more of learning than of forgetfulness. Maybe.

The Issues

The first question at issue is the following: what are the effects of economic conditions on the level and type of resources committed to the military?

This article was presented at a conference at the Center for Institutional Reform and the Informal Sector at the University of Maryland in November 1997 and was first published in *Institutional, Economic, and Organizational Basis of Military Capability*, ed. Anthony Lanyi and Kimberly Brickell (College Park, MD: The IRIS Center, University of Maryland, 1999). My thanks to the IRIS Center for its permission to republish this article.

This question is subject to fairly simple research, based on the experience over time in one country or a comparison of the record among a set of countries. The only conceptual challenge is to identify and control for other conditions that also affect the demand for military forces. The second question is much more difficult to address: what are the effects of the level and type of military forces on the level of military capability? Some understanding of the answers to both of these questions is necessary to answer the primary question at issue: what are the effects of economic conditions on the level of military capability? This paper presents some empirical results bearing on the first question and some plausible speculations about the other questions.

The revived interest in these issues seems to be based primarily on whether we should welcome or worry about the high economic growth in China and the expected recovery in Russia. At most, this paper can provide only the most general guidance on this issue. A more precise response to these specific concerns requires attention to the specific conditions in China and Russia and other considerations that are likely to affect the behavior of their governments.

The Available Data

My first reaction on deciding to write this paper was to bury myself in the unclassified data on *World Military Expenditures and Arms Transfers* recently published by the U.S. Arms Control and Disarmament Agency. This annual publication presents aggregate data on military and economic conditions, now for 172 countries through 1995. Military conditions are summarized by data on the number of active military personnel and by the level of military expenditures. The primary economic condition of interest is the level of the gross national product. The data on military expenditures and the GNP are both presented in millions of U.S. dollars; these dollar estimates are subject to considerable "noise," reflecting the problems of estimating both the military budget and national output of other countries and their dollar equivalent. As a rule, the dollar equivalent is based on the purchasing power parity basis for the currencies of largest countries and the average exchange rate for the smaller countries. The other variable of interest is the total population of the country. My focus is on the sample of 149 countries for which data for each of these four variables are available for 1995.

The Research Technique

My first objective is to estimate the effects of per capita GNP on three major dimensions of military capability: the number of active military personnel, the level of the military budget, and whether a country has at least some nuclear weapons. In order to isolate these effects, it is also necessary to control for other conditions that also affect these target conditions. For each country, thus, I control for the alliance or regional groups of which the country is a part and the total population of the country.

Four major alliance or regional groups are considered:

1. The United States, the other NATO countries, and the other countries to which the United States has made a security commitment,
2. Russia and the other countries of the former Soviet Union or Warsaw Pact,
3. other communist or former communist countries, and
4. all countries in the Middle East from Libya through India.

These groupings are identified by (1,0) dummy variables with a value of 1 if the country is in a specific group and 0 otherwise; the coefficients on these dummy variables are estimates of the effects of being in these specific groups relative to the average of all countries not included in any of these groups.

These several effects are estimated by weighted least-squares regressions on the sample of 149 countries for which data on all of these conditions are available for 1995. The common weight is the total population of each country; this has the effect of making the estimates much more accurate for the largest countries, even at the expense of somewhat less accurate estimates for the smallest countries.

Separate regressions, thus, are estimated for the three target conditions:

1. *LAMP* natural log: number of active military personnel
2. *LMEX* natural log: dollar level of military expenditures
3. *NWD* nuclear weapons dummy

Each of the three regressions, in turn, include the following common independent variables:

1. *C* constant
2. *USD* United States dummy
3. *SUD* Soviet Union dummy
4. *OCD* Other communist dummy
5. *MED* Middle East dummy
6. *LPCY* natural log: per capita GNP
7. *LPOP* natural log: total population

Although my primary interest is estimating the coefficients on per capita GNP, the estimates of the other coefficients are also of considerable interest.

Estimates of the economic and other effects on the major dimensions of military capability are summarized by Table 5.1.

First, a word about how to read this table. The coefficient on a group dummy is the proportionate increase in the target variable associated with a country in that group; the (population-weighted) number of military personnel in the U.S. group, for example, is 72 percent higher than if that country were not a member of any of these groups. The coefficients on *LPCY* and on *LPOP* are the "elasticities" of the target variables with respect to per capita GNP and total population; the (population-weighted) level of military expenditures, for example, increases by about the same percent as the percent increase in per capita GNP. The ratio of the coefficient to its standard error indicates the statistical significance of the coefficient; all of these coefficients, with the sole exception of the effect of per capita GNP on the probability that a country has some nuclear weapons, are highly significant. The R-squared statistic is the proportion of the variance of the target variable that is explained by the set of independent variables, and the S.E.R. statistic is the standard error of the unexplained residuals; notice that the S.E.R. of the population-weighted regression is substantially smaller in each case than the S.E.R. for the unweighted sample.

Military Personnel

The strongest effect on the number of active military personnel is the size of the total population but this effect, with an elasticity of .63, is less than proportionate. In contrast, the effect of per capita GNP, with an elasticity of .18, is relatively small, the net effect of an increase in the demand for military forces and an increase in the price of military personnel. One should not expect, therefore, that

Table 5.1
ESTIMATES OF THE EFFECTS ON MILITARY PERSONNEL, MILITARY EXPENDITURES, AND NUCLEAR WEAPONS

	Target Variables		
Independent Variables	*LAMP*	*LMEX*	*NWD*
C	0.976	−3.996	−1.246
	(0.368)	(0.393)	(0.244)
USD	0.722	0.412	0.541
	(0.17)	(0.181)	(0.113)
SUD	1.408	1.527	0.775
	(0.153)	(0.163)	(0.101)
OCD	1.154	0.433	0.352
	(0.105)	(0.112)	(0.07)
MED	0.822	0.54	0.426
	(0.113)	(0.121)	(0.075)
LPCY	0.182	1.035	0.002
	(0.047)	(0.05)	(0.031)
LPOP	0.627	0.933	0.265
	(0.036)	(0.038)	(0.024)
Weighted Statistics			
R-Squared	0.999	0.999	0.988
S.E.R.	0.581	0.62	0.385
Unweighted Statistics			
R-Squared	0.604	0.851	—
S.E.R.	1.087	0.906	0.692

NOTE: Numbers in parentheses are the standard errors of the coëfficients.

a combination of slow population growth and high economic growth leads to a substantial increase in military personnel.

Somewhat more surprising, several years after the end of the Cold War and the breakup of the Soviet Union and the Warsaw Pact, is that the level of military personnel is still strongly dependent on the regional or defense group of which the country is a part, with proportionate effects ranging from .72 for the U.S. group to 1.41 for those countries in the former Soviet group. These effects reflect some combination of continuing security concerns and a lagged response to the realities of the post–Cold War world.

Military Expenditures

The strongest effects on the level of military expenditures are the per capita GNP and the total population of the country, each with roughly unitary elasticities. An increase in total GNP, thus, is likely to lead to a roughly proportionate increase in military expenditures. Military expenditures are still strongly dependent on the regional or defense group of which a country is a part, with proportionate effects ranging from .41 for the U.S. group to 1.53 for the former Soviet group.

Nuclear Weapons

The strongest general effect on whether the government of a country has some nuclear weapons is the total population of the country; a country with twice the population of another has a 26 percent higher probability of having some nuclear weapons. More surprisingly, the level of per capita GNP has *no* significant effect on whether a country has some nuclear weapons. The probability that a country has some nuclear weapons is also dependent on the regional or defense group of which the country is a part, with probabilities ranging from 35 percent for the other communist group to 78 percent for the former Soviet group.

Some Speculation about the Military "Production Function"

The next step is to identify the relation between military capability and the major dimensions of military forces. This has been the task of military analysts and historians for many years, of course, but most such analysis is focused on specific conflict conditions. There is no relevant database to estimate a general military "production function" and, possibly, no meaning to this concept. My task, nevertheless, is to discuss the economic basis for military capability, so some speculation about the relation of military capability to the major dimensions of military forces is necessary to address this issue. For this reason, I have used the concept of a production function to estimate an index of military capability. The general form of this production function is the following:

$IMC = ae^{bNWD} AMP^{c} MEX^{d}$, where
IMC is an index of military capability,
NWD is the nuclear weapons dummy,
AMP is the number of active military personnel, and
MEX is the level of the military budget.

My speculation concerns the choice of parameters for this function. The parameter *a*, of course, is arbitrary; I have chosen values for this parameter so that the *IMC* for the United States is 100. For the parameter *b*, I have chosen a value of .095 so that the control of some nuclear weapons increases the *IMC* by 10 percent. For the parameters *c* and *d*, I have chosen two sets of values that are most likely to bracket military reality. For the *IMCA* index, both parameters are set at a value of 0.5.

For the *IMCB* index, the parameter *c* is set at a value of 2/3 and the parameter *d* at a value of 1/3. For the *IMCA* index, thus, the marginal proportionate effect of an increase in military personnel is the same as an increase in total military expenditures, and this index may better represent the capability for combat some distance from the home country. For the *IMCB* index, the marginal proportionate effect of an increase in military personnel is twice the effect of an increase in military expenditures, and this index may better represent the capability for sustained combat on or near the home country.

The alternate production functions, thus, are as follows:

$$IMCA = .0042ge.^{09SNWD} AMP^{.5} MEX^{.5}$$
$$IMCB = .01010e.^{095NWD} AMP^{(2/3)}\ MEX^{(1/3)}$$

Table 5.2 presents the index of military capability for selected countries based on each of these production functions.

As indicated by Table 5.2, the rankings of military capability are the same on each index (with the exception of South and North Korea), but the relative military capability of the poorer countries is higher on the second index. I will leave the reader to judge the index that may be more accurate.

Estimates of the Effects on the *Indices* of Military Capability

The final step is to estimate the effects of economic and other conditions on the indices of military capability. For this purpose, I

Table 5.2
The Index of Military Capability

Selected Countries	IMCA	IMCB
United States	100.0	100.0
Russia	48.6	58.9
China	64.3	90.8
Taiwan	10.1	13.5
South Korea	13.2	18.5
North Korea	10.7	18.8
Britain	13.1	13.5
France	23.1	25.5
Germany	16.3	17.4
Japan	14.9	14.4

use the natural log of *IMCA* and *IMCB* as the target variables and the same set of independent variables as in the first set of regressions.

Table 5.3 presents the weighted least-squares estimates of these effects, again using the total population of each country as the weighting variable.

The strongest effect on military capability is the total population of a country; a country with twice the population of another country, controlling for other conditions, should be expected to have a military capability 75 to 80 percent higher. The level of per capita GNP also has a strong but somewhat smaller effect; a country with twice the per capita GNP of another country, again controlling for other conditions, should be expected to have a military capability 47 to 61 percent higher. The ratio of the economic effect to the population effect, as expected, is higher the stronger the relative effect of military expenditures on military capability.

The effects of the four group dummies are surprisingly invariant to differences in the production function, probably because the variance of per capita GNP within each group is lower than the variance among the groups. A substantial part of the variance of military capability appears to be attributable to the regional or defense group of which the country is a part. Compared to countries that are not part of any of these four groups, the (population-weighted) index

Table 5.3
ESTIMATES OF THE EFFECTS ON MILITARY CAPABILITY

	Target Variables	
Independent Variables	LIMCA	LIMCB
C	−7.081	−5.395
	(.373)	(.370)
USD	.619	.670
	(.172)	(.171)
SUD	1.542	1.522
	(.155)	(.154)
OCD	.827	.947
	(.106)	(.106)
MED	.721	.769
	(.115)	(.114)
LPCY	.609	.467
	(.048)	(.047)
LPOP	.805	.754
	(.036)	(.036)
Weighted Statistics		
R-Squared	.999	.998
S.E.R.	.588	.588
Unweighted Statistics		
R-Squared	.792	.792
S.E.R.	.889	.927

NOTE: Numbers in parentheses are the standard errors of the coefficients.

of military capability is 62 percent higher for countries in the U.S. group, about 150 percent higher in the former Soviet group, about 90 percent higher in the other communist group, and 72 percent higher in the Middle East group. Some part of these group effects may reflect continuing security concerns, but some part surely reflects a lagged response to the change in conditions after the Cold War. My guess, maybe my hope, is that each of the group effects will be smaller in another five years.

Other Plausible Economic Effects on Military Capability

Enough data mongering; time for some pure speculation about other plausible economic effects on military capability. The composition of the economy differs as a function of per capita GNP and population, and these differences may affect military capability. The rich economies, for example, have a smaller share of the labor force in agriculture, forestry, and manufacturing; this may reduce the pool of fit young men with simple manual skills but increase the number with advanced technical skills. The share of the economy involved in international trade is also smaller as a function of the total population of the country; this may reduce the dependence of the largest countries on alliances to maintain the necessary imports.

Other conditions may jointly affect economic conditions and military capability. The social, economic, and political rules and institutions that favor economic growth may either weaken or strengthen military capability. For years, conservative strategic analysts have worried that rich countries risk "going soft," with a population less able to endure the rigors of combat, less responsive to orders, less willing to risk casualties. Maybe so. On the other hand, such countries are likely to have a larger pool of potential combatants who are tactically resourceful and strategically creative. More important, the conditions that favor economic growth are likely to make the population more supportive of the necessary military measures to maintain these conditions. Many countries are poor because the government is little more than the dominant local protection racket; such conditions do not promote loyalty beyond the group that specially benefits from this racket.

What are the lessons from history that bear on these other plausible relations between economic conditions and military capability? First, it is difficult to distinguish between the effects of economic conditions and the nature of the political regime. Over the past 150 years, most of the rich countries have also been democracies. During this period, there have been almost no wars between democratic governments, and the rich democracies have prevailed in most conflicts. Germany, Japan, and the Soviet Union, under totalitarian regimes, supported formidable military forces that did not prevail in the long run. This is encouraging but not inevitable. For example, the record of U.S. military forces in Korea and Vietnam, in combat with forces from very poor communist countries, was not impressive.

Conclusion

Military capability, controlling for other conditions, is likely to increase at about half the rate of per capita economic growth. But other conditions are not constant. Most important, the conditions that sustain economic growth are likely to make a country less threatening, even if they increase its potential military capability. For those who either welcome or worry about the high economic growth rate of China and the expected recovery of Russia: we should both welcome such economic growth *and* be very watchful about its side effects.

6. Creating Good Jobs and Good Wages

All in all, this seems like a strange time to be concerned about good jobs and good wages in the American economy. Total civilian employment has increased about 175,000 a month for more than seven years, and the employment rate is at a record high. As of October 1999, the unemployment rate was 4.1 percent, the lowest since the late 1960s, and the median period of unemployment was only 6.4 weeks. The number of major strikes has declined to an annual rate about one-tenth that of the 1960s. Although the growth of productivity and average real compensation was sluggish for many years, both have increased at a 2+ percent annual rate since 1995. Moreover, the inflation rate is at its lowest level since the early 1960s, increasing the prospect that these conditions may continue indefinitely. Current macroeconomic conditions in the United States are the envy of the world.

Now is an appropriate time, however, to focus on the longer-term trends and perceived problems in the U.S. labor market. Two conditions merit special attention:

1. The annual increases in (measured) productivity and average real compensation were unusually low in the period from 1974 through 1995.
2. The variance of wages by skill level increased substantially during this same period.

These two trends and the government policies that might affect them are the focus of this chapter.

This article was presented at a conference at the Aspen Institute in August 1998 and was first published in *A Working Nation: Workers, Work, and Government in the New Economy*, ed. David T. Ellwood (New York: Russell Sage Foundation, 2000). My thanks to the Russell Sage Foundation for its permission to republish this article.

Major Developments Affecting Employment and Earnings

Changes in consumer demand and relative productivity have led to substantial changes in the composition of employment. Agricultural employment declined from about 10 percent of total employment in the mid-1950s to less than 3 percent in the 1990s. Over this same period, employment in goods-producing industries, transportation, and public utilities declined from about 50 percent of nonagricultural employment to about 25 percent, and union membership declined from about 35 percent of private employment to about 10 percent (but increased substantially among government employees). The change in the composition of employment, in turn, is a major cause of both the rapid increase in employment opportunities for women and the decline in union membership.

Changes in the composition of employment, of course, may also affect average compensation, even if the relative compensation among sectors has not changed. The substantial reallocation of employment from agriculture, the goods-producing industries, transportation, and public utilities to the more heterogeneous service sector, however, does not appear to be a major cause of the increased variance of wages. (Valletta 1997a) Changes in production techniques that increase the demand for skilled workers appear to be the major cause. Early studies estimated the contribution of technological change only by a process of elimination, but recent direct evidence supports their conclusions. (Johnson 1997)

We seem to be at the dawn of a third industrial revolution, one based on the rapid development of digital technology and biotechnology. Applications for U.S. patents, for example, nearly doubled from 1985 to 1995. One important puzzle, however, must be sorted out. The past few decades have witnessed a rapid development of both information technology and biotechnology. From 1974 through 1995, however, the rate of growth of (measured) productivity was unusually low, and the variance of earnings by education increased. If these new technologies are so important, why were they not reflected in the productivity data? Why would new technology increase the variance of wages?

There are several answers to this puzzle. One answer is that our measures of output growth are biased downward for the same reasons that our measures of inflation are biased upward—inadequate measures of the value of new products, quality improvements, and product and outlet substitution. The Boskin Commission, for example, estimated that the consumer price index overstates the inflation rate by about one percentage point. Although this estimate has been the subject of some dispute, there is widespread agreement among economists that inflation has been overstated to some extent, which means that the real earnings of Americans have been rising faster than reported by the current statistics and that low-income workers in particular may not be suffering as large an erosion in their real earnings as has been commonly believed.

One issue that the Boskin Commission did not address is whether the inflation bias has increased over time, which some observers believe has occurred. If, however, the bias has been roughly constant over the past few decades, actual productivity growth has been higher than the measured rate but has declined by the same amount. In any case, whether or not the real earnings of low-skill workers have increased or declined, the variance of earnings has increased.

A more comprehensive answer is that slower growth of measured productivity and a higher variance of earnings may be characteristic of the early stages of a major technological change. Careful studies of the industrial revolutions in Britain and the United States find that measured productivity growth declined and the variance of earnings increased for the first 20 to 40 years after the introduction of the steam engine and, later, electrical power. (Greenwood 1997) Only later did major productivity benefits show up as firms and individuals learned how to use the new technologies to make old things in new ways and to come up with new things entirely. To be sure, the microprocessor has been with us for a quarter century, but firms and individuals are still learning to adapt to it, and most of its benefits probably lie in the future.

The two hypotheses that best fit this evidence have interesting implications for understanding recent experience: measured output understates actual output because it does not include the substantial investment involved in learning how to use the new technology. Educated workers have an advantage in implementing new technology, but the relative demand for educated workers will decline as the stock of learning increases. All of this suggests that measured U.S. productivity growth should increase and the variance of earnings should decline, as indeed has happened in the past few years. The puzzling combination of current economic conditions may be a basis for optimism that these recent conditions will continue.

Over the past 25 years, the share of international trade in U.S. gross domestic product roughly doubled. This has led many commentators, including some economists, to conclude that the increased variance of wages may be a consequence of increased international trade. And this relation is quite plausible. Increased trade increases the demand for high-skill labor that is more abundant in the United States than in the rest of the world and increases the effective supply of low-skill labor that is more abundant in the rest of the world than in the United States. The coincident increase in the variance of wages in the United States and the increase in unemployment in Europe suggests that increased international trade may cause problems for low-skill workers in high-wage countries, with the nature of these problems depending on the characteristics of each labor market.

Most trade economists tend to minimize the effect of trade on the increased variance of wages. As evidence, they note that most low-skill labor works in service sectors not directly affected by trade, that the relative prices of low-skill-intensive goods have declined only slightly, and that the relative employment of high-skill labor has increased in most sectors. At most, trade economists attribute only 10 to 20 percent of the increase of wage variance to increased trade. In contrast, some labor economists claim that the increase in imports of manufactured goods from low-wage countries has also induced part of the technological change in the traded goods sector, has indirectly reduced wages in other sectors, and may explain 50 to 100 percent of the increase of wage variance.

Both of these groups, however, reject protectionism in favor of skill development as the appropriate policy response. This issue is complex and contentious and is unlikely to be resolved soon, either among economists or in the policy community. For the moment, I share the judgment of Richard Freeman, who, summarizing a symposium on income inequality and trade, concludes, "trade matters, but it is neither all that matters nor the primary cause of observed changes" (Freeman 1995, 30).

A related and similarly contentious issue is the increase in immigration. Again, it is plausible that the increase in immigration, mostly from low-wage countries, may have reduced the real wages of low-skill labor in the United States. A recent survey of the empirical studies on this issue, however, concludes, "The weight of the empirical evidence is that immigration to the United States has not contributed much to reducing wages for low-skill native workers nor to changes in overall wage inequality" (Topel 1997, 5).

A neglected dimension of the plausible causes of the increased variance of wages is the change in the job-related skills and attitudes at any level of education. The available data on high school students who aspire to college are very disturbing. The average composite Scholastic Aptitude Test score declined substantially from the mid-1960s to 1980 and has since recovered only slightly. In 1995, 41 percent of freshmen at public two-year colleges and 22 percent of freshmen at public four-year colleges were required to take at least one remedial course. Apparently, a high school degree does not represent an adequate preparation for college.

Less is known about the change in job skills of those who do not attend college, but the indirect evidence is even more disturbing. A study of the wage variance among countries in the Organization for Economic Cooperation and Development (OECD) observed that the skills of those at the bottom of the U.S. wage distribution are lower than those of similar workers in Europe (Blau and Kahn 1996). The dramatic change in family structure clearly has contributed to a number of problems, including poor school performance, employment problems, and crime. From 1960 through 1995, for example, the percentage of births to single mothers increased from 2 to 25 percent among whites and from 22 to 70 percent among blacks. Many job skills are learned on the job, but the employment rate for young black males declined from 52 percent in 1954 to 28 percent in 1998. These demographic and employment trends have not yet been reversed and are likely to cast a shadow on the potential wages of low-skill workers for many years. An absolute reduction in job-related skills must explain some of the decline in the real wages of low-skill workers, although, to my knowledge, no direct estimate of this effect has been made.

One related development during this period merits more attention. Although the variance of wages by skill level increased, the variance of wages by sex and race declined. The wage differential between men and women fell from 37 percent in 1984 to 24 percent in 1995. At the same time, the wage gap narrowed from 27 to 18 percent, respectively, for white and black males and from 9 to 6 percent, respectively, for white and black females (Lerman 1997). In that sense, the American wage structure has become more meritocratic—more a function of acquired skills and less a function of conditions of one's birth.

Finally, changes in labor market institutions may explain part of the increased variance of wages. Three conditions have been studied: the decline in the percentage of private employees covered by union contracts, the decline in the real minimum wage, and the substantial reduction of economic regulation. One recent study attributes about one-third of the increase in the variance of wages during the 1980s to these conditions—with deunionization an important condition for men, the decline in the real minimum wage more important for women, and no significant effect of the reduction of economic regulation (Fortin and Lemieux 1997). One caveat is that this study ignores the employment effects of lower unionism and lower real minimum wages. Total employment increased rapidly during these years, especially for women, so the effect of these conditions on the variance of earnings is likely to be smaller than the effect on the variance of wage rates.

What Should Be Done about These Developments? A Personal Perspective

My strongest inclination is to reject the European model for the U.S. labor market. Although conditions differ somewhat among the European countries, the most important common characteristics of the European labor market are centralized wage-setting processes, government restrictions on firing, and relatively generous unemployment benefits of extended duration. The first characteristic leads to a compression of wages at the bottom of the wage distribution, increasing the lowest wages relative to the median wage; this increases the earnings of those employed, reduces the incentive of workers to improve their skills, and reduces the incentive of employers to hire the least skilled: The restrictions on firing also reduce the incentive to hire, transforming labor from a variable input into a capital input. The third characteristic reduces the incentive of the unemployed to find another job. The combination of these characteristics leads to low employment growth, high unemployment rates,

Table 6.1
EMPLOYMENT CONDITIONS IN EUROPE AND THE UNITED STATES, 1985–1995 (PERCENTAGE)

	Civilian Employment		Unemployment Rate	
Country	Rate 1995	Change 1985 to 1995	Rate 1995	Unemployed More Than One Year
France	48.8	3.3	11.7	45.6
Germany[a]	49.7	6.5	6.5	48.3
Italy	41.8	−2.4	12.0	62.9
Spain[b]	44.2	9.4	23.8	56.5
United Kingdom	56.7	6.2	8.8	49.8
United States	62.9	16.5	5.6	9.7

SOURCE: OECD figures, 1997.

[a] Former Federal Republic of Germany only.

[b] Rate in 1994 and change from 1984 to 1994.

unusually high long-term unemployment rates, and high government expenditures for unemployment and welfare. Table 6.1 summarizes these conditions for the major European countries and the United States.

Since 1995 employment conditions in Europe and the United States have continued to diverge. As of August 1999, the standardized unemployment rate was 9.2 percent in OECD Europe and only 4.2 percent in the United States. European labor policies have reduced the variance of wages in the bottom half of the wage distribution, but only at a great cost in employment conditions. I doubt that many Americans would prefer this combination of wage and employment conditions.

In that case, what, if anything, should be done about the increased variance of wages in the United States? There is a reasonable case that nothing should be done. People do not have a property right to the *value* of their skills and other assets. Moreover, they have no inherent right to claim a share of the income of other people who may have benefited relatively more from market developments. Any consensus on redistribution must be based on either the *ex ante* consent of the larger community regarding the rules for redistribution or the *ex post* consent of those from whom the transfers are made. There is a reasonable basis for assuming that "behind the veil of ignorance," most Americans would agree to some rule for redistribution, although the Constitution now provides no authority for such a rule. There is also a reasonable basis for assuming that those who benefit most from life's lottery would agree to some amount of some type of redistribution. One implication of either the contractarian or libertarian perspective, however, is that transfers should be focused on those near the bottom of the distribution for reasons largely not of their own choosing. This suggests that the proper focus is on the wages of the least skilled, not on the variance of wages. A reduction of the post-tax-and-transfer variance of wages may be an effect of the preferred policy but should not be its goal.

Finally, my priority is to remove those government barriers that restrict the opportunities of the least skilled. Such measures have the best prospect of being positive-sum games for all those with the relevant rights.

One of the two most important American domestic policy issues in the next several decades will be a profound reform of the organization of kindergarten through 12th-grade schooling. (The other major issue, the transition to a sustainable retirement income and health insurance program, must be faced by most of the OECD countries.) A growing concern about the quality of U.S. public schooling led to the creation of numerous official commissions, most notably summarized by a 1983 report, *A Nation at Risk*: "The educational foundations of our society are presently being eroded by a rising tide of mediocrity that threatens our very future as a Nation and a people" (National Commission on Excellence in Education 1983, 63). These commissions promoted a laundry list of reforms in the public school systems that are still under way, for the most part with little net benefit. For 50 years, real spending per student in the public schools has increased nearly 40 percent a decade, but most measures of student performance, especially for students in inner-city public schools, are lower now than in the mid-1960s.

In parallel with these commissions, fortunately, a number of scholars completed careful studies of the comparative performance of students in public and private schools, the most important of which was by James Coleman and his colleagues (Coleman, Hoffer, and Kilgore 1982). All of the comparative studies found that the cost per student is substantially smaller in Catholic schools than in public schools in the same area. The most controversial of the Coleman findings is that the performance of students from disadvantaged backgrounds is substantially higher in Catholic high schools than in inner-city public high schools. The most counterintuitive of the Coleman findings is that Catholic schools are more integrated by race than the characteristic public school that draws students only from the local area.

The Coleman study provoked a furious response from the educational community, but its primary conclusions have been confirmed by the broader body of "effective schools research" and have now become conventional wisdom. Building on this research, an influential 1990 book by two Brookings scholars made the case for a general system of tax-financed vouchers in which "Schools would be legally autonomous: free to govern themselves as they want, specify their own goals and methods, design their own organizations, select their own student bodies, and make their own personnel decisions. Parents and students would be legally empowered to choose alternative schools, aided by institutions designed to promote active involvement, well-informed decisions, and fair treatment" (Chubb and Moe 1990, 226). Since that time, a growing number of scholars and officials have endorsed some form of education voucher system.

And small tax-financed voucher programs are now under way in Milwaukee and Cleveland. In Milwaukee, about 1,500 children from low-income families get about $4,700 each to attend private secular schools, a program initiated in 1991. In Cleveland, about 1,300 children receive vouchers of up to $2,500 each to attend either secular or religious schools, a program initiated in 1996. The early experience led the state legislatures in both Wisconsin and Ohio to expand these programs, but the expansion has been delayed pending resolution of constitutional challenges initiated by the teachers' unions.

Both of these programs have been subject to careful testing. In Milwaukee, the average voucher student had reading scores 5 percentage points higher in the fourth year than public school students with similar backgrounds and had math scores 12 percentage points higher. A study of two schools in the Cleveland program found average gains in the first year of 5 percentage points on reading tests and 15 percentage points on math tests (Peterson and Hassel 1998). Moreover, a recent study of the broader experience with school competition indicates that "competition from private schools does not have a significant effect on public school spending per pupil [and] that if private schools in an area receive sufficient resources to subsidize each student's tuition by 1,000 dollars, then the achievement of public school students is higher, regardless of whether it is measured by test scores, ultimate educational attainment, or wages" (Hoxby 1998, 8).

A related development has been the rapid growth of privately financed school voucher programs for children of low-income families. These programs characteristically finance half or more of the tuition at private schools for children of poor households. In 1998 there were 36 such programs with more than 12,000 students enrolled and many times that number on waiting lists. In June 1998 two leading businessmen offered a challenge grant of $100 million to expand these programs by about 50,000 students. There has yet to be an evaluation of these private voucher programs other than the testimony of many grateful parents.

The barriers to tax-financed voucher programs may be reduced soon. In June 1998 the Wisconsin Supreme Court approved a plan to expand the Milwaukee voucher program to include church-affiliated schools, but this decision will surely be appealed. On that same day, Congress approved a tax-free education savings account that parents could have used for private school tuition if the bill had not been vetoed. My judgment is that school choice will expand quickly and will prove to be the most effective policy to improve the quality of elementary and secondary schooling and to restore the inner city.

Vocational Training and the Transition from School to Work

In the United States the transition from school to work has little structure and is not very effective, but there is little agreement on what might work better. Training systems based on the German model might seem to be an attractive alternative; in the countries that use this system, a majority of those ages 16 through 19 spend most of the workweek in work site training, augmented by 1 or 2 days of related school studies. In Germany, more than 20 percent of employers participate in this system, and about 60 percent of young people choose their vocation and their first job based on these apprenticeships. American educators and employers, however, both reject the German model, reflecting a concern about the early tracking and narrow vocational specialties that characterize this system.

A recent report by an employers group, for example, recommends a combination of improved general academic standards, the development of interactive skills based on actual or simulated work experience, and a network of intermediary organizations that link schools and employers, but the report acknowledges that the limited experience with this model is not encouraging (Committee for Economic Development 1998). My guess is that the American school-to-work transition process will continue to be unsatisfactory. The only effective alternatives seem to be either better general academic training or earlier tracking to work-based vocational training.

American employers, again, prefer employees with better general academic skills to those with school-based vocational training. According to a recent survey, the proportion of American businesses providing remedial basic education for employees increased from 18 percent in 1984 to 43 percent in 1995; these costs could be saved if school performance were better (Smith 1996). More specific vocational training is best provided on the job, and American businesses would provide more vocational training if not for the unusual turnover among young workers. The average American worker has held more than seven jobs by age 29. The major alternative policies to induce a more optimal amount of vocational training are tax-financed training programs and some form of indenture contract to reduce turnover. Tax credits and wage subsidies, however, have not proved to be an efficient policy for encouraging employers to participate in training programs (Office of Technology Assessment 1995).

And the many government training programs for low-skill workers, except for adult women, also have a discouraging record (Friedlander, Greenberg, and Robins 1997). For much of American history, most young employees, especially immigrants, worked under an indenture contract for a period until their employers recouped the costs of transportation and training. This practice has largely disappeared, except for expensive specialized military and medical training, maybe because an employee who chafes at the indenture is not worth maintaining, maybe because the courts will no longer enforce an indenture contract. In any case, the once-common arrangement for providing vocational training is no longer acceptable, the many new experiments with tax-financed training have not been effective, and the losers have been those who leave school without either good academic or work skills. On this issue, I have yet to read a creative proposal.

Opportunities for the Least Skilled

Many government policies affect the employment and earnings opportunities of the least skilled. The most important of these is the earned income tax credit (EITC), a federal program that augments the earnings of workers in low-income households. For a household with two or more children, in 1996 this program subsidized earnings at a 40 percent rate up to an annual income of $8,890 and phased out this subsidy at a 21 percent rate on incomes above $11,610. This program has a high participation rate, low administrative costs, an undesirably high rate of overclaims, and an annual budget cost of about $28 billion. It has been especially effective in helping women substitute work for welfare. Over the phaseout range, however, many EITC recipients face a combined marginal tax rate of more than 50 percent—the sum of the phaseout rates for EITC and food stamps, the payroll tax rate, and the federal and state income tax rates—a rate that significantly reduces work, especially by secondary workers in low- to middle-income households. The cost of this program has increased rapidly and the political support has narrowed, but the EITC should be considered an essential component of welfare reform.

Other measures that would increase the opportunities for low-skill workers include the repeal or rejection of government barriers to work. A repeal of the minimum wage should be at the top of the list. The misleading rationale and tortured evidence for the minimum wage no longer merit serious attention. An increase in the minimum wage would significantly reduce the legal employment of the least-skilled workers, probably by about 0.2 times the percentage increase in the real minimum wage, and most of the benefits of the wage increase would accrue to secondary workers in nonpoor households. For the same reason, the government should reject the recurrent proposals for mandates on employers to provide health insurance, family leave, and other benefits that would disproportionately increase the cost of hiring the least-skilled workers. One local government measure that would especially help the more entrepreneurial of low-skill workers would be to repeal the limits on the number of taxicabs and street vendors and on the licensing of certain occupations such as barbers and beauticians.

Labor Law

Most of my remaining suggestions bear on what policies should *not* be approved in the name of good jobs and good wages. Labor law is a good place to start. For the most part, the U.S. labor market works very well. Over the past several decades, however, a gradual erosion of the "employment at will" doctrine, largely by state courts, has contributed to significant differences in employment growth by state. In effect, this doctrine set the default rule on firing; in the absence of an explicit labor contract, employers were presumed to have the right to fire any employee without cause and without notice. In effect, the accumulation of exceptions to this doctrine substituted a state-designed labor contract for the pattern of explicit and implicit private employment arrangements and increased the expected cost of hiring new employees. State legislators should evaluate the effects of these exceptions on labor market conditions in their state.

One recent development in federal labor law merits attention. Over the past several years, the National Labor Relations Board has declared that "quality circles" in several nonunion firms are in fact company unions and therefore illegal under the Wagner Act. (Quality circles are problem-solving work teams focused on improving quality or productivity.) This represents an artificial restriction on a structure of work relations that has proved both productive and popular in other firms. These decisions should be reversed. At the same time, it is important to reject the recurrent proposals to mandate or subsidize changes in the structure of work relations. Decision sharing or profit sharing may increase productivity in some firms, but there is no reason to expect the government to have superior information about these effects or for a specific structure to be best for all firms.

Macroeconomic Policy

The record of the past 40 years should be sufficient evidence of a *positive* relation between unemployment and inflation in the long term. The primary policy implication of the new macroeconomics is that monetary policy should be designed to stabilize a path of aggregate demand such that the expected inflation rate is about zero. Fiscal policy should be designed for long-term objectives, not as an instrument of discretionary macroeconomic policy.

Social Policies

A range of social policies could have important effects on the number and economic prospects of low-skill workers. The most important social policy objective, I suggest, would be to reduce the number of births to single mothers—a condition that now contributes to low school performance, employment problems, and a high crime rate; I have yet to read a creative proposal to address this condition. Young workers, especially blacks, and two-worker households should expect a very low return from social security; allowing workers to divert most of their payroll tax to personal retirement accounts would especially benefit these groups. Social services to low-wage workers, such as those employed in childcare, should be provided, if at all, by a tax-financed, means-tested subsidy, not by mandates on employers.

Taxes

Several changes to the federal income tax should also be considered. Increasing the personal exemption would sharply reduce the marginal tax rate faced by those with wages in the phaseout range for the EITC and other benefits. The federal income tax, like the Social Security retirement program, is also biased against the two-worker household, by making the marginal tax rate of the second worker dependent on the income of the first worker; broadening the 15 percent tax bracket may be the most efficient way to reduce this bias. The tax treatment of health insurance is still biased against the self-employed, permitting a deduction of only 40 percent of the premiums in 1997, with this deduction scheduled to increase to 80 percent by 2006. A broader reform would be necessary to provide equal tax treatment of the self-employed and employees not covered by an employer plan. In general, these tax changes would be most important for those trying to move up into the middle class.

A more general tax reform would be necessary to reduce the severe bias against saving and investment and the misallocative effects of a complex tax base and multiple tax rates.

Trade and Immigration

Finally, a growing chorus of commentators has promised to protect American workers against increased international trade, investment, and immigration. So far, as long as total employment is growing, there has been little popular response to this noisy crowd. This group, however, represents a potentially harmful coalition of the populist left and right when the U.S. economy next turns down. The policies proposed by this group to limit international trade and investment should be strongly rejected in favor, if necessary, of measures to assist those workers who are specifically threatened by the global economy. Similarly, proposals to restrict immigration should be rejected in favor, if necessary, of an increase in the share of skilled workers in the total immigration quotas.

Conclusion

In general, the American labor market works very well—with a low unemployment rate, a rapid reallocation of labor in response to changes in demand and supply, and compensation that is closely related to productivity. Over the past several decades, however, the outcomes of the U.S. labor market reflected two major new conditions: from 1974 through 1995, the growth of (measured) productivity and average real compensation were unusually low, and the level of real compensation and, probably, the skills of the least-skilled workers declined. The primary causes of these two conditions are not fully understood, but both conditions can be reduced or alleviated by identifiable changes in public policies. We need both a broader understanding of the strengths of the U.S. labor market and a broader consensus for the policy changes that would improve the outcomes of this market.

References

Blau, Francine D., and Lawrence M. Kahn. (1996) *Wage Inequality: International Comparisons and Its Sources.* Washington: AEI Press.

Chubb, John E., and Terry M. Moe. (1990) *Politics, Markets, and America's Schools.* Washington: Brookings Institution Press.

Coleman, James S., Thomas Hoffer, and Sally Kilgore. (1982) *High School Achievement: Public, Catholic, and Private Schools Compared.* New York: Basic Books.

Committee for Economic Development. (1998) *The Employer's Role in Linking School and Work.* New York and Washington: Committee for Economic Development.

Fortin, Nicole M., and Thomas Lemieux. (1997) "Institutional Charges and Rising Wage Inequality: Is There a Linkage?" *Journal of Economic Perspectives* 9(3): 15–33.

Freeman, Richard B. (1995) "Are Your Wages Set in Beijing?" *Journal of Economic Perspectives* 9(3): 15–33.

Friedlander, Daniel, David H. Greenberg, and Philip K. Robins. (1997) "Evaluating Government Training Programs for the Economically Disadvantaged." *Journal of Economic Literature* 34(4): 1809–55.

Greenwood, Jeremy. (1997) *The Third Industrial Revolution: Technology, Productivity, and Income Inequality.* Washington: AEI Press.

Hoxby, Caroline M. (1986) "The Economics of School Reform." *NBER Reporter* (Spring): 6–12.

Johnson, George E. (1997) "Changes in Earnings Inequality: The Role of Demand Shifts." *Journal of Economic Perspectives* 11(2): 41–54.

Lerman, Robert I. (1997) *Meritocracy without Rising Inequality?* Washington: Urban Institute Press.
National Commission on Excellence in Education. (1983) *A Nation at Risk*. Washington: National Commission on Excellence in Education.
Office of Technology Assessment. (1995) *Learning to Work*. Washington: U.S. Congress.
Peterson, Paul E., and Bryan Hassel. (1998) *Learning from School Choice*. Washington: Brookings Institution Press.
Smith, Nelson. (1996) *Standards Mean Business*. Washington: National Alliance of Business.
Topel, Robert H. (1997) "Factor Proportions and Relative Wages: The Supply-Side Determinants of Wage Inequality." *Journal of Economic Perspectives* 11(2): 55–74.
Valetta, Robert G. (1997) "The Effects of Industry Employment Shifts on the Wage Structure, 1979–1995." *Economic Review* 1: 16–32.

7. Should the Ex-Im Bank Be Retired?

The U.S. Export-Import Bank is now 65 years old and should soon be retired—but not before completing one remaining task. As summarized in an appendix to the annual *Budget of the United States Government* for Fiscal Year 2001:

> The purpose of the Export-Import Bank (Em-Im Bank) is to aid in the financing and promotion of U.S. exports. To accomplish its objectives, the bank's authority and resources are used to: assume commercial and political risks that exporters or private institutions are unwilling or unable to undertake; overcome maturity and other limitations in private sector export financing; assist U.S. exporters to meet officially sponsored foreign export credit competition; and provide leadership guidance in export financing to the U.S. exporting and banking communities and to foreign borrowers.

My assessment of the Ex-Im Bank is complicated only by a tension between two of the above objectives. On the one hand, I regard the market-failure rationale for Ex-Im as wholly spurious, and the activities based on this rationale are best described as "Aid to Dependent Corporations."

The "Market-Failure" Rationale

Let me be the first to acknowledge that private credit markets are not perfect. The fact that private credit is sometimes not available on terms that a potential foreign buyer and U.S. exporter would prefer, however, is not sufficient evidence of a market failure. The

---

This article was presented at a conference at the Institute for International Economics in May 2000 and was first published in *The Ex-Im Bank in the 21st Century: A New Approach?* ed. Gary C. Hufbauer and Rita M. Rodriguez (Washington: Institute for International Economics, 2001). My thanks to the Institute for International Economics for its permission to republish this article.

terms on which credit is available from a private lender reflect the costs, taxes, and regulations to which that lender is subject; its assessment of the commercial and political risks of a specific loan; and the expected return on alternative loans. In a competitive credit market among lenders that face the same costs and alternatives, the best terms will be offered by the potential lender that is *most optimistic* about the commercial and political risks of a specific loan. The lack of private credit on terms acceptable to a foreign borrower is not an example of market failure but an important signal of the risks of lending to that borrower, even by the Ex-Im Bank.

In rare cases, some activity in another country generates sufficient benefits to the United States to merit some U.S. subsidy. Such cases might include an increase in the military equipment of a U.S. ally or an investment that improves the U.S. environment in some way. In such cases, however, it is important to recognize that the external benefit of these activities is independent of whether the equipment is purchased from a domestic firm, a U.S. firm, or a third-country firm. In other words, the benefit to the United States is a function of the level of some foreign activity, not of the purchases from a U.S. firm. U.S. interests are best served by purchases from the most efficient supplier. Such cases may merit some U.S. military or environmental assistance, but not Ex-Im credit. More often than not, however, the external-benefits argument is only a thinly disguised rationale for another export subsidy; in fiscal year 1996, for example, the U.S. government spent $7.9 billion to help U.S. companies secure just over $12 billion in agreements for new international arms sales (Hartung 1999).

As a rule, there is no reason to expect the value of Ex-Im credit to be higher than the opportunity cost of the private credit that it displaces. No external benefits are specific to U.S. exports, and the managers of the Ex-Im Bank do not have better incentives or more accurate information than the managers of private financial institutions. Two government agencies with a reputation for careful analysis and language have concluded that it is highly doubtful that the Ex-Im Bank generates any net benefits to the U.S. economy. A Congressional Research Service study (cited by George Kourous and Tom Barry of the Interhemispheric Resource Center, 1996, 3) noted:

> Most economists doubt . . . that a nation can improve its welfare over the long run by subsidizing exports. Internal

> economic policies ultimately determine the overall level of a nation's exports. . . . By providing financing or insurance for exporters, Ex-Im Bank's activities draw from the financial resources within the economy that would be available for other uses. Such opportunity costs, while impossible to estimate, potentially could be significant.

Similarly, a senior official at the U.S. General Accounting Office testified:

> Government export finance assistance programs may largely shift production among sectors within the economy rather than raise the overall level of employment in the economy.

Does this sound too good to be true? That is because it *is* too good to be true. There is no way to meet these noncommercial policy objectives without a subsidy. Although these market window operations receive no annual appropriation, the commercial export credit agencies (ECAs) borrow at little more than the cost of funds to the government, and they pay little taxes and no dividends. The U.S. financial institutions that most closely approximate these commercial ECAs are the several huge government-sponsored enterprises that now dominate the mortgage market, which are financed by a total debt that will soon be larger than the explicit debt of the federal government. Gillespies invites us to consider the commercial ECAs not a "competitive threat, but rather an opportunity. It is an opportunity to embrace a model that ultimately addresses customer needs—exporter and foreign buyers alike." As an American, I can hardly imagine worse advice than to create another huge government-sponsored enterprise, in this case to provide general trade finance.

The "Other Governments Do It" Rationale

I share the broader concern that U.S. firms should not have to compete with governments, either at home or abroad. Moreover, I apply this standard to both exporters and financial institutions. U.S. exporters should not have to compete with foreign firms that are supported by subsidized credit from other governments. And U.S. financial institutions should not have to compete with an export credit bank financed by our own government. A "level playing field" among the national export credit agencies is a necessary condition to meet the first criterion. Reducing the common level of export credit subsidies, preferably to zero, is the necessary condition to meet the second criterion. A fine essay by Peter Evans and Kenneth Oye concludes that

> the United States competes on a reasonably even footing on terms, conditions, and implicit levels of subsidization in formal ECA activities regulated under the [1978] OECD Arrangement and in sectors regulated by annexes to the Arrangement. The U.S. strategy of regulation and retaliation has been a qualified success. But in areas that are not regulated under the Arrangement, U.S. practices differ markedly from those of other industrial countries. And many of these differences operate to the detriment of potential U.S. exports.

Fortunately, the governments of the countries that belong to the Organization for Economic Cooperation and Development have recognized that competition among the export credit agencies serves no one's interests and is costly to taxpayers. The OECD Arrangement, in that sense, is similar to an arms control agreement, an attempt to constrain counterproductive, costly competition. The Arrangement, moreover, has been unusually effective in constraining competition in the broad area that it covers. As with any arms control agreement, some governments have initiated or maintained favorable terms in areas where the Arrangement is silent, subject to interpretation, or not enforced. But in my judgment, the areas not covered by the Arrangement seem relatively minor.

The important issue is where we should go from here. Maintaining common terms on subsidized export credit protects our exporters but is still costly to our taxpayers. What is the best strategy to reduce the current roughly equal level of export credit subsidies? As developed in Robert Axelrod's elegant book *The Evolution of Cooperation* (Axelrod 1984), the best opening move in a prisoner's dilemma game (of an uncertain number of plays and in which no one play is "lethal") is a cooperative move, made in hopes of eliciting cooperative moves by the other players in response. In a similar spirit, Evans and Oye write:

> Even without substantial U.S. pressure, Japanese and European positions may evolve toward the American position in some areas. This is particularly true for project risk and untied ODA, because of growing internal financial constraints. The growing Japanese fiscal crisis and continuing

> European budgetary constraints have already compelled reappraisals of the more expensive export financing activities discussed above. European and Japanese countermeasures against each other are having an effect. Even without aggressive U.S. matching, it seems likely that the next financial crisis in emerging markets may become an object lesson on the virtue of conservative project risk standards.

So the first move should be a unilateral *reduction* of U.S. export credit subsidies, accompanied by a commitment to a series of further reductions if the governments of the other OECD nations respond in kind and in magnitude.

Axelrod further counsels that subsequent moves should be on a tit-for-tat basis. If the other governments respond cooperatively, our government should make another reduction of export credit subsidies, and so on. If the other governments, however, do not respond with a corresponding reduction of their export credit subsidies, some countermeasure by the U.S. government is the appropriate next step. The most effective countermeasure may not be the restoration of the prior level of U.S. export credit subsidies. This conventional response puts the few foreign firms that would benefit from maintaining a differential export credit subsidy at odds only with their taxpayers, a contest that the taxpayers usually lose.

My suggestion is to change the nature of the U.S. countermeasure—*from* a measure that merely neutralizes a differential export credit subsidy by some government in third markets *to* a measure that penalizes all exports from that country to the U.S. market. Such a measure, for example, might be a uniform 10 percent incremental U.S. tariff on all goods and services imported from any country for which the government maintains an export credit subsidy in third markets. This response would put the few firms that would benefit from maintaining a differential export credit subsidy at odds with all firms from that country that export to the U.S. market, a contest that the few firms would usually lose.

The U.S. government has a huge, almost unique advantage in implementing this type of response: For most countries, the benefits of general "most favored nation" access to the huge U.S. market are much larger than the benefits to those few firms with exports that are supported by a credit subsidy in third markets. In effect, this measure would apply a countervailing duty to all imports by the

United States from any country for which the government maintains subsidized export credits in third markets. This type of U.S. response, of course, would require the approval of other governments belonging to the World Trade Organization for a narrow exemption from the most-favored-nation standard of world trade—but the benefits would be substantial to all countries. This measure, I suggest, is the only type of U.S. response that has any prospect of leading to progressive reduction, and possible elimination, of export credit subsidies by all governments.

The Export-Import Bank was established in 1934, initially to provide export credit to the Soviet Union. The Soviet Union has collapsed, and there is now an opportunity to end the continuing cold war of export credit subsidies. At such time that the U.S. government is prepared to broaden the use of countervailing duties as the countermeasure for export credit subsidies by other governments, the Ex-Im Bank should be retired with the rare honors due an agency that has actually completed its major mission.

References

Axelrod, Robert. (1984) *The Evolution of Cooperation.* New York: Basic Books.

Evans, Peter, and Kenneth A. Oye. (2001) "International Competition in Government Financing." In *The Ex-Im Bank in the 21st Century: A New Approach?* ed. Gary Clyde Hufbauer and Rita Rodriguez, 113–58. Washington: Institute for International Economics.

Hartung, William D. (1990) "Corporate Welfare for Weapons Makers: The Hidden Costs of Spending on Defense and Foreign Aid." Cato Institute Policy Analysis no. 350.

U.S. General Accounting Office. (1997) "Key Factors in Considering Ex-Im Bank Reauthorization." Testimony by JayEtta Hecker to the Subcommittee on Banking, Housing, and Urban Affairs.

8. On the Death of the Phillips Curve

There is no evidence of a Phillips curve showing a trade-off between unemployment and inflation. The function for estimating the nonaccelerating inflation rate of unemployment (NAIRU) has been incorrectly formulated. Indeed, the unemployment rate is a positive function of the inflation rate with a lag of a year or two. An alternative formulation of the relation between unemployment and inflation leads to an estimate that the NAIRU is about 3.7 percent and can only be achieved by a sustained inflation rate of zero. Moreover, this relation appears to have been stable for over four decades.

The Simple Relation between Unemployment and Inflation

For several decades now, macroeconomists have confused each other, generations of students, and too many policymakers by their search for the elusive Phillips curve, a presumed negative relation between unemployment and inflation (Phillips 1958). For a while, U.S. data beginning in the late 1950s seemed consistent with the hypothesis that there is an inherent trade-off between the unemployment rate and the inflation rate. The Phillips curve became the critical link between the nominal (current dollar) variables and the real (inflation-adjusted) variables in the new macroeconomic models developed during this period and was the basis for recommendations that policymakers should choose that point on this relation that minimizes the sum of the costs of unemployment and inflation. And since the cost of unemployment always seemed larger and more urgent to reduce than the cost of inflation, this perspective contributed some part of the rationalization for the policies that led to the higher inflation rates of the 1970s.

This article was first published in the *Cato Journal* 22, no. 2 (2002). My thanks to the *Cato Journal* for its permission to republish this article.

Figure 8.1
WHERE IS THE PHILLIPS CURVE?
1960–2001

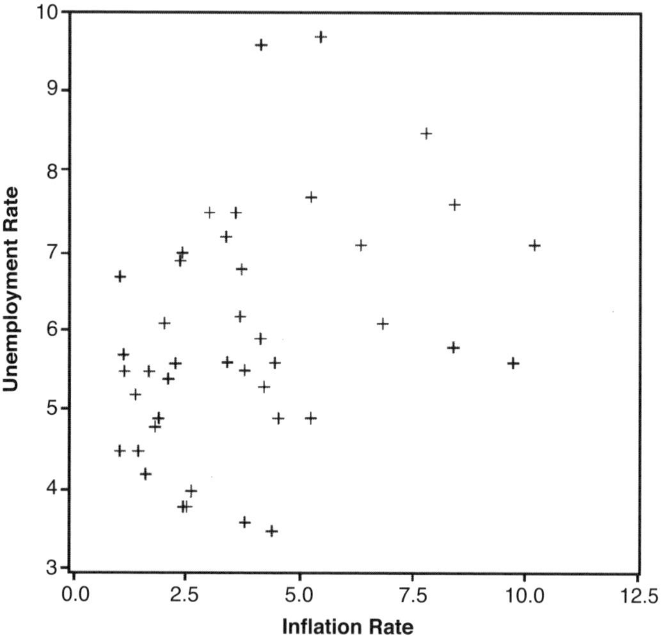

But a strange thing happened on the road to this social engineering nirvana: Both inflation and unemployment increased in the 1970s, a condition that came to be described as "stagflation." This provoked an unproductive search for what might have caused the Phillips curve to shift; the favorite explanation at the time was the oil shock of the mid-1970s. But there was no obvious explanation consistent with a Phillips curve for the nearly continuous reduction of both unemployment and inflation after 1982. The futility of this search is illustrated by Figure 8.1, which presents the raw data on the unemployment rate and the inflation rate by year for the years 1960 through 2001, a relation that is close to white noise. The concept of a Phillips curve should be considered empty when most of the variation in the data must be explained by shifts in this presumed relation. In any case, the Phillips curve proved to be a poor basis for forecasting and a worse guide to policy.

Figure 8.2
THE ELUSIVE NAIRU
1960–2001

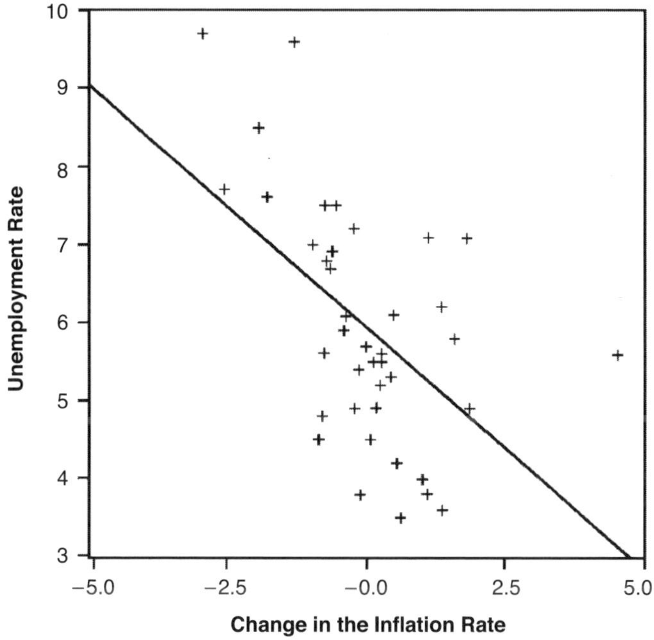

The Elusive Search for the NAIRU

A more productive development was the reformulation of the Phillips curve by Ed Phelps (1967) and Milton Friedman (1968) as a negative relation between the unemployment rate and the change in the inflation rate. This formulation implies that the unemployment rate would decline in response to an increase in the inflation rate but would be invariant to any steady-state rate of inflation. As Figure 8.2 illustrates, there was at least a weak negative relation of the unemployment rate and the change in the inflation rate over the past four decades. This formulation led to a search for the lowest unemployment rate that could be maintained without an increase in the inflation rate, a number described by that dreadful acronym NAIRU.

Figure 8.2 suggests that this rate is about 6 percent, but it also reveals that there has been a wide range of unemployment rates

Figure 8.3
THE LONG-TERM RELATION
1960–2001

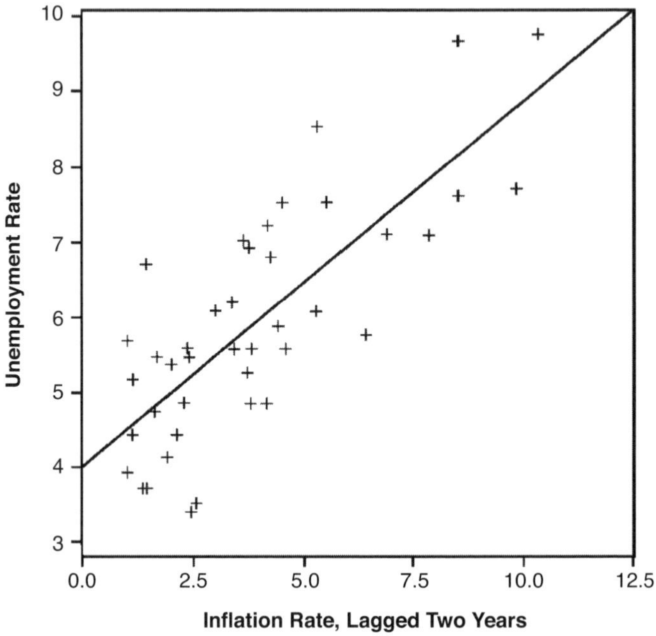

consistent with little change in the inflation rate. The U.S. unemployment rate, for example, ranged from 4 to 6 percent since 1994 with little variation in the inflation rate. The uncertainty about the NAIRU also led to an unproductive search for what may have caused this relation to shift and reduced its value as a guide to policy.[1]

The Long-Term Relation between Unemployment and Inflation

The most important lesson from this examination is that there is a strong positive relation between the unemployment rate and the inflation rate lagged one or two years, as illustrated by Figure 8.3, a condition that Milton Friedman anticipated in his 1976 Nobel lecture (Friedman 1987). This finding is inconsistent with both the Phillips curve and the NAIRU reformulation of the relation between unemployment and inflation. There are at least several plausible reasons for a positive long-term relation between unemployment and inflation.

First, since the tax code is not fully indexed, inflation increases effective tax rates, especially on the income from capital, and thus reduces output and employment. Second, inflation may confuse the relative price and wage signals on which an efficient labor market is dependent. Third, after a year or so, a high rate of inflation may trigger monetary restraint that temporarily increases the unemployment rate. The relative magnitude of these and other possible effects is not now known, but it is important not to dismiss this clear evidence of a positive long-term relation of unemployment and inflation.

A New Alternative Formulation

The relation between the unemployment rate and the inflation rate is better described by the following model:

$$(1) \qquad U^* = a - bI + cI_{-1} + u$$

$$(2) \qquad (U - U_{-1}) = d(U^* - U_{-1}) + v$$

$$(3) \qquad U = ad - bdI + cdI_{-1} + (1 - d)U_{-1} + (du + v).$$

Equation 1 expresses the equilibrium unemployment rate as a negative linear function of the current inflation rate and a positive linear function of the inflation rate lagged one year; this would be identical to the NAIRU relation if the coefficients b and c are equal. Equation 2 expresses the rate of change of the unemployment rate as a linear function of the difference between the equilibrium rate and the unemployment rate in the prior year; the actual rate converges on the equilibrium rate by the coefficient d per year. Equation 3, thus, is the result of inserting Equation 1 into Equation 2 and then solving for U.

An ordinary least-squares regression on Equation 3 yields the following:

$$(4) \qquad U = \underset{(.450)}{1.487} - \underset{(.086)}{.229}I + \underset{(.091)}{.464}I_{-1} + \underset{(.077)}{.594}U_{-1} + (du + v)$$

Adjusted R-squared = .814

S.E.R = .642

Durbin-Watson = 1.955.

The sample is annual U.S. data from 1960 through 2001. The lessons from this regression are that there is a small negative relation between unemployment and inflation in the same year, a larger positive relation with the inflation rate in the prior year, and that the unemployment rate adjusts only slowly to the equilibrium rate. All of the coefficient estimates are strongly significant, and this relation appears to have been stable over the whole sample.

An estimate of Equation 1 can then be derived from the above regression, yielding the following:

$$U^* = 3.672 - .564I + 1.144I_{-1} + u. \qquad (5)$$

The important lessons from this equation are that the level of the NAIRU has been stable over this period at about 3.7 percent, and that the only steady-state inflation rate consistent with this level of the unemployment rate is a zero rate.

Conclusion

The major lessons of this examination for macroeconomic policy are the following:

- There is no trade-off of unemployment and inflation except in the same year.
- In the long term, the unemployment rate is a positive function of the inflation rate.
- The minimum sustainable unemployment rate is about 3.7 percent, and can be achieved only by a zero steady-state inflation rate.

In conclusion, a monetary policy targeted to achieve a steady growth of aggregate demand at a zero inflation rate is also consistent with the lowest possible sustainable unemployment rate.

References

Friedman, M. (1968) "The Role of Monetary Policy." *American Economic Review* 58 (March) 1–17.

______. (1987) "Inflation and Unemployment." (The 1976 Nobel Lecture.) In *The Essence of Friedman*, ed. K. R. Leube, pp. 347–69. Stanford, CA: Hoover Institution Press.

Phelps, E. S. (1967) "Phillips Curve, Expectations of Inflation, and Optimal Unemployment over Time." *Economica* 34 (August): 254–81.

Phillips, A. S. (1958) "The Relationship between Unemployment and the Rate of Change of Money Wages in the United Kingdom, 1861–1857." *Economica* (November): 283–99.

"Symposium: The Natural Rate of Unemployment." (1997) *Journal of Economic Perspectives* 11, no. 1 (Winter): 3–108.

Note

1. For a summary of recent economic perspectives on this issue, see "Symposium: The Natural Rate of Unemployment," *Journal of Economic Perspectives* 11, no. 1 (Winter 1997): 3–108.

9. The Economic Burden of Taxation

The many burdens of government include those attributable to taxation, monetary policy, regulations, and restrictions on civil liberties. This paper is specific to the economic burden of taxation, without in any way minimizing the other types of burdens.[1]

The Model

The economic burden of taxation is a function of three conditions: the level of the average tax rate, the relation of the marginal tax rate to the average tax rate, and the response of the tax base to changes in the marginal tax rate.[2] Start with the basic relation of the size of the economy to the two major fiscal decisions:

$$Y = aG^b(1 - R)^c \quad (1)$$

where Y = GDP per potential worker,
G = expenditures for government services (excluding defense) per potential worker, and
R = the *average* tax rate.

The two major fiscal decisions, of course, are the level of expenditures for government services (excluding defense) and the level of the average tax rate. This equation is expressed in terms of output per potential worker to capture the effects of G and $(1 - R)$ on both hours worked per potential worker and on output per worker hour. The implicit assumption in this equation is that government expenditures for defense, transfer payments, interest payments, and subsidies have no significant net effect on the output per potential worker; there is ample evidence, of course, that most transfer payments

This article was first published in *The Legacy of Milton and Rose Friedman's Free to Choose: Economic Liberalization at the Turn of the 21st Century, Proceedings of a Conference Sponsored by the Federal Reserve Bank of Dallas*, October 2003, pp. 93–98. My thanks to the Federal Reserve Bank for its permission to republish this article.

reduce output per potential worker. The elasticity c, as I will demonstrate, reflects the combined effects of the relation of the marginal tax rate to the average tax rate times the elasticity of Y with respect to 1 minus the marginal tax rate. For the moment, pay no attention to the G variable; at the end of the paper, I will return to discuss the effects of the combination of G and R on the optimal size of government.

Given Equation 1, tax revenues per potential worker are

$$(2) \qquad T = RY = aG^bR(1 - R)^c$$

and the output per potential worker net of taxes is

$$(3) \qquad N = Y - T = aG^b(1 - R)^{(1+c)}.$$

The marginal economic burden of taxation, thus, is the change in net output per unit increase in tax revenues. Some manipulation of Equations 1 and 2 yields the following equation for the marginal economic burden:

$$(4) \qquad \delta N/\delta T = - [(1 + c)(1 - R)]/[1 - (1 + c)R].$$

Equation 4, plus the observed data for the average tax rate and an estimate of the elasticity c, thus, is sufficient to estimate the quantitative magnitude of the marginal economic burden of taxation. If the elasticity $c = 0$, of course, the reduction in net GDP is equal to the increase in tax revenues, and there is no deadweight loss of the additional taxes. The marginal cost of taxation, however, increases rapidly as a function of both c and R.

Before presenting my estimates of the relevant parameters, however, I promised to address the effects of the structure of the tax system, more specifically the relation between the marginal and average tax rates. A more precise formulation of Equation 1 would include the marginal tax rate M rather than the average tax rate R in the term in parentheses. For two reasons, however, I have chosen to use the average tax rate R: There are no available data on the income-weighted aggregate marginal tax rate or agreed procedures for estimating this rate. And, since $T = RY$, the average tax rate must be used in Equation 2, adding an undetermined variable to the model. If the marginal tax rate M, however, is a function of the average tax rate R, the average tax rate can be used in both equations. For example, if

(5) $$M = -x + yR,$$

then

(6) $$(1 - R)^c = (1 + x - yR)^z$$

and the relation between c and z is

(7) $$c = yz[(1 - R)/(1 + x - yR)].$$

The elasticity c, thus, is seen to be the product of the marginal effect of R on M and the marginal effect of $(1 - M)$ on Y. An increase in the elasticity c may reflect either an increase in the progressivity of the tax structure (the parameter y) or an increase in the adverse economic effect of the marginal tax rate (the parameter z).

The Elasticities

For this study, the elasticities b and c of Equation 1 are estimated by two independent techniques. The first technique is to estimate the long-term relation between fiscal choices and economic outcomes in the United States. For this purpose, several economic growth equations were estimated by two-stage least-squares regressions, based on a sample of annual U.S. data from 1964 through 1999. Equations were estimated for the annual change of three dimensions of economic growth:

1) real GDP per potential worker,
2) output per hour in the business sector, and
3) hours worked in the business sector per potential worker.

The primary fiscal measures in these regressions are the annual change in real expenditures for government services (excluding defense) per potential worker, 1 minus the average tax rate, and 1 minus the average tax rate in the second prior year. The first equation is sufficient to estimate the elasticities for this study, but the other equations were estimated to identify the relative effects of the fiscal choices on productivity and hours worked.

The second technique is to estimate the elasticities b and c that are implicit in the actual levels of G and R for the United States in 1996, given the model of the fiscal choices of democratic governments developed in my book. In effect, this involves solving my model of democratic government backward from the known fiscal choices in 1996 to the elasticities that are consistent with these choices. The

Table 9.1
ESTIMATES OF THE ELASTICITIES OF THE FISCAL EFFECTS ON ECONOMIC GROWTH

	Estimated	Implicit
b	.200 (.036)	.220
c (short run)	.748 (.127)	.772
c (long run)	1.212 (.164)	

NOTE: Numbers in parentheses are the standard errors of the estimates from the regression equation.

finding that the elasticities estimated by these two techniques are quite close may be an indirect validation of my model of the fiscal choices of democratic governments.

Table 9.1 presents the estimates of the elasticities of fiscal effects from these two techniques.

The other regressions on the changes in productivity and hours worked suggest that about half of the effect of tax changes on short-run economic growth operates through changes in productivity and about half through changes in hours worked. The estimated effect of the after-tax rate on hours worked is consistent with a large number of other studies, most of which have neglected to estimate the effect on productivity. In the long run, however, about two-thirds of the effect of tax changes on economic growth operates through changes in productivity, because there is no significant difference between the short-run and long-run effects on hours worked. The finding that the implicit estimate of the elasticity *c* is quite close to the short-run estimate from the time-series regression may suggest that our government takes into account only the short-run effects on output of changes in taxes.

The Marginal Economic Burden of Taxation

Now we can address the primary topic of this paper. Table 9.2 presents estimates of the marginal economic burden of taxation from Equation 4 for a range of the variable *R* and the elasticity *c*. These

Table 9.2
THE MARGINAL ECONOMIC BURDEN OF TAXATION

	R		
	.2	.3	.4
c			
.4	1.556	1.690	1.909
.8	2.250	2.739	3.857
1.2	3.143	4.529	11.000

numbers, again, are the marginal reduction in output (or income) after taxes per additional dollar of government tax revenue.

Given that the elasticity c implicit in recent U.S. fiscal conditions is about 0.8 and the average tax rate is about 0.3, the marginal cost of government spending and taxes in the United States may be about $2.75 per additional dollar of tax revenue. One wonders whether there are *any* government programs for which the marginal value is that high. Given the estimate of the long-term elasticity c from the U.S. time-series data, the marginal cost of government spending and taxes may be as high as $4.50 at the current average tax rate. The cost estimate in a benefit-cost study of any program financed by general taxes should be multiplied by the relevant number from this table. All of these estimates, of course, increase as a function of both c and R and approach infinity as R nears the revenue-maximizing tax rate.

Some Other Interesting Estimates

The model and the empirical estimates of Equation 1 also provide a basis for estimating several other interesting magnitudes: the revenue-maximizing average tax rate, the net output maximizing level of G, and the net excess burden of maintaining a 30 percent average tax rate given the optimal level of G.

The maximum average tax rate is determined from Equation 2 by setting the derivative of T with respect to R equal to zero; this yields the following equation for the maximum R:

$$R = 1/(1 + c). \tag{8}$$

As the equation indicates, the revenue-maximizing average tax rate declines with an increase in the elasticity c, whether caused by

Table 9.3
SOME OTHER INTERESTING ESTIMATES

	Maximum R	Optimal G/Y	Net Burden
c			
.4	.714	.143	.247
.8	.556	.111	.350
1.2	.455	.091	.437

an increase in the progressivity of the tax system or an increase of the elasticity of output with respect to 1 minus the marginal tax rate.

The level of G that maximizes net output is determined from Equation 3 by setting the derivative of N with respect to G equal to zero; this yields the following equation for the optimal ratio of G to Y:

$$G/Y = b/(1 + c). \tag{9}$$

As this equation indicates, the optimal domestic spending share of GDP increases with the elasticity b and declines with the elasticity c. This has always presented somewhat of a dilemma for tax reformers; a reduction of the progressivity of the tax structure is likely to lead to an increase in the relative size of government spending because it reduces the marginal cost of additional spending. My own suggestion is that approval of any broad-based, flat-rate tax reform should be accompanied by a change of the voting rule to require a supermajority vote for any subsequent increase in the base or rate.

The net excess burden of taxation is also estimated from Equation 3 by calculating the net output if $R = .3$ (roughly what it has been in the United States for some years) relative to the net output if R is sufficient to finance only the optimal level of G. This is a rough estimate of the loss of net output from setting an average tax rate sufficient to finance government spending for defense, transfer payments, and so on, in addition to the optimal level of G.

Table 9.3 presents these other interesting estimates for several levels of the elasticity c. All of the calculations of the optimal level of G/Y and the net excess burden are based on the elasticity $b = .2$, as there seems little uncertainty about this elasticity.

As expected, the revenue-maximizing average tax rate declines sharply with an increase in the elasticity c; this rate would be the peak of any Laffer curve expressed in terms of the average tax rate and is the ultimate limit on the sustainable level of government spending relative to GDP. The optimal level of expenditures for government services (excluding defense) relative to GDP also declines with an increase in the elasticity *c* but to a level that is not much lower than recent experience; in 2001, for example, government consumption expenditures and gross investment, excluding defense, were 14.5 percent of GDP. Given an estimate of the elasticity *c* that reflects the effects of the after-tax rate on both the supply of labor and on productivity, the optimal level of *G* is about 10 percent of GDP, a relative level of *G* that Milton Friedman has supported for many years. The net excess burden of taxation beyond that necessary to finance the optimal level of *G*, however, increases with the elasticity *c*. This column indicates that the net economic cost to the economy of a level of total spending and taxes beyond that necessary to finance the optimal level of *G* increases from about 25 percent of net potential output if $c = .4$ to about 44 percent of net potential output if $c = 1.2$. This does not suggest that there is no value to government spending above the optimal level of *G*, only that the net cost to the economy of this spending is much higher than the direct expenditures for these programs.

For those of you who may wish to pursue these issues in the larger context of the fiscal choices of alternative political regimes, I encourage you to read my book.

Notes

1. Most of this paper is a summary of some footnotes in my new book, *Autocratic, Democratic, and Optimal Government: Fiscal Choices and Economic Outcomes* (Cheltenham, U.K.: Edward Elgar, 2004).

2. The standard reference article on this issue is by Edgar K. Browning, "The Marginal Welfare Cost of Taxation," *American Economic Review* 77 (1987): 11–23.

10. Increasing Individual Responsibility Would Improve Retirement Security

Consideration of the current financial picture of the Social Security, Medicare, and Medicaid programs leads to the conclusion that increasing individual responsibility for retirement income and health care financing would actually bolster retirement security and reduce the cost to future taxpayers. In other words, the Ponzi scheme is over; there is no longer any politically feasible way to maintain retirement and health care security by tax-financed means.

The Looming Retirement Crisis

Social Security

According to the 2004 annual report of the Social Security trustees, Social Security now faces a net liability of about $12 trillion.[1] Benefits are expected to be higher than tax revenues by 2018, and the trust fund is projected to be exhausted in 2042, after which benefits will have to be reduced by about 27 percent. The tax increases or benefit cuts necessary to put Social Security on a sustainable basis are huge. Either the payroll tax would have to be increased from the current 12.4 percent to 19.4 percent by 2080, an equivalent amount of revenue would have to be raised through other taxes, or benefit provisions would have to be scaled back by an equivalent amount.

The tax increases or benefit reductions necessary to put Social Security on a sustainable basis, however, will not be enough to correct the major biases in the current system. Young workers will earn a rate of return of less than 2 percent, far less than what they could get in a private retirement account. For workers with the same

---

This article first appeared in *In Search of Retirement Security: The Changing Mix of Social Insurance, Employee Benefits, and Individual Responsibility*, ed. Teresa Ghilarducci, et al. (New York: The Century Foundation Press, 2005). My thanks to the Century Foundation for its permission to reprint this article.

earnings profile, Social Security is strongly biased against those, such as blacks, with a lower expected life span. And Social Security is most strongly biased against the increasingly prevalent two-worker families because the spousal benefit, equivalent to 50 percent of the retiree's benefit, favors single-earner families, especially those with higher salaries.

Medicare and Medicaid

According to the December 2003 report on "The Long-Term Budget Outlook" by the Congressional Budget Office, expenditures for Medicare and Medicaid are estimated to increase from 3.9 percent of GDP in 2003 to 11.5 percent in 2050, not even counting the increase in state government expenditures for Medicaid.[2] This may be an optimistic estimate, based on an assumption that annual expenditures per Medicare enrollee will increase only 1 percent a year faster than per capita GDP; in fact, annual expenditures per enrollee have increased 3 percent faster than per capita GDP since 1970, excluding the growth related to demographic changes. If annual expenditures per enrollee increase 2.5 percent faster than per capita GDP, federal expenditures for Medicare and Medicaid alone could be 21.3 percent of GDP by 2050. For comparison, total federal revenues have averaged 18.3 percent of GDP over the past 40 years. As the above estimates indicate, the projected increase in federal expenditures for health care is substantially larger than that for Social Security, overwhelms the rest of the federal budget, and will severely limit public tolerance of any tax increase to finance Social Security. Our political system, however, still seems committed to adding to federal medical expenditures, as indicated by the recent approval of prescription drug benefits for the Medicare program and the nearly unanimous endorsement of broader, tax-financed health insurance by the candidates for the Democratic presidential nomination.

Despite the huge increase in the projected federal spending for Medicare and Medicaid, there will still be substantial problems with each program. Both are defined benefit programs, and some potentially desirable treatments are never likely to be covered. Congress has often curtailed the increase in payment rates to providers, a form of price control that limits the access of some Medicare patients to some benefits. Federal matching of state spending for Medicaid makes federal expenditures dependent on the scope of benefits approved by state governments. And, despite the huge outlays for these programs, there are still about 40 million Americans who do not have any health insurance.

Some Suggested Alternatives

Social Security

In a July 1998 speech, President Clinton acknowledged that the only ways to keep Social Security solvent are to raise taxes, cut benefits, or garner a higher rate of return through private capital investment.[3] In testimony before the Senate in January 1999, Henry Aaron agreed that "increased funding to raise pension reserves is possible only with some combination of additional tax revenues, reduced benefits, or increased investment returns from investing in higher-yield assets."[4]

The Cato Institute has been promoting individual, private retirement accounts invested in higher-yield assets as an alternative to Social Security for about 25 years. Its distinguished advisory committee on privatization has recently approved a proposal with these provisions:

1. Individuals would be allowed to divert 6.2 percent of the payroll tax to privately owned investment accounts. Those choosing to do so would forgo all future accrual of Social Security retirement benefits.
2. The remaining 6.2 percent of the payroll tax would be used to fund disability and survivor's benefits and would contribute to funding the transition costs as well.
3. Workers choosing the individual account option would receive a zero-coupon "recognition bond" equal to 95 percent of the accrued value of their lifetime benefits to date. These bonds, redeemable at retirement, would be fully tradable in secondary markets.
4. Contributions to individual accounts would be initially deposited in a balanced fund of 60 percent stocks and 40 percent bonds. Workers would be allowed to choose from a wider array of investment options as the size of their accounts increased.
5. At retirement, workers could choose to purchase an annuity providing yearly income equal to 120 percent of the poverty

level, a programmed withdrawal option, or the combination of an annuity and a lump-sum payment.

6. The federal government would provide a safety net ensuring that no worker's retirement income would be below 120 percent of the poverty level. Workers whose accumulations under the private investment option fell below an amount required for purchasing an annuity of that level would receive a supplement sufficient to allow them to do so. This safety net would be financed from general revenues.
7. Those who wished to remain in the traditional Social Security system would be free to do so and would receive a level of retirement benefits payable on a sustainable basis, given the current revenue projections.

The Cato advisory committee proposal includes no explicit provision about how to finance the transition costs above dedicating the remaining 6.2 percent of the payroll tax. Even if this share of the transition costs is financed entirely by a temporary increase in the explicit federal debt, the sum of the explicit debt) would decline over time with the shrinking number of retirees receiving Social Security benefits.

Medicare and Medicaid

Most policy analysts, including those at Cato, are not yet ready to endorse a specific proposal to deal with the problems of Medicare and Medicaid. The reasons for the extraordinary growth of spending per enrollee are not very clear. The absolute magnitude of the projected expenditures suggests that no conventional reform would prove sufficient. The CBO report "The Long-Term Budget Outlook," for example, discusses a number of standard options for slowing spending growth and characteristically concludes that" . . . even relatively dramatic policy change would do little to address the long-term fiscal challenge facing Medicare."[5] And there still appears to be broad political support for tax-financed health insurance, at least for the retired and the poor.

An eyes-open perspective on this issue, however, suggests the following:

1. Broad, tax-financed health insurance is part of the problem, not part of the solution. The relative price of medical care has increased much more rapidly since 1965, apparently because

an increasing number of people now face lower prices for medical care, principally through third-party payment arrangements. The necessary condition to reduce the growth of tax-financed medical expenditures is that more individuals be exposed to higher prices for medical care.

2. Any tax-financed health insurance should take the form of a defined contribution plan (in which the insured receives a fixed amount of money rather than an open-ended entitlement to benefits) to replace both the Medicare and Medicaid defined benefit plans. Under a defined contribution plan, each individual, not some government agency or insurance company, chooses the treatment option on the advice of his or her physician. An individual's payment for medical care would depend on the price and number of treatments chosen and the plan's deductible and copayment, not on whether the treatment is covered benefit.
3. Each individual would choose his or her own defined contribution plan, insurance company, and physicians.
4. The primary fiscal support of these plans would be a lump-sum premium subsidy. The amount of this premium subsidy would decline with the individual or household income and increase with the individual's age. The primary fiscal decisions affecting these plans, thus, would be setting the income and age parameters of the premium subsidy. The one tax-financed defined benefit that it is tempting to maintain would be a lump-sum payment for one physician visit per year, in the expectation that this would reduce the third-party cost of contagious diseases.

As indicated by the general nature of the proposals presented here, there is still a long way to go in the process of working out the details of an alternative to Medicare and Medicaid. And Cato has yet to consider the problems of a transition from the current programs. On one issue, however, the Cato analysts agree: the current programs are fiscally explosive, so it is a matter of urgency to stop adding fuel to the fire.

Enhancing Retirement Security

Social Security

The proposal substitution of individual retirement accounts for Social Security would improve retirement security in several ways:

1. The average real rate of return on the proposed initial portfolio would be about 5 percent, based on the real returns for equities and corporate bonds and the administrative costs now assumed by the Social Security actuaries. This portfolio would be subject to some market risk, depending on the timing of the individual worker's retirement. A study of historical, long-term market returns by the Congressional Research Service, however, found that this portfolio would have outperformed Social Security for the vast bulk of all retirees since the late 1960s and would have earned only slightly less than the average real return to Social Security for the remainder.
2. The average real rate of return on Social Security is estimated to be about 2 percent for workers now age 30 and lower for future workers, assuming payroll taxes are increased to meet the promised benefits. This return, however, is subject to considerable political risk since reluctance to increase taxes may lead to some reduction in the benefits now promised (such as raising the age for full retirement benefits or the scope of the now restricted income tax on future benefits).
3. The individual retirement accounts would have several additional benefits. The rate of return on these accounts would not be biased against those with a shorter expected life span because any accruals in these accounts upon death would become property of the heirs. The rate of return on these accounts would not be biased against two-worker families, which could lead to greater labor force participation by the lower-wage spouse. And, as private property, these accounts would probably be subject to less political manipulation than promises of the government to which people have no legal claim.

Medicare and Medicaid

The proposed substitution of individual defined contribution health insurance policies for Medicare and Medicaid would enhance retirement security in several ways:

1. Each individual would choose his or her own health insurance plan, insurance company, and physicians. Individuals, on the advice of their physician, would choose the level and frequency of their medical treatments. An increasing number of these choices would no longer be biased by the nature and magnitude

of the tax-financed health insurance. These conditions would almost surely lead to a more efficient utilization of medical care, a lower rate of increase in the relative price of medical care, and a slower rise in tax-financed expenditures for medical care.

2. In contrast, there is no politically plausible prospect that the federal government would increase taxes by an amount sufficient to finance the indefinite extension of Medicare and Medicaid. As a consequence, the most likely political responses are restrictions on those eligible for these programs, the range of benefits, the approved providers of covered care, and the reimbursement rates of suppliers. Those who continued to be dependent on these programs would face a Soviet-style system of medical care: low quality, long waiting times, and situations in which complaining and political influence are the only ways to obtain satisfactory care.

Conclusion

There is no longer any acceptable trade-off of further government expenditures for retirement security and no way to bolster retirement security by increasing tax financing of retirement income and health insurance. The most promising way to better retirement security is to promote individual responsibility through major changes in policies that would also reduce the role of government and its outlays.

Notes

1. The *2004 Annual Report of the Board of Trustees of the Federal Old-Age and Survivors Insurance and the Disability Insurance Trust Funds*, Social Security Administration, March 23, 2004, http://www.ssa.gov/OACT/TR/TR04.pdf.
2. Congressional Budget Office, "The Long-Term Budget Outlook," December 2003, http://www.cbo.gov.showdoc.cfm?index=4916&sequence=0.
3. President Clinton, speech at the Concord Coalition/AARP Social Security Forum, town hall meeting, University of New Mexico, Albuquerque, July 27, 1998.
4. Henry J. Aaron, testimony before the Senate Subcommittee on the Budget 106th Congress, 2nd sess., January 19, 1999, p. 3.
5. Congressional Budget Office, "Long-Term Budget Outlook."

11. An Unnecessary War Is an Unjust War

The war in Iraq was unjust because it was unnecessary to protect the vital interests of the United States. Let me summarize the argument that I first made in a televised debate with James Woolsey, a former director of the CIA, on December 13, 2001.[1] That may have been the first public statement against the then prospective war in Iraq. At that time, like almost everyone else, I assumed that Iraq had some biological and chemical weapons. However, I had accepted the 1997 judgment of the International Atomic Energy Agency that "[t]here are no indications that there remains in Iraq any physical capability for the production of amounts of weapon-usable nuclear material of any practical significance."[2]

The subsequent failure to find any such "weapons of mass destruction" only strengthens the argument that I made in this debate.

1. There was no evidence that Iraq supported the September 11, 2001, attack on the United States.[3]
2. Iraq did not have the capability for a direct attack on the United States, lacking any long-range bombers or missiles or an ocean-going navy.[4]
3. Iraq's only capability to attack the United States would be to provide dangerous weapons to some terrorist group.[5] Four conditions, however, limited the relevance of this capability for an indirect attack:
   - The potential for an indirect threat from Iraq was in no way distinctive from that by a dozen or so other governments not friendly to the United States that were also presumed to have some dangerous weapons.[6]

This article is based on my televised debate with James Woolsey, a former director of the CIA, on December 13, 2001, and was first published in *NEXUS*, vol. 9, 2004. My thanks to NEXUS for its permission to republish this article.

- Iraq had no record of supporting al Qaeda or other terrorist groups '... of a global reach,' President Bush's own initial description of the potential targets for a U.S. response.[7]
- The leadership of al Qaeda regarded the secular Iraqi government as infidels for failure to impose a theocratic state.[8]
- Any terrorist attack that can be clearly traced to support by a national state could probably be deterred by a preannounced threat to retaliate. As it turns out, of course, Iraq did not have any "weapons of mass destruction" to arm some terrorist group.

4. A war in Iraq would probably weaken our capability for the far more important war against terrorism for the following reasons:
   - Critical intelligence resources would be diverted to support the war in Iraq, since the U.S. government had relatively few intelligence agents who speak Arabic and had a specialized knowledge of the region.[9]
   - A war in Iraq that is not supported by most other governments may reduce the willingness to share intelligence with us and to arrest or extradite suspected terrorists in their countries.
   - A war in Iraq may increase the incentive of militant Muslims to attack U.S. targets, both at home and abroad.
5. One major cost of a war in Iraq would be to weaken the general reservation against preventive wars that has been a part of international law since the 1648 Treaty of Westphalia.[10] At some future time, Iraq could be an imminent threat against the United States that would justify *preemptive* military action. However, that was not the case at the time, and Iraq was in no way distinctive from other countries that may someday pose an imminent threat.

What has happened in the past two years that would change my argument that a war in Iraq was unnecessary to protect the vital interests of the United States? Not much, I suggest. The failure to find any weapons of mass destruction weakens one of the major rationales for the war. The rapid destruction of the Iraqi army was evidence of the awesome capability of the U.S. military, but the unexpected period of extended guerilla combat weakens the case for the war. So far, fortunately, there has not yet been another terrorist attack in the United States. There was an attack on an American residential compound in Riyadh,[11] however, and, because we put our military in harm's way, daily terrorist attacks in Iraq, many of which are apparently by non-Iraqi fedeyeen.

One lesson is that the Bush administration and other supporters of the war were unwilling to be judged by any one rationale for the war. Instead, they invented some new "rationale of the month" as conditions developed. Some of the rationales were based on undisputed conditions that preceded the war:

- Saddam Hussein was a tyrant who was dangerous to the Iraqi people and to neighboring countries. The issues are why the overthrow of petty foreign tyrants is a vital interest of the United States and why Saddam was a priority.[12]
- Iraq clearly defied a number of U.N. resolutions.[13] But who made the United States the U.N.'s enforcer, especially since the U.N. did not endorse the recent war and the American public would not accept such a general responsibility?
- One of the recurrent rationales was based on fantasy—the prospect that a peaceful, prosperous, and democratic state in Iraq would have a positive domino effect throughout the region, resolving bitter and longstanding disputes—some of which go back to the Crusades, some to the creation of the state of Israel.

One spurious rationale that the second Bush administration fortunately did not make, in contrast to the position of the first Bush administration, is that the war in Iraq was necessary to protect our access to oil from the Middle East. Many of the critics of the war assumed that this was the dominant rationale, maybe because none of the other rationales seemed to make much sense.

The major long-term benefit of the war in Iraq, I suggest, is that it will substantially reduce the prospect that the United States will soon embark on another preventive war, even against the other nations that Bush identified as part of "the axis of evil."[14]

War is always an unjust *instrument* because the acts of war, by their nature, are not subject to the consent of the many innocent parties. For that reason, it is important to set a very high threshold of grievances to authorize a war, such as suggested by the Weinberger-Powell doctrine.[15] One of the minor tragedies of the war in Iraq is that Colin Powell was party to undermining this doctrine.[16]

But war and a credible threat of war may serve just ends, such as to preserve our own freedom and reduce the prospect of future wars. The major open question is whether replacing an oppressive foreign regime is such a just end that makes it one of our vital interests, even if that regime is not an imminent threat to the United States. So it is important to question whether each announced objective of a war is consistent with our vital interests, rather than deciding on a war and then rationalizing it on other grounds.

Again, the war in Iraq was unjust because it was unnecessary to protect the vital interests of the United States.

Notes

1. James Woolsey and William Niskanen, "Should the United States Go to War against Iraq?" debate, December 13, 2001, http://www.cato.org/events/011213pf.

2. International Atomic Energy Agency, *Fourth Consolidated Report of the International Atomic Energy Agency to the United Nations Security Council*, October 8, 1997, at 21.

3. The House Permanent Select Committee on Intelligence and the Senate Select Committee on Intelligence, *Report on the Joint Inquiry into the Terrorist Attacks of September 11, 2001*, H. Rpt. No. 107-792 (2nd Sess. 2002).

4. Hearing on the CIA National Intelligence Estimate of Foreign Missile Development and the Ballistic Missile Threat through 2015 Before the Senate Subcomm. on Int'l Sec., Proliferation and Fed. Services, 107th Cong. (March 11, 2002) (statement of Robert Walpole, CIA strategic and nuclear programs officer), available at http://www.senate.gov/gov_affairs/031102walpole.pdf (last visited February 1, 2004).

5. "Saddam's a Threat, but Is it Imminent?" *Orange County Register*, Feb. 6, 2003, available at 2003 WL 6986858.

6. Randall Forsberg, "Curbing Saddam Without War," *Boston Globe*, Mar. 15, 2003, available at 2003 WL 3385728.

7. John J. Mearsheimer and Stephen M. Walt, "An Unnecessary War," *Foreign Policy*, Jan. 1, 2003, available at 2003 WL 13316197.

8. Douglas Jehl, "The Struggle for Iraq: Washington Memo; More Proof of Iraq-Qaeda Link, or Not," *New York Times*, Nov. 20, 2003, (Late edition), at 18.

9. Susan Schmidt and Allan Lengal, "Help Still Wanted: Arabic Linguists, Agencies Rushed to Fill Void, But Found Screening New Hires Takes Time," *Washington Post*, Dec. 27, 2002.

10. The Treaty of Westphalia is a peace settlement enacted in 1648. This treaty ended the war between Spain, the Dutch, and Germany. It created sovereign territories that effectively weakened the power of the Holy Roman Empire and the Diet. "Peace of Westphalia," *Encyclopedia Britannica* (2004), at http://www.britannica/eb/article?eu=78730 (last visited Feb. 1, 2004).

11. Neil MacFarquhar, "Blast Shatters Housing Enclave in Saudi Capital," *New York Times*, Nov. 9, 2003, (Late edition), at 1.

12. Shibley Telhami, "Who Knows What a Desperate Saddam Might Do?" *Los Angeles Times*, Mar. 3, 1999 (Record edition), at 9.

13. U.N. SCOR, 4644th mtg. U.N. Doc. S/Res/1441 (2002).

14. President George W. Bush used the term "axis of evil" to describe the terrorist regimes. President George W. Bush, State of the Union Address, (Jan. 29, 2002), available at http://www.whitehouse.gov/news/releases/2002/01/2 0020129-11.html (Jan. 29, 2002).

15. The Weinberger-Powell Doctrine expresses the idea that the U.S. should only use military force for vital interests and should only be a last resort. Caspar W. Weinberger, *Fighting For Peace: Seven Critical Years In the Pentagon* (Warner Books, 1990).

16. Colin Powell currently serves as the U.S. Secretary of State. Additionally, Secretary Powell is a highly decorated Army General who was in charge of Operation Desert Storm.

12. Major Policy Lessons from the Corporate Scandals

Congress should

- clarify that the criminal penalties in the Sarbanes-Oxley Act (SOA) require proof of malign intent and personal responsibility for some illegal act;
- address the potential problem of the delisting of foreign and small firms from the American stock exchanges, maybe by exempting such firms from the regulatory requirements;
- *eliminate* the expensive and wholly unnecessary Public Company Accounting Oversight Board, preferably before it establishes new precedents and creates some special interest;
- consider the wholesale *repeal* of the SOA on the basis that it is unnecessary, harmful, and inadequate to address the major problems in the U.S. corporate economy;
- *eliminate* the current roles of the Financial Accounting Standards Board (FASB), the Securities and Exchange Commission (SEC), and Congress in setting accounting standards, allowing each stock exchange to set the accounting standards for corporations listed on that exchange;
- delay implementation of the FASB ruling that would require the expensing of stock options until the issue of the authority to set accounting standards is resolved;
- encourage the development of a parallel system of the primary *nonfinancial* indicators of the earnings potential of a firm;

This article was first published in the *Cato Handbook on Policy* 2005. This article briefly summarized the book for which I was the contributing editor, *After Enron: Lessons for Public Policy* (Lanham, MD: Rowman & Littlefield, 2004). My thanks to the Cato Institute for its permission to republish this article.

- allow each stock exchange to set the disclosure rules for corporations listed on that exchange, to select and monitor the independent public auditors of those corporations, and to establish a market for the voting rights in the shares of those corporations;
- consider broadening the certification provisions of the SOA to include the accountants, bankers, and lawyers who abet the misrepresentation of a corporation's financial condition;
- consider a rule that a lawyer must report a possibly illegal act by a corporate client to a senior partner in his firm and to the board of the corporation;
- eliminate the authority of the SEC to designate credit-rating agencies as nationally recognized statistical rating organizations (NSROs);
- reduce and eventually eliminate the reliance of regulators on credit ratings;
- reduce the standard-setting role of the SEC but increase its effectiveness by modernizing its reporting and review process;
- repeal the $1 million limit on the salary and bonus that may be deducted as a current expense, and repeal the SOA ban on loans to corporate officers;
- *replace* the corporate income tax with a broad-based tax on the net cash flow of all nonfinancial businesses; and
- *repeal* the Williams Act of 1968 and other restrictions on the market for corporate control.

The Flawed Governmental Response to the Corporate Scandals

A $7 *trillion* decline in the value of American equities, a wave of corporate accounting scandals, and the bankruptcy of Enron, WorldCom, and several other large corporations led Congress, the Securities and Exchange Commission, and a gaggle of state attorneys general to implement the most comprehensive new regulation of corporate behavior since the 1930s. Unfortunately, most of the new regulations authorized by the hurriedly assembled Sarbanes-Oxley Act are unnecessary, harmful, or inadequate to address the major problems of the corporate sector.

Unnecessary

Because the stock exchanges had already implemented most of the SOA changes in the rules of corporate governance in their new listing standards, the SEC had full authority to approve and enforce accounting standards, the requirement that CEOs certify the financial statements of their firms, and the rules for corporate disclosure; and the Department of Justice had ample authority to prosecute executives for securities fraud. The expensive new Public Company Accounting Oversight Board (PCAOB) is especially unnecessary. Its role is to regulate the few remaining independent public auditors, but it has no regulatory authority beyond that already granted to the SEC. Moreover, the audit firms still have a potential conflict of interest, because they are selected by and paid by the public corporations that they audit. The PCAOB may also be unconstitutional, because it is a private monopoly that has been granted both regulatory and taxing authority.

Harmful

The SOA is harmful because it substantially increases the risks of serving as a corporate officer or director, the premiums for directors' and officers' liability insurance, and the incentives, primarily for foreign and small firms, not to list their stock on an American exchange. The ban on loans to corporate officers eliminates one of the more efficient instruments of executive compensation. And the SOA may also reduce the incentive for corporate executives and directors to seek legal advice.

Inadequate

The SOA failed to identify and correct the major problems of accounting, auditing, taxation, and corporate governance that have invited corporate malfeasance and increased the probability of bankruptcy.

Unfortunately, the Sarbanes-Oxley Act, the new SEC regulations, and the extortion suits by the state attorneys general are better examples of the incentive for public officials to be seen doing something about a perceived problem than of a patient and informed reflection about the origins of the problem.

Lessons

The major policy lessons that were illustrated by the collapse of Enron and other corporate scandals are the following:

Don't Count Too Much on Financial Accounting

Financial accounting is backward looking, unusually complex, subject to subjective interpretation, vulnerable to several controversial accounting doctrines, and an invitation to manipulation. More important perhaps, many changes in nonfinancial conditions, which are never recorded on the balance sheet, may affect the value of a firm for better or for worse. For these reasons, corporate financial accounts do not provide accurate or sufficient information to corporate managers, investors, or regulators. This leads us to recommend that the SEC allow each stock exchange to set the accounting standards for all firms listed on that exchange and to promote the development of industry-specific nonfinancial accounts to complement the financial accounts.

Don't Count Too Much on Auditing

The most important lesson of the Enron collapse is that *every* link in the audit chain—including the audit committee and the board, the independent public auditor, the bankers and lawyers that aided and abetted the misrepresentation of Enron's financial condition, the credit-rating agencies, and the Securities and Exchange Commission—failed to deter, detect, and correct the conditions that led to that collapse. Although not a part of the formal audit chain, most of the market specialists in Enron stock and the business press were also late in recognizing Enron's financial weakness. Moreover, this is a characteristic pattern in many other bankruptcies.

This leads us to recommend that most of the audit functions be assigned to the stock exchanges, the only institution with the potential to capture the third-party benefits of a good audit. Each stock exchange would set the disclosure rules for the corporations listed on that exchange and select, monitor, and compensate the independent public auditor of each firm.

I also recommend new rules for the accountants, bankers, and lawyers that contribute to the misrepresentation of a corporation's financial condition, a reduced role for the credit-rating agencies, and a more focused role for the SEC.

Our Tax System Is a Major Part of the Problem

Our tax system encourages too much debt and overly risky investments, the characteristic conditions that lead to bankruptcy. American corporations use too much debt because interest payments are a deductible expense but returns to equity are not. Until the implementation of the 2003 tax law, retained earnings and investment within the corporation were too high because the individual tax rate on long-term capital gains was much lower than on dividends. The effects of those characteristics are magnified by the fact that the combined federal and state U.S. tax rate on corporate income is now among the highest of the industrial nations, second only to that in Japan. The limit of $1 million for salary and bonus as a deductible expense, combined with the increase in the top marginal tax rates on earnings and the reduction of the long-term capital gains rate, strongly increased the incentive to compensate corporate officers by stock options, a form of compensation that encourages risk taking. Our tax system, much like the Generally Accepted Accounting Principles and for much the same reasons, is extraordinarily complex, inviting attention to the many types of legal tax shelters used by Enron. Those characteristics of the current tax system lead me to recommend that the $1 million limit on the deductibility of salary and bonus be repealed and that the corporate income tax be replaced by a broad-based tax on the net cash flow of all nonfinancial corporations.

The U.S. Rules of Corporate Governance Do Not Now Adequately Protect the Interests of General Shareholders

Over the past four decades, beginning with the federal Williams Act of 1968, the combination of federal and state legislation and court rulings and rules approved by corporate boards has led to an accumulation of takeover defenses, even though firm performance is negatively related to the number of such defenses. This has increased the power of incumbent managements relative to their boards and general shareholders, increased the number of unprofitable acquisitions by large corporations, increased executive compensation, and almost destroyed the market for corporate control. The primary policy lesson that we can draw from this experience is that the federal government should withdraw from *any* role in establishing the rules of corporate governance and disclosure, returning this role to the state governments and stock exchanges. The policy actions that would be most helpful in restoring an effective market for corporate control would be for Congress to repeal the Williams Act and for the SEC to allow a market for the voting rights of shares that are separable from the ownership rights.

Conclusion

The corporate scandals illustrated by the Enron collapse were a serious problem, undermining trust in the accounts and the behavior of all corporations and the political support for free-market policies. At the same time, it is important to recognize that the more serious corporate malfeasance was apparently limited to a few dozen of the 12,000 U.S. public corporations and that the general performance of the stock market and the U.S. economy has been better than that of most other industrial nations, both in the last several years and in the last two decades. So it is important not to overreact by such measures as the Sarbanes-Oxley Act.

This chapter, in contrast, advocates addressing the problems illustrated by the Enron collapse by *reducing* and *focusing* the role of government.

References

Culp, Christopher L., and William A. Niskanen, eds. (2001) *Corporate Aftershock: The Public Policy Lessons from the Collapse of Enron and Other Major Corporations.* Hoboken, NJ: John Wiley & Sons.

Litan, Robert E., with George Benston, Michael Bromwich, and Alfred Wagenhofer. (2003) *Following the Money: The Enron Failure and the State of Corporate Governance.* Washington: AEI-Brookings Joint Center for Regulatory Studies.

Niskanen, William A., ed. (2005) *After Enron: The Major Lessons for Public Policy.* Lanham, MD: Rowman & Littlefield.

13. An Unconventional Perspective on the Greenspan Record

On his nomination as chairman of the Federal Reserve Board, Ben Bernanke stated, "My first priority will be to maintain continuity with the policies and policy strategies established during the Greenspan years." For that statement to provide much information, however, it is useful to understand the record of the Greenspan years.

The Greenspan Record

The most important summary statistic of this record is that the *trend* rate of increase of aggregate demand—measured by nominal final sales to domestic purchasers—from the third quarter of fiscal year 1987 through the first quarter of fiscal year 2006 was 5.4 percent a year. This increase in demand reflected an increase of real final sales to domestic purchasers of 3 percent a year and an average inflation rate of 2.4 percent. Thus, during the Greenspan era, the trend rate of increase in demand was only slightly too high to meet a 2 percent inflation target. From my perspective this was the appropriate trend rate of increase in demand during this period.

The variation around this trend, displayed in Figure 13.1, provides valuable additional information about "the policies and policy strategies established during the Greenspan years." Although the standard deviation of demand around this trend was only 1.3 percent, this variation had significant effects on asset prices and the real economy, and most of this variation was a consequence of the Fed's response to financial crises.

The Fed's Response to Financial Crises

The Fed's characteristic response to a financial crisis during this period was to put a lot of money in the market quickly and then

This article was first published in the *Cato Journal* 26, no. 2 (2006). My thanks to the *Cato Journal* for its permission to republish this article.

Figure 13.1
NOMINAL FINAL SALES TO DOMESTIC PURCHASERS

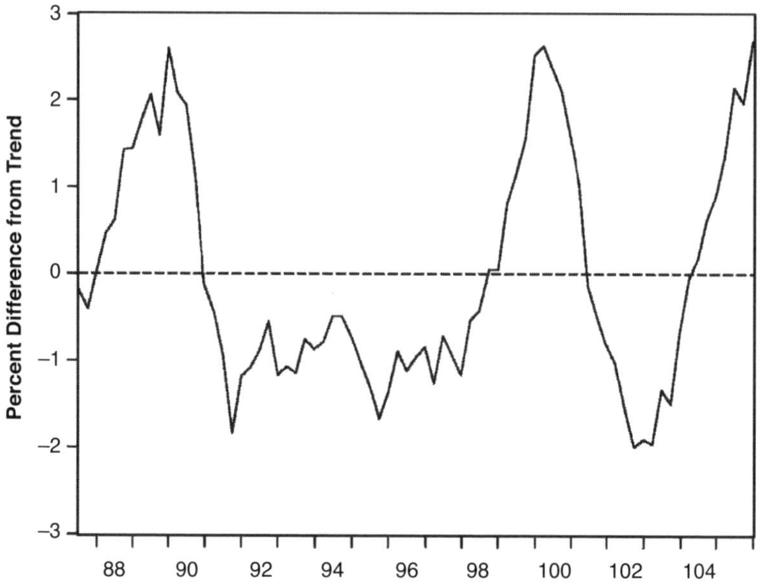

slowly take it out. The first unusually large increase in demand was clearly a consequence of the Fed's response to the large decline in U.S. equity prices in October 1987, only two months after Greenspan's confirmation. This response led to higher real economic growth in 1988 and 1989 than most experts had forecast. In turn, Fed tightening to deflate this demand bubble was the primary cause of the shallow recession of 1991.

The second unusually large increase in demand was clearly a consequence of the Fed's response to a series of foreign and domestic financial crises beginning with the Asian crisis in 1997, sustained by the collapse of Long Term Capital Management and the Russian default in 1998, and ending with the Brazilian devaluation and the anticipated Y2K crisis in 1999. The Fed's easy money policy led to a bubble in aggregate demand that was nearly synchronous with the equity bubble, and Fed tightening to deflate the demand bubble contributed to the sharp reduction in equity prices and the shallow recession of 2001.

It is less clear what triggered the third large increase in demand. Some have suggested that the September 11, 2001, crisis led to this increase, but this view is implausible because demand did not begin to increase rapidly until 18 months later. In any case, the recent increase in demand is too high—a 7.4 percent annual rate over the past two years (2004/I–2006/I)—to maintain Bernanke's apparent inflation target of 1 to 2 percent. As a result, the general inflation rate increased to 3.1 percent during 2005. One of Bernanke's first major challenges will be to reduce the increase in demand to a sustainable 4 to 5 percent range without another recession.

Some Policy Lessons

The major lesson from Figure 13.1 is that most of the variation in demand has been triggered by the Fed's response to financial crises. A second lesson is that the Fed seems to overreact. A reasonable standard by which to judge the Fed's response to a financial crisis would be to avoid a *decline* in the growth of aggregate demand relative to the target path. Instead, the Fed has let demand increase relative to the target path. A third lesson is that the deflation of the demand bubbles caused by overreacting to financial crises led to the two shallow recessions during the Greenspan years.

Institutional Problems

Some of the more important institutional problems that the Bernanke Fed should address are whether and how much to respond to a financial crisis. For example, the Fed did not respond to the Mexican financial crisis in the winter of 1985, but did respond to the several financial crises during the Greenspan era. The conventional perspective on this issue is that the Fed faces a trade-off between avoiding the potential near-term contagion effects of a financial crisis and the longer-term problem of moral hazard and that the Fed is biased in favor of reducing the near-term contagion effects. The record of the Greenspan years suggests that there is another potential long-term cost of responding to a financial crisis—the increased probability of a recession caused by deflating the demand bubble caused by the Fed's overreaction to a crisis.

Conclusion

I do not mean to imply that the Fed should never respond to a financial crisis. My objective is to induce more analysis about how to minimize the combined effects of a financial crisis and the Fed's response to it on the Fed's primary mission: to maintain a steady increase in aggregate demand consistent with a low target rate of inflation.

14. The Several Costs of Responding to the Threat of Terrorism

This paper describes several dimensions of the cost of the U.S. response to the threat of terrorism. Following an evaluation of the nature and magnitude of the threat of terrorism against the United States, the paper describes the restrictions on our civil liberties that make no contribution to the defense against terrorism but are rationalized on that ground, and the effects on our language and the potential for civil discourse of an extended defense against terrorism.

Most of us have come to expect the government to protect us from foreign and domestic threats to our life, liberty, and property. And when there is significant increase in a threat to our life, most of us are prepared to sacrifice some liberty and property to counter this threat. The issue about which there is some disagreement is one of relative magnitude: how much liberty and property are we willing to sacrifice to counter a specific increase in a threat to our life?

Let us start with the official definition of terrorism in Title 22 of the United States Code, Section 2656f(d):

> The term terrorism means premeditated, politically motivated violence perpetrated against noncombatant targets by subnational groups or clandestine agents, usually intended to influence an audience.

This definition includes violence against military personnel who at the time of the incident are unarmed or not on duty and attacks on military installations or on armed military personnel when a state of military hostilities does not exist at the site, both in the United States and abroad. The official definition also recognizes that the

---

This article was presented at a conference at George Mason University in May 2006 and was first published in *Public Choice* 126, no. 5 (2006). My thanks to *Public Choice* for its permission to republish this article.

primary objective of a terrorist act may not be the direct damage of the act but its influence on a broader audience. For the most part, except for the rare kidnapping, the direct damage of terrorist acts to Americans has been to liberty and property. The other dimensions of the costs of terrorism are almost completely a function of the *response* to terrorism, and that is the focus of this paper.

The Nature and Magnitude of the Terrorist Threat to Americans

For a decade now, starting with the truck bombing of the federal building in Oklahoma City in 1995 and greatly amplified by the attacks on the World Trade Center and in the Pentagon on September 11, 2001, there has been a substantial increase in the *perception* of a threat of terrorism in the United States, a perception reinforced by the 2005 terrorist bombings in London and in the Sinai. There is no apparent trend, however, in the actual threat of terrorism to Americans, either at home or abroad.

The U.S. Government has greatly *overreacted* to the terrorist threat to Americans, creating "a false sense of insecurity" (Friedman 2005 and Mueller 2004). Over the past decade, fewer than 400 Americans a year have died as a consequence of domestic and foreign terrorism, about the same number who drown from using a bathtub and less than 1 percent of the number who die from traffic accidents. Moreover, the relatively vulnerability of Americans to terrorist attacks is not likely to increase *if terrorist groups do not acquire nuclear weapons*. The highest priority must be to assure that terrorist groups do not obtain nuclear weapons, because the relative effectiveness of biological and chemical weapons has been vastly overblown (Easterbrook 2002). The 2001 anthrax attack in the United States, the origins of which are apparently still unknown, killed five people. If the purpose of terrorists, however, is not to destroy but to terrify, they have chosen the right types of weapons and targets. The late Senator Patrick Moynihan observed that "terrorism succeeds when people become terrified" (*Washington Post*, September 16, 2001). How much Americans are terrified by terrorism, however, depends, primarily on the nature of our public and private responses to a terrorist act, not on the direct damage done by the act. Most of the costs of terrorism to the United States are the anxiety of Americans and the costs of the measures to reduce the prospect of future terrorist acts.

These same costs, however, increase the political benefits to terrorists of a future attack.

The War of Terrorism Has Led to a Significant Reduction of Our Civil Liberties

Some of the threats to civil liberties have been based on an interpretation of laws in place *before* September 11, 2001:

- the imprisonment of American citizens in military brigs without a charge or access to an attorney,
- increased eavesdropping on attorney-client conversations,
- trials before military commissions,
- unusually strict enforcement of the immigration laws,
- the Total Information Awareness database by the Pentagon, and
- a database of all students aged 16 through 25.

Shortly after 9/11, the Bush administration proposed an omnibus (and ominous) package of additional authority and demanded quick congressional approval (Lynch 2005). The congressional leadership cooperated by holding closed hearings and scheduling a final vote before copies of the bill were available to members of Congress, naming the final bill the USA Patriot Act; the bill passed the Senate with only one dissenting vote.

The authority for several of the most serious threats to liberty in the Patriot Act would have expired in December 2005 had Congress not voted to extend this authority. Section 215 authorizes federal agents to seize any tangible item from a person's home, following a court order that a judge is required to issue when the executive branch claims it is conducting a terrorism investigation; more shocking, Section 215 makes it a crime for anyone to tell another person about the exercise of this authority. Section 505 bypasses the Constitution's search warrant procedure by authorizing federal agents to subpoena transactional records without a court order. Section 218 broadens the reach of the Foreign Intelligence Surveillance Act by authorizing the government to conduct electronic surveillance of citizens and resident aliens if foreign intelligence is only a significant purpose of the investigation, a change that now authorizes such surveillance of many ordinary criminal matters.

But several other disturbing provisions of the Patriot Act are not subject to the sunset provisions. Section 213, the so-called "sneak and peek" power, authorizes federal agents to conduct covert entries into homes and businesses following a judicial search warrant, but without informing the property owner about the entry for days or weeks later. Another section authorizes the sharing of grand jury information among federal agencies without the approval of a federal judge. A third section broadens the network of businesses other than banks that are required to report suspicious financial transactions to include mortgage companies, pawn brokers, used car dealerships, and many other businesses under penalty of substantial fines for failure to provide sufficient assistance in a money laundering investigation.

As with many post-9/11 policy changes, the Patriot Act authorizes a collection of powers that the government had wanted for some time but was approved as a package only because of widespread anxiety about terrorism. Congress reviewed the Patriot Act in July 2005, under the threat of a Bush veto if they did not renew the entire act. Moreover, the Senate Intelligence Committee had proposed to add a number of new investigative tools, including an administrative subpoena that would allow the Federal Bureau of Investigation to gain access to anyone's financial, medical, employment, and even library records without the approval of a judge. Shortly after the London bombings, the House and Senate approved somewhat different versions of a renewed Patriot Act, and a consensus bill was expected to be approved in September.

The record to date, however, did not support the case for these expanded powers. As of June 2005, 330 persons were on the Justice Department list of terrorism prosecutions, but only 73 had been convicted of any crime, only 39 of which had been convicted of terrorism or some other national security crime. The median sentence was just 11 months, often for such minor crimes as making false statements or violating immigration laws (Eggan and Tate 2005). It is not clear that the powers authorized by the Patriot Act were necessary for any of these convictions.

Some of the Most Visible Home Security Measures Are Irritating, Quite Ineffective, and Seem to Be Designed to Convince the Broader Public That the Government Is Doing Its Job

The airport search procedures implemented by the Transportation Security Administration are probably the most dramatic example.

These procedures cost taxpayers about $5 billion a year and air travelers up to one additional hour per trip. But they are not necessary to prevent the type of 9/11 attack, and they are not very effective as a defense against attempts to destroy commercial aircraft. First, some facts of life:

It is *easy* to prevent the type of 9/11 attack in which terrorists take control of an aircraft to use as a guided bomb by the following actions:

- securing cockpit doors so that they may not be opened from the cabin,
- a rule that pilots may not reenter a cabin in flight for any reason, and
- arming the pilots.

All commercial aircraft using U.S. airports or crossing U.S. airspace would have to meet these conditions. The cockpit doors of all commercial aircraft have already been strengthened.

It is very *difficult* to prevent a determined terrorist, even one who is not prepared to sacrifice his own life, from destroying a commercial aircraft. Screening of passengers and baggage is time-consuming and irritating, but is moderately effective. But current surveillance technology does not detect hidden explosives, and air cargo is not screened. A defense against the most serious threat has not been implemented, namely, the proliferation of shoulder-fired anti-aircraft missiles. Over 500,000 of such missiles have been produced. They can be purchased on the military arms black market for as little as $5,000. More than two dozen terrorist groups, including al Qaeda, are believed to possess such weapons. The FBI estimates that there have been 29 attacks by such missiles resulting in 550 deaths, none so far including an attack on a U.S. airliner. At least 25 of the reported attacks have been attributed to nonstate actors. Laser-jamming infrared countermeasures now used on U.S. military aircraft are a quite effective defense against these missiles but are expensive. Equipping all U.S. commercial aircraft with this technology is estimated to cost $11 billion plus $2.1 billion recurring annual cost (Pena April 2005). An alternative ground-based system has recently been developed that promises to be much less expensive but would protect only those aircraft using the airports at which this system is installed (Karp 2005).

One silly example of an ineffective anti-terrorist measure is the national color-coded alert system. Raising the alert level probably causes some combination of confusion, anxiety, and cynicism but provides no useful information to anyone.

For those who live or work in the District of Columbia, local traffic management provides other examples. All vehicle traffic on Pennsylvania Avenue and E Street next to the White House has now been blocked. The U.S. Capitol Police have now initiated a random process of investigating all vehicles within a block of the Capitol building. In both cases, diverting all *trucks* and *buses* to streets a block or so away would provide adequate protection against an explosion and would restore car traffic.

In an October 2001 interview, Osama bin Laden claimed that "freedom and human rights in America are doomed. The United States government will lead the American people into an unbearable hell and a choking life" (CNN News 2002). Fortunately, that is still far from the case. As observed by *Washington Post* columnist Melanie Scarborough, however, "some changes in recent years are worrisome. Long lines, searches, and identification requirements are becoming routine. Unwarranted intrusion and inconvenience are becoming an American way of life" (Scarborough 2005).

Most of the Fiscal Cost of the War on Terrorism Is the Cost of Programs That Make No Contribution to a Defense against Terrorism but are Rationalized on That Ground

For this paper, I will avoid the contentious issue about whether the war in Iraq reduced or increased the threat of terrorism against Americans. Other elements of the defense budget provide less controversial examples. The total defense budget has increased nearly $100 billion since 9/11, in addition to the cost of military operations in Afghanistan and Iraq. The fiscal year 2005 defense budget, for example, was described as including "robust readiness and acquisition funding, important legislative initiatives, and other essentials for winning the global war on terrorism" (Department of Defense Fiscal 2005 Budget Release).

A large part of the increase in the defense budget, however, is for new high-tech weapons systems that would make no contribution to defense against terrorism: a ballistic missile defense system that has not yet been successfully tested, new nuclear submarines that cost nearly $3 billion each, a new class of expensive tilt-rotor aircraft that has proved unsafe in testing (Pena March 2005). The U.S. military has not yet come to terms with the view that an effective war on terrorism requires good intelligence, good intelligence sharing, and good local police work but not much of a military contribution beyond small, high-quality special operation forces.

A smaller example is the new program of first responder grants, an understandable policy response to the extraordinary heroism of the New York City police and firemen on 9/11. The funding for this program is now $3.4 billion a year. The problem is that this program has become a general federal grant to local police and fire departments, rather than a program targeted to develop the equipment and skills to respond to a local terrorist threat in the most vulnerable cities (de Rugy 2005).

A final example: the outrageous agriculture legislation of 2002, of course, was titled "The Farm Security Act."

Finally, the Response to an Extended Threat of Terrorism Threatens to Undermine the Civil Discourse That is Necessary for an Informed Democracy

Writing about the extended Peloponnesian War, the Greek historian Thucydides may have been the first to observe that

> To fit in with the change of events, words, too, had to change their usual meanings. What used to be described as a thoughtless act of aggression was now regarded as the courage one would expect to find in a party member; to think of the future and wait was merely another way of saying one was coward; any idea of moderation was just an attempt to disguise one's unmanly character; ability to understand a question from all sides meant that one was totally unfitted for action. Fanatical enthusiasm was the mark of a real man, and to plot against an enemy behind his back was perfectly legitimate self-defense. Any one who held violent opinions could always be trusted, and anyone who objected to them became a suspect. . . . As a result . . . there was a general deterioration of character throughout the Greek world. The plain way of looking at things, which is so much the mark of noble nature, was regarded as a ridiculous quality and soon ceased to exist. Society became divided into camps in which no man trusted his fellow (quoted in Cahill, 2003).

May we pray that fellow Americans still have the time and wisdom to avoid this potential effect of an extended threat of terrorism.

References

Cahill, T. (2003) *Sailing the Wine-Dark Sea: Why the Greeks Matter*. Doubleday: London.

Easterbrook, G. (October 7, 2002) "Weapons of Mass Destruction Meaningless." *New Republic.*

Eggan, D., and Tate, J. (June 12, 2005) "U.S. Campaign Produces Few Convictions on Terrorism." *Washington Post.*

Friedman, B. (July/August, 2005) "Homeland Security." *Foreign Policy.*

Karp, J. (June 14, 2005) "Protecting Jets from Missiles." *Wall Street Journal.*

Lynch, T. (2005) "The Patriot Act." *Cato Handbook on Policy* Cato Institute: Washington.

Mueller, J. (Fall 2004) "A False Sense of Insecurity." *Regulation.*

Pena, C. V. (March 28, 2005) "$400 Billion Defense Budget Unnecessary to Fight War on Terrorism." Cato Institute Policy Analysis No. 539.

______. (April 19, 2005) "Flying the Unfriendly Skies: Defending Against the Threat of Shoulder-Fired Missiles." Cato Institute Policy Analysis No. 541.

Rugy, V. de (April 1, 2005) "What Does Homeland Security Spending Buy?" Working Paper 107, American Enterprise Institute, Washington.

Scarborough, M. (June 29, 2005) "The Security Pretext: an Examination of the Growth of Federal Police Agencies." Cato Institute Briefing Paper No. 94.

15. The Failure to "Starve the Beast"

For nearly 30 years, many Republicans have argued that the most effective way to control federal government spending is to "starve the beast" by reducing federal tax revenues. Moreover, two Nobel laureate economists, Milton Friedman and Gary Becker, have endorsed this argument. Friedman (2003) summarized this perspective as follows:

> How can we ever cut government down to size? I believe there is one and only one way: the way parents control spendthrift children, cutting their allowance. For governments, this means cutting taxes. Resulting deficits will be an effective—I would go so far as to say, the only effective—restraint on the spending propensities of the executive branch and the legislature. The public reaction will make that restraint effective.

Becker and his colleagues Ed Lazear and Kevin Murphy (2003) described this effect as "the double benefit of tax cuts." (Lazear is the recently appointed chairman of the Council of Economic Advisers.) This argument has been effective in unifying the Republican Party in favor of reducing federal taxes, but at the cost of undermining the more traditional Republican concern about fiscal responsibility.

Problems with "Starve the Beast"

There are three major problems with the starve-the-beast argument: (1) it is not a plausible economic theory; (2) it is inconsistent with the facts; and (3) it has diverted attention away from the political reforms needed to limit government growth.

This article was first published in the *Cato Journal* 26, no. 3 (2006). My thanks to the *Cato Journal* for its permission to republish this article.

Figure 15.1
Federal Spending and Receipts as a Percent of GDP

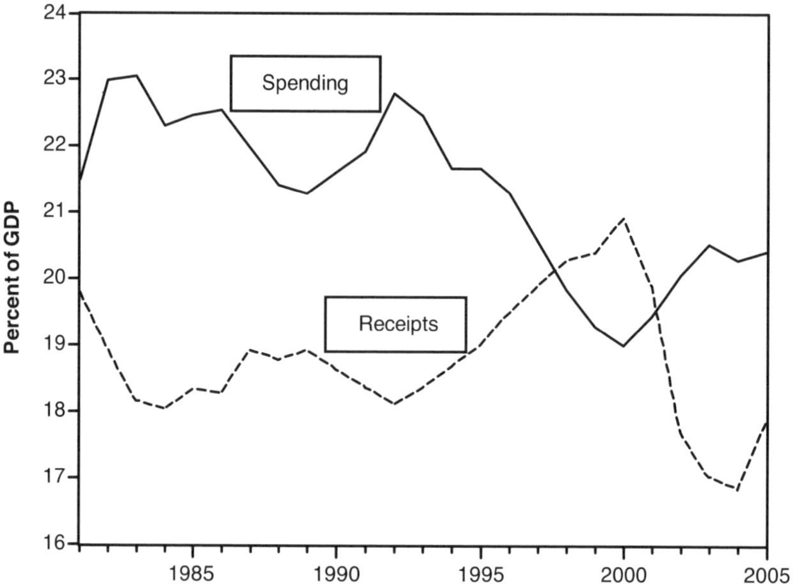

The Implausibility Issue

It is most implausible that reducing the current tax burden of federal spending would *reduce* the amount of federal services that voters demand. Orthodox price theory, of which Friedman and Becker are among the leading exponents, is unambiguous in concluding that reducing the price of a good or service increases the amount demanded. Reducing the current tax burden of federal spending has much the same effect as a price control, increasing the amount demanded relative to that supplied from current revenues, an effect that Friedman and Becker have consistently and correctly opposed in private markets.

The Facts

Second and more important, the starve-the-beast hypothesis is not consistent with the facts, at least since the beginning of the Reagan administration. Figure 15.1 shows current federal spending and receipts as a percent of gross domestic product by calendar year from 1981 through 2005. As this figure illustrates, most of the changes in the relative level of federal spending were coincident with changes in the relative federal tax burden in the *opposite* direction.

What is going on? One condition that contributes to this pattern is the variation in the unemployment rate, since an increase in the unemployment rate increases federal spending and reduces federal tax receipts. So any estimate of the relation between changes in federal spending and the level of current receipts should control for changes in the unemployment rate. Second, one should also control for the change in net interest payments as a percentage of GDP because interest payments are a fixed expenditure that is independent of the conditions that affect other spending.[1]

The relation between current federal spending and receipts from 1981 through 2005 is best summarized by the following least-squares regression:

$$D\,(S) = \underset{(.848)}{2.761} - \underset{(.045)}{0.145}\,R + \underset{(.055)}{0.598}\,D\,(U) + \underset{(.197)}{0.514}\,D\,(I) + u,$$

$$\text{Adjusted } R^2 = .848 \quad \text{S.E.R.} = .223 \quad \text{D.W.} = 2.386$$

where

D (*S*) is the change in current federal spending as a percent of GDP,

R is the *level* of current federal receipts as a percent of GDP,

D (*U*) is the change in the unemployment rate,

D (*I*) is the change in net interest payments as a percent of GDP, and the figures in parentheses are the standard errors of the estimated coefficients.

The most important finding from this regression is that the level of current federal receipts as a percent of GDP has a significant *negative* effect on the change in current federal spending as a percent of GDP. A 1 percentage point increase in current federal receipts as a share of GDP apparently reduces the change in current federal spending as a share of GDP by about one-seventh of 1 percent a year indefinitely. As expected, the change in the unemployment rate has a strong positive effect on the change in current federal spending, and the change in net interest payments also has a significant positive effect.[2] Using the sample 1949 through 1980 produced an estimated coefficient on the federal tax share of GDP that is also negative but not statistically significant.

Using both sample periods (1949–80 and 1981–2005), I found no significant relation between the change in the current federal spending share of GDP and the lagged federal deficit as a percent of GDP. In sum, there is no significant evidence that a recent high deficit ever had an effect similar to that of reducing a child's allowance; the difference is that the federal government has a credit card with no effective debt limit. Federal spending is better described as buying government services at a discount equal to the deficit, the costs of which will be borne by someone sometime in the future. For no extended period did these estimates reveal a significant positive relation between the change in federal spending as a percent of GDP and the level of federal receipts as a percent of GDP, the necessary condition for the starve-the-beast hypothesis to be confirmed. *Starve the beast just does not work.*

Another value of the above regression is that it provides a basis for estimating the current federal receipts share of GDP at which there would be no change in the current federal spending share. Assuming no change in the unemployment rate or in the interest payments share of GDP, federal receipts of about 19 percent of GDP would be necessary to stabilize current federal spending as a percent of GDP. Since federal receipts were 17.8 percent of GDP in 2005, a tax increase of about 1.2 percent of GDP would be necessary to prevent a continued increase in the federal spending share of GDP.

Given that total federal spending was 20.4 percent of GDP in 2005, however, even current receipts of 19 percent of GDP would not be sufficient to balance the budget, unless expenditures for defense and net interest payments are reduced by about 1.4 percent of GDP. Assuming no change in the defense and net interest spending shares of GDP, current receipts of 19.9 percent of GDP—a tax increase of about 2.1 percent of GDP relative to 2005—would be necessary to balance the budget within five years. A reduction of defense spending on completion of the U.S. military role in Iraq may be the only way to balance the budget without increasing current federal receipts above 19 percent of GDP. This reduction is well within the range of recent experience: spending for defense and net interest payments declined by 1.2 percent of GDP from 1992 to 1994 and by 3.3 percent of GDP from 1992 to 2000.

The Problem of Fiscal Discipline

The third problem, of course, is that the starve-the-beast perspective has led too many conservatives and libertarians to be casual about the sustained political discipline necessary to control federal spending directly, succumbing to the fantasy that tax cuts would solve this problem. President George W. Bush, for example, has proposed and won the approval of most congressional Republicans for large increases in federal spending for agriculture, defense, education, energy, homeland security, medical care, and transportation, and he has yet to veto a single spending bill. As a consequence, real per capita federal spending during the Bush administration has increased at the highest rate since the Johnson administration.

What to Do?

Why not balance the budget without a tax increase? From my perspective, that would be desirable but most unlikely in the near term. As long as the tax burden of federal government is lower than about 19 percent of GDP, the above estimates suggest that our political representatives would resist a net reduction in federal spending as a percent of GDP. If our political system is biased in favor of larger government spending than a majority of the voters prefer, as is surely the case, we need to identify and correct these biases. My favorite rule to reduce these biases would be a constitutional amendment requiring that total federal spending in any fiscal year not exceed 110 percent of total federal receipts in the second prior fiscal year without the approval of a supermajority, say 60 percent, of the total members of each house of Congress or in any year in which a declaration of war is in effect. The 110 percent rule would lead to a small annual surplus in strong economic years, a small annual deficit in recession years, and a roughly balanced budget over time.

A 10 percent growth of federal spending over two years would maintain the federal spending share of GDP about constant, consistent with an annual increase of real GDP of 3 to 3.5 percent and an inflation rate of 1.3 to 1.8 percent, well within the range of recent experience. The 110 percent rule would require that tax cuts be matched with spending reductions within two years, and there would be strong incentives to increase economic growth and to maintain a low inflation rate.

Conclusion

If our political system then leads to decisions that roughly reflect voter preferences, the longer-term challenge for those of us who favor limited constitutional government is to try to convince voters to reduce their demand for the services financed by federal spending. Until that time, some increase in federal taxes appears to be a necessary part of a fiscal policy to balance the budget.

References

Becker, G. S., Lazear, E. O., and Murphy, K. (2003) "The Double Benefits of Tax Cuts." *Wall Street Journal*, October 7.

Friedman, M. (2003) "What Every American Wants." *Wall Street Journal* (January 15).

Niskanen, W. A. (1992) "The Case for a New Fiscal Constitution." *Journal of Economic Perspectives* 6 (2): 13–24.

______. (2002) "Comment on Tax Policy from 1990 to 2001." In *American Economic Policy in the 1990s*, ed. J. A. Frankel and P. R. Orszag. Cambridge, MA: MIT Press.

Notes

1. I am indebted to Robert Raynsford for a suggestion about how to test this relation, based on his correct judgment that interest payments, but not defense expenditures, were exogenous during this period.

2. Somewhat to my surprise, another regression (not shown) indicates that current defense spending had no significant effect on total federal spending during this period, indicating that the increase in defense spending reduced some other components of spending by a roughly equal amount.

Part II

Public Choice

16. Autocratic, Democratic, and Optimal Government: A Sketch

How are the level of government spending and the average tax rate related to the type of government? How many of the differences in economic conditions among nations are attributable to differences in the basic structure of their governments? How much are these fiscal decisions and economic conditions a function of the fiscal horizon of the government?

Only a few economists have even addressed these questions. Conventional public finance addresses the effects of fiscal decisions but not their causes.[1] For the most part, modern public choice addresses the second-order characteristics of democratic governments. Joseph Schumpeter was one of the few economists with the intellectual breadth and curiosity to address the broader choice among the several major types of political economies, most importantly in his classic 1942 book on *Capitalism, Socialism, and Democracy*. The modern classic in this tradition is Mancur Olson's 1982 book on *The Rise and Decline of Nations*. In the end, for somewhat different reasons, both Schumpeter and Olson were pessimistic about the long-run viability of the combination of democracy and capitalism. The analysis in these two classics, however, was developed in a literary form that is not a sufficient basis for quantitative estimates of the effects they describe. More recently, Francis Fukuyama revived the concept of "Universal History" in a 1992 book that concludes that liberal democracy and a market economy may be the best conceivable forms of social organization—"the end of history." The general pessimism of Schumpeter and Olson and the refreshing optimism of Fukuyama,

---

This article was first published in *Economic Inquiry* 35, no. 3 (1997). My thanks to *Economic Inquiry* for its permission to republish this article. I later expanded this article into a book with the same title, published by Edward Elgar in 2004.

however, may both have been a reflection of the periods in which these books were written: Schumpeter during a period when the liberal democracies were threatened by both Nazism and Stalinism, Olson following the U.S. defeat in Vietnam and the "stagflation" of the late 1970s, and Fukuyama following the dramatic collapse of communism beginning in 1989. A more objective evaluation of the several major types of government may require a more formal analysis that is less influenced by the prevailing intellectual mood of a specific period of history.

This paper addresses the "Schumpeterian" questions about the effects of different types of political economies with the simplest possible tools of modern economic analysis. The impetus for this paper was an invitation to comment on a 1991 paper by Mancur Olson on "Autocracy, Democracy, and Prosperity." The focus of this stimulating paper is the set of historical conditions that led to the progression from anarchy to autocracy to, more recently and selectively, democracy. Olson's own motivation to write this paper was to understand why some autocracies were broadly popular and why, in general, the general population wished the autocrat a long life and a peaceful succession. (One memorable phrase in this paper is Olson's description of autocrats as "stationary bandits.") On first reading the Olson paper, I thought that autocratic, democratic, and optimal governments could each be analyzed by a simple model. As it turned out, this proved to be more complex than I expected. The present paper is the result of that analytic exploration, the early growth from the seed that Olson planted.[2]

The section entitled "Models of Government" develops simple models of autocratic, democratic, and optimal governments, where each model includes two common functions relating economic conditions and tax revenues to the primary fiscal decisions by each type of government. This provides a basis for comparing the fiscal decisions and economic conditions resulting from each type of government. The next section, "The Parameters," presents several sets of parameters for these models, each estimated from recent economic and fiscal conditions in the United States. The section entitled "Some Suggestive Quantitative Results" presents the solutions of these models for each type of government and set of parameters. And the conclusion summarizes the major lessons from this analysis and the major remaining issues for further analysis.

Models of Government

The Common Functions

All types of government face a common set of primary fiscal decisions: choose the level of government expenditures and the rate of taxation that best serve the interests of those who control the government. Each type of government, thus, must have a rough understanding of the effects of these fiscal choices on the level of output and, in turn, on the level of tax revenues in the specific economy in which they operate. For each of the several major types of government, these effects are represented by the following two common functions:

$$Y = a(1 + G)^b(1 - R)^c, \tag{1}$$

and

$$T = RY = a(1 + G)^b R(1 - R)^c, \tag{2}$$

where Y is the level of output per person, G is the level of government expenditures per person (excluding external defense, transfer payments and subsidies, and net interest payments), R is the average tax rate, and T is the level of tax revenues per person. For these two functions, the parameter a is the level of output per person in a baseline economy where both G and R are zero, and the parameters b and c are the elasticities of both output and tax revenues with respect to the level of government expenditures and the after-tax rate. For this analysis, the level of the population under each type of government is assumed to be constant but may not be the same. Also, unless otherwise mentioned, the budget of each type of government is assumed to be balanced.

Each of the major types of government is defined by who controls the government and by the economic and fiscal conditions that best serve their interests. The terms used to describe each of the three major types of government, of course, should probably be in quotes. Any real government has other important but second-order characteristics, some of which will be described and evaluated below. Most political scientists and historians would probably describe my simple model of the first-order characteristics of each of these major types of governments as "crudely reductionist" or "economistic." For the moment, I will acknowledge the accuracy of such descriptions without apology. My objective is to analyze the effects of the first-order characteristics of these major types of government. The second-order characteristics are nuances that are best analyzed by modifying the simple models developed in this paper.

Autocratic Government

Autocratic government is defined as one controlled by a specific autocrat. And the interests of this autocrat are defined in terms of the difference between the level of tax revenues and the level of total government expenditures for goods and services. In other words, the autocrat is assumed to have no marginal benevolence or malevolence with respect to the general population that he rules, and the autocrat provides some level of government services only to increase the net amount that he can extract from the economy. For autocratic government, thus, the objective function is defined as

$$NA = T - (F + G), \quad (3)$$

where NA is the net output per person that the autocrat may use to serve his own interests, and F is the "fixed" cost per person for defense and net interest payments. Concern about a potential coup, of course, would lead the autocrat to share this net revenue with other members of the ruling class, but only the potential for a revolution would deter an autocratic government from maximizing the net revenues from the population subject to its rule.

Substituting Equation 2 for per capita tax revenues T expresses this objective function in terms of the fixed cost F, government expenditures on services G, and the average tax rate R.

$$NA = a(1 + G)^b R(1 - R)^c - (F + G) \quad (4)$$

For the autocrat, the tax rate that best serves his interests is the revenue-maximizing tax rate,

$$R = 1/(1 + c). \quad (5)$$

The level of $(1 + G)$ that maximizes NA, in turn, is equal to

$$(1 + G) = bT = (abR)^{[1/(1-b)]}. \quad (6)$$

The implications of these solutions for specific values of the parameters a, b, and c are developed below in "Some Suggestive Quantitative Results."

Democratic Government

The question of who controls a democratic government is somewhat less obvious than for an autocratic government. It is not enough to say that the "people" select or control democratic government; the analysis of democratic government must specify which people and the nature of their interests.

For this paper, the effective decisionmaker in a democracy with majority rule is assumed to be the median voter.[3] And given a broad-based franchise, the median voter is assumed to be from a median-income household.[4] The interests of the median voter, in turn, are defined in terms of the sum of his income minus taxes plus transfer payments received.

Including Transfer Payments. For a democracy with net transfer payments, thus, the objective function is defined as

$$ND = dY - eT + f\,[T - (F + G)], \tag{7}$$

or

$$ND = dY + (f - e)T - f\,(F + G), \tag{8}$$

$$T > (F + G).$$

The parameter d is the ratio of the median household income to the average household income. The parameter e is the ratio of the taxes paid by the median income household to the average taxes per household. The parameter f is the ratio of the transfer payments received by the median-income household to the average transfer payments per household; in the limit, this parameter is equal to $1/s$, where s is the share of the voters necessary to elect a government or approve fiscal legislation.

A number of interesting conditions can be evaluated by changing these parameters. Changes in the distribution of income, for example, can be evaluated by changing the income and tax parameters d and e. Changes in the progressivity of tax payments can be evaluated by changing the parameter e, the ratio of median to average taxes; if tax payments are proportional to income, for example, the parameter e is equal to the parameter d, the ratio of median to average income. The evaluation of changes in the effective voting rule on the major fiscal decisions involves changes in each of the parameters d, e, and f, reflecting income, tax, and transfer payment effects.

One of the more interesting characteristics of this objective function is that the coefficient on tax payments per household, given that the ratio of median to average transfer payments is greater than the ratio of median to average taxes paid, is positive; in other words, the median voter benefits from a higher level of tax payments per household because this voter's share of transfer payments is higher than his (or her) share of taxes. Another interesting implication is that increasing the fixed costs (such as for defense and net interest payments) reduces transfer payments by an equal amount and has no effect on G, R, T, or Y. This may help explain why the American Right embraced a combination of higher defense spending and deficit financing at a time roughly coincident with the rise of the modern welfare state. In this limited case, increases in defense expenditures and net interest payments are free to the minority that pays most of the taxes and receives no transfer payments.

Substituting Equation 1 for per capita output Y and Equation 2 for per capita tax revenue T expresses this objective function in terms of F, G, and R.

$$(9) \qquad ND = ad(1 + G)^b(1 - R)^c + a(f - e)(1 + G)^b R(1 - R)^c - f(F + G),$$

or

$$(10) \quad ND = a(1 + G)b\,[d + (f - e)R](1 - R)^c - f(F + G).$$

Solving Equation 10 for the tax rate that maximizes the net benefits to the median voter yields

$$(11) \qquad R = (f - e - cd) / [(1 + c)(f - e)].$$

Since the median voter is concerned about both his income after taxes and transfer payments received, this rate is substantially lower than the revenue-maximizing tax rate that is characteristic of autocratic government. Similarly, the level of $(1 + G)$ that maximizes the net benefits to the median voter is

$$(12) \quad (1 + G) = \{[(ab)/f]\,[d + (f - e)R]\}^{[1/(1-b)]}(1 - R)^{[c-(1-b)]}.$$

A democratic government, thus, will spend more for government services than an autocratic government because an increase in these services over some range increases both the income after taxes and the transfer payments received by the median voter. Substituting the values of R and $(1 + G)$ from Equations 11 and 12 into equations 1 and 2 yields the levels of Y and T, and the level of transfer payments is equal to $T - (F + G)$.[5]

Excluding Transfer Payments. Equations 11 and 12 describe the fiscal behavior of democratic governments, however, only when the effective constitution allows transfer payments and when the combination of parameters generates tax revenues that are larger than the sum of fixed costs and expenditure for government services. If the effective constitution, however, does not authorize transfer payments or the tax rate resulting from Equation 11 does not generate sufficient tax revenues to cover fixed costs and the expenditures for government services, the objective function of a democratic government is

$$ND = dY - eT, T = (F + G). \tag{13}$$

In this case, a democratic government faces only one major fiscal decision, since R and G are jointly determined and are a function of the level of fixed costs. The calculation of the values of R and G that best serve the interest of the median voter is also substantially more complicated in this case.

Substituting Equation 2 for per capita tax revenue T in the equality $T = (F + G)$ yields

$$(F + G) = a(1 + G)^b R\,(1 - R)^C. \tag{14}$$

This leads to a relation between G and R for which the graph is like an egg balanced on its large end. In this case, there is no way (apparent to me) to solve directly for the values of government services expenditure G, and the tax rate R, that maximize Equation 13.

For values of the R above the minimum tax rate, however, the relation between G and R can be almost perfectly approximated by

$$(1 + G) = gR^h(1 - R)^i. \tag{15}$$

The parameters of Equation 15 can be estimated from a log-linear regression, based on a sample of G and R from Equation 14 that excludes those values in the range below the minimum value of R. Substituting the estimated Equation 15 into Equations 1 and 2, and the resulting equations for Y and T into Equation 13, thus yields an objective function expressed entirely in terms of the tax rate R.

(16) $ND = ad[gR^h(1 - R)^i]^b(1 - R)^c - ae[gR^h(1 - R)^i]^bR(1 - R)^c,$

or

(17) $ND = adg^b R^{bh}(1 - R)^{(bi+c)} - aeg^b R^{(bh+1)}(1 - R)^{(bi+c)}.$

Solving Equation 17 for the value of R that maximizes the interests of the median voter yields the following quadratic equation in R:

(18) $$[b(h + 1) + (1 + c)]eR^2 - [(bdh) + (bh + 1)e + (bi + c)d]R + bdh = 0.$$

In the specific case of proportional taxes (where $e = d$),

(19) $$R = (bh) / [b(h + i) + (1 + c)].$$

The value of the tax rate from Equations 18 or 19 is then substituted into Equation 14 to find the corresponding level of government expenditures.

At this point, let me acknowledge that this simple model does not incorporate many of the characteristics of democratic government. Among the more important characteristics that are not incorporated are legislatures, the judiciary, the executive veto, the role of agenda setters, the potential cyclicality of majority rule, the division of roles between national and regional governments, and the role of money in politics. These characteristics are important to evaluate the differences among democratic governments but, I contend, are second-order characteristics for evaluating the difference between democratic and other major types of governments.

Optimal Government

For this model, the effective decisionmaker in an optimal government is assumed to be a representative person "behind the veil of ignorance" about his or her future income and relative political influence.[6] Moreover, this person is assumed to be risk-neutral with respect to future income after taxes; as a consequence, this model assumes that no government-financed social insurance would be approved at the constitutional stage.[7] For this definition of optimal government, then, the objective function is

(20) $$NO = Y - T.$$

Substituting Equations 1 and 2 into Equation 20 yields

(21) $$NO = a(1 + G)^{b}(1 - R)^{(1+c)}.$$

Solving for the optimal levels of (1 + G) and R involves the same process as described above for a democratic government without transfer payments. The optimal level of R turns out to be

(22) $$R = (bh) / [b(h + i) + (1 + c)],$$

the same as in democratic government with proportional taxation and no transfer payments. In the limit, as G increases relative to F, the optimal tax rate converges to

(23) $$R = b / (1 + c).$$

The optimal level of (1 + G), in turn, is found by substituting the value of R from Equation 22 into Equation 14.

At this point, one should recognize that the government described above is optimal but not perfect. More specifically, levels of (1 + G) and R are optimal only for the specific values of the parameters *a*, *b*, and *c*. An increase in the general productivity in a nation would increase the parameter *a*, the optimal level of G, and the resulting income after taxes. An increase in the productivity of government services would increase the parameter *b*, the optimal levels of G and R, and the resulting level of income after taxes. Similarly, a reduction in the misallocative effects of the tax code would reduce the parameter *c* and increase the optimal levels of G and R and the resulting level of income after taxes. No real government, of course, is either optimal or perfect. The primary value of defining the characteristics and outcomes of optimal government is to provide a basis for comparison with the major types of real governments, given the same observed levels of the relevant parameters.

The Parameters

Most of the parameters in the models of government described above can be estimated from observed data. The several sets of parameters used in this paper are estimated from recent U.S. data.

The two exceptions to the above generalization bear on the productivity and transfer payments parameters *a* and *f*. For this paper, the productivity parameter *a* is set equal to 100 in all calculations to provide an easy basis for comparing the output per person in the several models. The transfer parameter *f* is derived from the effective voting rule in democratic governments. Majority rule, for example, requires the median voter to share the level of transfer payments equally with at least half of the population; in the limit, thus, $f = 2$ for majority rule. Similarly, in the limit, $f = 1.667$ for a 60 percent voting rule. In practice it is not usually possible to limit transfer payments to the minimum effective current coalition, so these values of f somewhat overestimate their actual values.

"Some Suggestive Quantitative Results," the following section, presents estimates of the model results for three alternative sets of the parameters b, c, h, and i, representing productivity of government services, misallocation induced by the tax code, and the relationship between government services expenditure and the tax rate. The X set derives the productivity and tax code parameters b and c from the model of democratic government with transfers, given the level of the other relevant parameters and the observed levels of $(1 + G)$, R, and Y for the United States in 1989; in other words, these parameters are selected to replicate the actual tax rate of R, $(1 + G)/Y$, and F/Y in the United States in 1989. Specifically, for this case,

$$b = [(1 + G) / Y]\{f / [d + (f - e)R]\} \tag{24}$$

and

$$c = [(f - e)(1 - R)] / [d + (f - e)R]. \tag{25}$$

In the Y and Z sets, the estimates of the productivity and tax code parameters (b and c) are from my 1993 study of the "Fiscal Effects on U.S. Economic Growth." These parameters are estimates of the elasticities of U.S. real GNP per adult in response to the real (federal, state, and local) government purchases of goods and services (excluding defense) per adult and the combined after-tax rate, controlling for a set of other conditions and based on an annual sample of the years 1951–1989. The Y parameters are the first-year effects; the Z parameters are the long-term effects. My hope is to focus attention on the models of government, using my own estimates of the parameters b and c only to illustrate the effects of alternative forms of government. Those readers who may prefer other estimates of the parameters b and c are encouraged to substitute them for my estimates and examine the results. In each set, the parameters h and i (not shown), relating to government service expenditure and the tax rate, are estimates from Equation 15, based on a restricted sample of observations from Equation 14, as described in the above section.

Table 16.1
THE MODEL PARAMETERS

	X	Y	Z
a	100	100	100
b	0.205	0.251 (.040)	0.394 (.074)
c	0.767	0.938 (.178)	1.472 (.314)

	Democratic Government Majority Rule	60 Percent Rule
d	0.792	0.936
e	0.584	0.888
f	2.000	1.667

NOTE: The *X* parameter set replicates the actual fiscal and economic conditions in the United States in 1989; the *Y* set is the estimate of first-year effects; the *Z* set comprises the long-term estimates.

The parameters *d* and *e* reflect the distribution of income and tax payments. For majority rule, *d* is the ratio of the median money income of households to the average money income of households in the United States for 1989; similarly, *e* is the ratio of the personal taxes paid per consumer unit in the third quintile to the average taxes per consumer unit, in this case for 1988. For a 60 percent voting rule, the estimation of *d* and *e* is slightly more complex. The estimate of *d* is the ratio of the money income of families at the top of the third quintile over the average money income of households, multiplied by the ratio of the median money income of households over the median money income of families. The estimate of *e* is the ratio of the average personal taxes paid in the third and fourth quintiles of consumer units over the average tax per consumer unit.[8]

Table 16.1 presents the three sets of parameters and the special parameters specific to democratic government. The numbers in parentheses are the standard errors of those parameters that are estimated by regression analysis.

Some of these parameter estimates merit comment at this point. The *X* parameters for *b* and *c*, in column *X*, as described above, are derived from the model of democratic government with transfers and are calculated to replicate the actual set of fiscal and economic conditions in the United States in 1989. These estimates are not significantly different from the first-year estimates of b and c in column Y but are substantially and significantly lower than the long-term estimates of these parameters in column Z.

There are three alternative explanations of the differences in these estimates: the model of democratic government with transfer payments may not accurately describe the behavior of American government. My model may be correct, but American government may somehow be stuck in a short-run equilibrium. Or the estimates of the long-term b and c parameters in the Z set may be biased upward.[9] It is not obvious (to me) which of the alternative explanations of the differences between the actual (X) and long-term (Z) estimates may be correct. Analyses of both voting and net migration data suggest that average tax rates in the United States, for whatever reason, are higher than those that would best serve the interests of the median voter.[10] There is also reason to believe that democratic political processes may discount future effects at too high a rate. The annual adjustment rate in the regression estimates, however, is .631 (with a standard error of .062); this implies that about 89 percent of the long-run effects of a current fiscal decision are realized within four years, so one might hope that fiscal decisions at the beginning of a presidential term would be based on at least this much of the long-term effects of these decisions. There is also the possibility that the estimates of b and c in both the Y and Z sets may be biased if some variable omitted from my regression equation, such as the cost of government regulation, is correlated with G / Y and $(1 - R)$. Since the ambiguity about which set of parameters best describes the economic effects of fiscal actions is not easily resolved, estimates of the model results are presented in the next section for each of the three sets of parameters.

Some Suggestive Quantitative Results

The models of government developed in "Models of Government" and the model parameters described in "The Parameters" now provide a basis for suggestive quantitative answers to the several questions posed at the beginning of this paper. The differences in the fiscal decisions and economic outcomes among the several major types of government are striking. Moreover, these results suggest that democratic governments face a serious dilemma in the long run: specifically, transfer payments to the effective majority coalition must be either phased out or accepted by the larger community as part of the fixed costs of government. Some ambiguities remain, however, and merit further analysis.

Several comments are appropriate before presenting the model results. The distribution of tax payments, unless otherwise specified, is assumed to be the same as the recent distribution in the United States. The level of fixed costs (for external defense, net interest payments, etc.) is assumed to be the same in all cases, and this level is selected to replicate the fixed cost share of total output in the United States in 1989, for conditions specific to the *X* parameters. And a new variable *P* is introduced to designate the level of transfer payments per person, where $P = T - (F + G)$. Again, readers are cautioned to recognize that the quantitative results presented in this section are specific to the parameters presented in Table 16.1. Readers are encouraged to develop the implications of their own best estimates of the critical *b* and *c* parameters; the major qualitative conclusions of this section, however, are invariant to substantial variation in these parameters.

Outcomes Based on the X *Parameters*

Table 16.2 presents the fiscal and economic outcomes of the major types of government for the conditions summarized by the *X* parameters. As described in "The Parameters," these parameters are calculated to replicate the major fiscal decisions by government in the United States in 1989. The numbers in parentheses are the shares of total output (GNP) for each of the fiscal variables. The major results of these conditions are summarized below:

1. An autocratic government is a great benefit to the autocrat but a disaster for the general population. The autocrat captures about 34 percent of total output, leaving about 43 percent for the general population. For these conditions, the autocrat would probably have to spend part of his surplus to maintain the general population in effective slavery. One should not be surprised that the children of Israel chose to wander in the desert for 40 years rather than stay in the land of the Pharaohs.
2. The substitution of democratic for autocratic government generates large net benefits to the general population. Total output

Table 16.2
FISCAL AND ECONOMIC OUTCOMES OF ALTERNATIVE GOVERNMENTS

	Autocracy	Democracy	Optimum
Y	84.1	132.5	144.0
F	10.3 (0.122)	10.3 (0.078)	10.3 (0.071)
G	8.8 (0.104)	17.0 (0.128)	9.2 (0.064)
P	28.6 (0.340)	15.5 (0.117)	
T	47.6 (0.566)	42.8 (0.323)	19.5 (0.135)
Net Income			
Average	36.5	89.6	124.6
Median	38.8	111.0	102.6

is increased about 58 percent, and the majority coalition captures nearly 12 percent of total output in transfer payments. The average net income is increased by about 145 percent, and the median net income (including transfer payments) is increased by about 186 percent.

3. The substitution of optimal government for democratic government substantially increases average net income but at some loss to the majority of the population. Total output is increased about 9 percent. The average net income is increased by about 39 percent. Median net income, however, declines about 8 percent.
4. Comparisons across the major types of government indicate that total output and average net income increase with each step toward an optimal government, transfer payments and tax rates decline, and that government expenditures are highest in a democratic government. In summary, democratic government may be better than any relevant alternative even though it generates the highest outcomes only to those who supply government services or receive transfer payments.

Table 16.3
OUTCOMES OF FISCAL DECISIONS BASED ON THEIR FIRST-YEAR EFFECTS

	Autocracy		Democracy	
	First Year	Long Term	First Year	Long Term
Y	95.0	92.2	171.1	232.1
F	10.3	10.3	10.3	10.3
	(0.108)	(0.111)	(0.060)	(0.044)
G	11.3	11.3	23.4	23.4
	(0.119)	(0.122)	(0.137)	(0.101)
P	27.5	26.0	8.3	23.4
	(0.289)	(0.282)	(0.049)	(0.101)
T	49.0	47.6	42.0	57.1
	(0.516)	(0.516)	(0.246)	(0.246)
Net Income				
Average	46.0	44.6	129.1	175.0
Median	46.5	45.2	127.5	197.2

Outcomes of Fiscal Decisions Based on Their First-Year Effects

For several reasons, the fiscal and economic outcomes presented in Table 16.2 are not satisfactory. As explained above, the parameters *b* and *c* in the *X* set are substantially and significantly lower than the estimates of the long-run effects of the fiscal variables from a regression analysis on postwar U.S. data. And the *X* parameters do not provide a basis for estimating the effects of time on the fiscal decisions and economic outcomes. For these reasons, all of the subsequent analysis is based on the *Y* and *Z* parameter sets.

Estimation of the effects of time on the primary fiscal decisions and economic outcomes involves two dimensions: the time horizon of economic effects on which the fiscal decisions are based, and the period over which the economic effects are measured. Table 16.3 presents the fiscal and economic outcomes of autocratic and democratic governments that base their fiscal decisions only on their first-year economic effects, as measured by the *Y* parameters. An optimal government, of course, would base its fiscal decisions on their long-run economic effects; for this reason, the corresponding outcomes for an optimal government are not included in this table. For autocratic and democratic governments, Table 16.3 presents both the first-year and long-term outcomes of fiscal decisions based on their first-year effects. In both cases, the fiscal decisions are based on the *Y* parameters. The economic outcomes, in turn, are based on the *Y* parameters to measure the first-year effects and on the *Z* parameters to measure the long-term effects. This provides a basis, thus, for estimating the changes in economic outcomes over time by autocratic and democratic governments with a myopic fiscal horizon.

The major patterns of the outcomes presented in Table 16.3 are the following:

1. The long-term effects of a myopic autocrat are slightly lower than the first-year effects for all parties. Total output and tax revenues are about 3 percent lower. The average level of transfer payments from each person to the autocrat is about 5 percent lower. Average net income and median net income are about 3 percent lower. Moreover, even a myopic autocrat captures about 28 percent of total output, leaving about 48 percent for the general population.
2. The long-term outcomes of a myopic democracy, however, are substantially better than the first-year effects. Total output and tax revenues are about 36 percent higher. The average level of transfer payments is about 182 percent higher. Average net income is about 36 percent higher, and median net income is about 55 percent higher.
3. A comparison across the two types of government, both of which make fiscal decisions based only on their first-year effects, indicates that democratic government leads to substantially higher total output, higher expenditures for domestic government services, and a lower tax rate. In the long run, total output is about 152 percent higher, and government spending for domestic services is about 107 percent higher .The average tax rate is lower by about 52 percent (27 percentage points). Average net income is about 292 percent higher, and median net income is about 336 percent higher. Even a myopic democracy is much superior to an autocracy for everyone except, of course, the autocrat and those who receive special favors from the autocrat.

4. A comparison of these results for a myopic democracy with the actual recent fiscal decisions in the United States (summarized by the numbers in parentheses in the middle column of Table 16.2) suggests that the current rate of government spending for domestic services, the current rate of transfer payments, and the current average tax rate may each be too high, in each case measured by the interests of the median voter.[11] One wonders about the reason for these differences. American government may not serve the interests of the median voter as well as even a myopic democracy.

Outcomes of Fiscal Decisions Based on Their Long-Term Effects

For each type of government, the outcomes of fiscal decisions that are based on their long-term effects are superior to those based on their first-year effects, even in the short term. For this case, the fiscal decisions are based on the *Z* parameters. Estimates of the first-year effects, then, are based on the *Y* parameters and the long-term effects are based on the *Z* parameters. For this case, a new variable must also be introduced: *D* is the first-year deficit necessary to finance the long-term level of government expenditures at the long-term tax rate. Table 16.4 presents the outcomes for both the first year and the long term, given that each type of government bases its fiscal decisions on their long-term effects.[12] A comparison of these outcomes with those presented in Table 16.3 thus reveals the differences in the fiscal decisions and economic outcomes that are attributable to the fiscal horizon of each type of government.

The outcomes presented in Table 16.4 reflect several common patterns. For each type of government, total output, government expenditures for domestic services and the net income of all persons are substantially higher if the primary fiscal decisions are based on their long-term effects. Average tax rates are also substantially lower. The patterns of outcomes specific to each type of government are summarized below:

First, for an autocratic government with a long fiscal horizon, total output is about 22 percent higher than in the first year and about 86 percent higher than if fiscal decisions are based on their first-year effects. Government spending is about 132 percent higher than in a myopic autocracy. The autocrat, however, faces one trade off: average extractions by the autocrat are about 25 percent lower in

Table 16.4
OUTCOMES OF FISCAL DECISIONS BASED ON THEIR LONG-TERM EFFECTS

	Autocracy		Democracy		Optimum	
	First Year	Long Term	First Year	Long Term	First Year	Long Term
Y	140.8	171.2	230.3	370.3	228.0	364.5
F	10.3	10.3	10.3	10.3	10.3	10.3
	(0.072)	(0.060)	(0.045)	(0.028)	(0.045)	(0.028)
G	26.2	26.2	60.8	60.8	54.9	54.9
	(0.186)	(0.153)	(0.264)	(0.164)	(0.241)	(0.151)
P	20.5	32.7				
	(0.145)	(0.191)				
T	57.0	69.2	44.2	71.1	40.8	65.2
	(0.405)	(0.405)	(0.192)	(0.192)	(0.179)	(0.179)
D		26.9		24.4		
		(0.117)		(0.107)		
Net Income						
Average	83.9	101.9	186.1	299.2	187.2	299.3
Median	78.2	95.0	156.5	25 1.6	156.7	250.5

the first year and about 26 percent higher in the long run than in a myopic autocracy. The average tax rate is lower by about 22 percent (11.1 percentage points).

Most of the benefits of an autocracy with a long fiscal horizon, however, accrue to the general population, not to the autocrat. Average net income is about 21 percent higher than in the first year and about 128 percent higher than in a myopic autocracy. Median net income is about 21 percent higher than in the first year and about 110 percent higher than in a myopic autocracy. "Long live the king" is a rational political position for the general population only if the alternative is another autocrat with a short fiscal horizon. Autocracy is clearly the worst form of government, only barely better than a baseline economy even in the long term.

Second, the most important general outcomes of a democracy with a long fiscal horizon are the following: *No transfer payments would be authorized unless they are regarded as fixed expenditures for social insurance.* This may help explain the progressive change in the rhetoric used to describe these payments from "charity" to "welfare" to "entitlements" to "human rights." And, with no transfer payments, the outcomes are very close to optimal for all concerned. These two results are probably the most important results from the analysis in this paper.

Total output is about 61 percent higher than in the first year and about 60 percent higher than in a democracy with a short fiscal horizon. Government spending for domestic services is about 160 percent higher than in a myopic democracy. The average tax rate is lower by about 27 percent (5.4 percentage points). A democratic government with a long horizon, however, must run a substantial first-year deficit to finance the long-term level of government expenditures at the long-term tax rate. The benefits of a long fiscal horizon, however, are substantial. Average net income is about 61 percent higher than in the first year and about 71 percent higher than in a myopic democracy. Median net income is also about 61 percent higher than in the first year and about 28 percent higher than in a myopic democracy. A large share of the benefits of a long fiscal horizon (and the ability to borrow to finance short-run deficits), thus, accrues to the minority who pay most of the taxes.

Third, a comparison across the several types of government indicates very large net benefits from replacing an autocracy with a democracy and, for this case, very small net benefits of further steps toward an optimal government. Total output in a democracy is about 116 percent higher than in an autocracy, and government spending for domestic services is about 132 percent higher. The average tax rate is lower by about 53 percent (21.3 percentage points). Average net income is about 194 percent higher, and median net income is about 165 percent higher. Optimal government would have a slightly lower total output, government spending, and tax rate in comparison to a democratic government with a long fiscal horizon and no transfer payments, and the average and median net income would not be significantly different.

Fukuyama may be correct. Liberal democracy may be the best conceivable type of government—"the end of history." At this point, however, one should make three tentative qualifications to this conclusion. Fiscal decisions may not be based on their long-term effects.

All modern democracies finance a high level of transfer payments. And the simple model of democracy developed in "Models of Government" may not incorporate some features of actual democracies that limit their potential.

Further Evaluation of Democratic Government

Democratic government merits further evaluation. Our own government is a constitutional democracy, and democratic government is the most distinctive and now more prevalent type of government in the modern age. The model of democratic government developed in "Models of Government" is not sufficient for an evaluation of the many second-order characteristics of democratic government. The model, however, is sufficient to evaluate differences or changes in the distribution of income and tax payments, the effective voting rule, and whether transfer payments are fixed obligations for social insurance or are variable outcomes of specific political and economic conditions. The outcomes of these several types of changes can be estimated by changing the parameters of this model.

Start with the outcomes of democratic government presented in Table 16.3, the outcomes of fiscal decisions based on their first-year effects. The effects of changing to a proportional tax system (in the range of the median income) can be estimated by setting the ratio of taxes paid by median and average households equal to the ratio of median and average household income (parameter e equal to the parameter d). The effects of a 60 percent voting rule on the primary fiscal decisions can be estimated by substituting the income, tax distribution, and transfer payments parameters (d, e, and f) specific to this rule that are presented in Table 16.1. Estimates of the long-term effects of fixed transfer payments are derived by adding the level of transfer payments in Table 16.3 to the level of fixed costs in Equation 14 and then estimating new values of the expenditures and tax rate parameters h and i. For each set of fiscal decisions, the long-term effects are based on the b and c parameters from the Z set.

Table 16.5 presents the outcomes of democratic government for several combinations of the fiscal horizon, the distribution of tax payments, the voting rule, and whether transfer payments are fixed or variable. The outcomes presented in the first column are the long-term outcomes presented in Table 16.3, and the outcomes presented in the fifth column are the long-run outcomes from Table 16.4 to

Table 16.5
LONG-TERM OUTCOMES OF ALTERNATIVE DEMOCRATIC GOVERNMENTS

Horizon	First Year			Long Term	
Voting Rule	50%	50%	60%	50%	50%
Taxes	Progressive	Proportional	Progressive	Progressive	Progressive
Transfers	Variable	Variable	Variable	Fixed	Variable
Y	232.1	248.1	252.0	248.7	370.3
F	10.3 (.044)	10.3 (.041)	10.3 (.041)	10.3 (.041)	10.3 (.028)
G	23.4 (.101)	22.1 (.089)	19.7 (.078)	29.0 (.117)	60.8 (.164)
P	23.4 (.101)	17.0 (.069)	11.9 (.047)	23.4 (.094)	
T	57.1 (.246)	49.4 (.199)	41.8 (.166)	62.6 (.252)	71.7 (.192)
Net Income					
Average	175.0	198.7	210.2	186.0	299.2
Median	197.2	191.33	194.9	207.0	251.6

provide a basis for comparing the intermediate outcomes. The major results from these comparisons are summarized below:

1. A proportional tax system (in the range of the median income) would increase total output about 7 percent in the long run. Government spending for domestic services would be lower by about 6 percent, and transfer payments would be lower by about 27 percent. The average tax rate would be lower by about 19 percent (4.7 percentage points). Average net income would be higher by about 14 percent, but median net income would be lower by about 3 percent. Democratic governments, however, are not likely to select a proportional tax system. A progressive tax system in contrast, is likely to be politically popular even though it increases the average tax rate and reduces both total output and average net income.

2. Substituting a 60 percent voting rule on the major fiscal decisions would increase total output (relative to the first column) by about 9 percent in the long run. Government spending for domestic services would be lower by about 16 percent, and transfer payments would be lower by about 49 percent. The average tax rate would be lower by about 37 percent (8 percentage points). Average net income would be higher by about 20 percent, but median net income would be slightly lower. Again, normal democratic politics would probably not select a 60 percent voting rule, but such a rule might be selected at the constitutional stage.
3. For a democratic government that bases its fiscal decisions on their long-term effects and regards transfer payments as a fixed obligation, total output would be about 7 percent higher than in a similar government with a short-term fiscal horizon. Government spending for domestic services would be about 24 percent higher, and the average tax rate would be higher by about 2 percent (0.6 percentage point). Average net income would be about 6 percent higher, and median net income would be about 5 percent higher. These results indicate the benefits of conditions that lead a democratic government to base its fiscal decisions on their long-term effects, even if transfer payments are regarded as a fixed obligation.
4. A democratic government, even with progressive taxation and majority rule, that bases its fiscal decisions on their long-term effects and does not regard transfer payments as a fixed obligation for social insurance would not authorize any transfer payments. In this case, total output would be about 49 percent higher than with fixed transfer payments and about 60 percent higher than for a democratic government with a short-term fiscal horizon. Government spending would be about 110 percent higher than with fixed transfer payments and about 160 percent higher than with a short-term fiscal horizon. The average tax rate would be lower by about 24 percent (6 percentage points) than with fixed transfer payments and about 22 percent (5.4 percentage points) lower than with a short-term fiscal horizon. Average net income would be about 61 percent higher than with fixed transfer payments and about 71 percent higher than with a short-term fiscal horizon. Median net income would

> be about 22 percent higher than with fixed transfer payments and about 28 percent higher than with a short-term fiscal horizon. For fiscal decisions that are based on their long-term effects, the outcomes of proportional taxation or a 60 percent voting rule (not shown) are not significantly different from the above outcomes.

A democratic government defined by the characteristics listed in the fourth column provides a level of social insurance equal to 9.4 percent of total output. The cost of this social insurance is the difference in net income between the fourth and fifth columns. Financing this level of social insurance, thus, reduces average net income by about 38 percent and median net income by about 18 percent. For the United States, where transfer payments were 11.7 percent of GNP in 1989, the cost of social insurance is surely higher.[13] At the constitutional stage, a political community may or may not choose to authorize social insurance, a decision that is dependent on the distribution of natural endowments and the relative preference for income and leisure as well as the expected cost of social insurance.[14] An estimate of the expected cost of social insurance, thus, is a necessary input to this decision but is not a sufficient basis for the constitutional decision. There is reason to expect that different political communities, over generations or among nations, would make different decisions on this important constitutional issue. The U.S. Constitution, for example, provides no explicit authority for transfer payments by the federal government, but now most democratic governments, including the U.S. government, finance a high level of transfer payments. The demand for transfer payments may have its origin in normal democratic politics, but an implicit or explicit constitutional consensus is necessary to sustain these payments as the fixed cost of social insurance. In the end, the question whether democratic government closely approximates an optimal government depends critically on whether there is a constitutional consensus on the powers of the government. There is ample reason for both Schumpeter's pessimism about the probable outcome and Fukuyama's optimism about the potential of democratic government.

Conclusion

Every type of government has had its defenders, not all of whom were paid apologists. A comparison of the major type of governments, however, has been complicated by two conditions: the conceptual case for each major type of government was often made on different grounds; and a comparison of the outcomes of actual governments is complicated by different initial conditions and different economic effects of the primary fiscal decisions. For these reasons, an evaluation of the major types of governments should be based on a common standard, the same initial conditions, and the same economic effects of the fiscal decisions. That has been the objective of the analysis summarized in this paper. The strength and breadth of the conclusions from this analysis suggests that this has been a worthwhile endeavor.

Autocratic government, on any basis other than the interests of the autocrat, produces substantially lower outcomes than any alternative. Mancur Olson was correct to describe the characteristic autocrat as a "stationary bandit." Olson was also correct to recognize that the interests of the general population are very dependent on the horizon over which the autocrat makes his fiscal decisions. For the general population, however, the outcomes of autocratic government with a long-term fiscal horizon are inferior to those of even a myopic democracy.

Democratic government provides substantially higher net income than autocratic government for every set of conditions. Alternative conditions among democratic governments, however, produce substantially different outcomes depending on the fiscal horizon, the voting rule, the distribution of tax payments, and whether transfer payments are a fixed or variable cost. Normal politics in a democratic government with a short-term fiscal horizon, for example, produces a substantial level of transfer payments to members of the majority coalition. For this case, a proportional tax system or a 60 percent voting rule reduces the level of transfer payments and generates a somewhat higher average net income and a slightly lower median net income. A democratic government that bases its primary fiscal decisions on their long-term effects, however, will authorize no transfer payments unless they are treated as the fixed costs of social insurance. *For a level of transfer payments somewhat lower than the recent U.S. level, average net income is nearly 40 percent lower than if no transfer payments are authorized, the best estimate of the cost of treating transfer payments as social insurance. Moreover, if no transfer payments are authorized, a democratic government with a long-term fiscal horizon produces outcomes that are very close to that produced by optimal government, even with progressive taxation and majority rule. These are clearly the most important conclusions from the analysis in this paper.*

These conclusions have several important implications bearing on the choice of specific second-order characteristics of democratic government. First, democratic governments face an inherent tradeoff between the benefits of frequent elections and the benefits of a long-term fiscal horizon. Frequent elections are valuable to reflect changes in popular concerns, correct bad policy choices, and replace bad governors. On the other hand, this may lead democratic governments to be permanently shackled with a short-term fiscal horizon. In this case, there is more reason to consider such changes as a proportional tax system or a 60 percent voting rule on the primary fiscal decisions. One alternative is to strengthen the role of the political parties in selecting candidates, because the parties have more reason to be concerned about the long-term effects of fiscal decisions than do individual politicians.

It is also important to resolve whether there is a broad consensus for treating the level of transfer payments as the fixed cost of social insurance. The modern welfare state in the United States has developed in response to normal democratic politics without any amendment to the Constitution that would authorize these programs, so this issue is not clear. If there is a broad consensus for these programs, the current structure of democratic government may be close to optimal, despite the high cost of this social insurance. If the major programs of the modern welfare state would not meet a constitutional test, these programs should be phased out. In that case, a democratic government with a long fiscal horizon would generate a substantially higher average and median net income without changing the tax structure or the voting rule. Fukuyama concludes that liberal democracy may be "the end of history" because he cannot conceive of a structure of government that would be generally superior. The analysis of this paper suggests that there is still ample opportunity for constitutional entrepreneurship.

From an analytic perspective, the most encouraging conclusion of this paper is that a simple model of each major type of government, based on observable parameters, is sufficient to estimate its primary fiscal decisions and economic outcomes. This type of analysis, however, is not complete and merits extension in at least three dimensions. There is some evidence that transfer payments have a direct negative effect on total output that is independent of the effects of other government spending and the average tax rate; incorporating this effect would somewhat reduce the total output of democratic government below that estimated in this paper.

The effects of population change should also be incorporated. Autocratic governments have an incentive to expand the population they rule, either by expanding their domain or attracting immigrants, because the income of the autocrat is proportional to the population minus the cost of measures to bring more people under his rule. This may be the primary reason why autocratic governments have been unusually aggressive. In contrast, democratic governments have an incentive to increase the population served only if they face substantial costs, such as for defense, that do not increase in proportion to the population.

Finally, the basic creativity and productivity of a political community may be dependent on the type of government. This effect is difficult to evaluate but may be more important than any of the effects addressed in this paper. There is still ample opportunity for intellectual creativity bearing on the effects of the basic structure of governments, a challenge to which several types of scholarship can make a contribution.

References

Buchanan, James. (1985) "Coercive Taxation in Constitutional Contract." Working Paper, George Mason University.

Buchanan, James, and Gordon Tullock. (1962) *The Calculus of Consent.* Ann Arbor: University of Michigan Press.

Fukuyama, Francis. (1992) *The End of History and the Last Man*. New York The Free Press.

McGuire, Martin C., and Mancur Olson. (1996) "The Economics of Autocracy and Majority Rule: The Invisible Hand and the Use of Force." *Journal of Economic Literature* (March): 72–96.

Niskanen, William. (1986) "A Constitutional Approach to Taxes and Transfers." *The Cato Journal* 6(1): 347–52.

———. (1992) "The Case for a New Fiscal Constitution." *The Journal of Economic Perspectives* (Spring): 13–24.

———. (1993) "Fiscal Effects on U.S. Economic Growth." In *Taxation in the United States and Europe*, ed. Anthony Knoester, pp. 137–55. New York: St. Martin's Press.

Olson, Mancur. (1982) *The Rise and Decline of Nations.* New Haven: Yale University Press.

———. (1991) "Autocracy, Democracy, and Prosperity." In *Strategy and Choice*, ed. Richard J. Zeckhauser, pp. 131–57. Cambridge, MA: MIT Press.

———. (1993) "Dictatorship, Democracy, and Development." *American Political Science Review* (September): 567–76.

Rawls, John. (1973) *A Theory of Justice*. Cambridge: The Belknap Press of the Harvard University Press.

Schumpeter, Joseph. (1942) *Capitalism, Socialism and Democracy.* New York: Harper and Brothers.

Zeckhauser, Richard. (1974) "Risk Spreading and Distribution." In *Redistribution Through Public Choice*, ed. Harold Hochman and George Peterson, pp. 206–28. New York: Columbia University Press.

Notes

1. One referee observed that public finance also provides a normative theory of what services government should provide. I do not find this normative theory very useful in explaining what governments actually do.

2. Olson has also developed his analysis in articles published in 1993 and (with Martin McGuire) in 1996.

3. The reason for this assumption, now standard in public choice analysis, is that the median voter must be part of any stable majority coalition.

4. A broad-based franchise, of course, is a more recent development than the basic structure of democratic government. If voter participation is a positive function of income, the income of the median voter would be somewhat higher than the median income.

5. In this specific case, this model somewhat overestimates the resulting levels of Y and T if transfer payments reduce the supply of output.

6. This phrase, of course, is that suggested by Rawls [1973] and is similar to the general approach to the analysis of constitutional decisions by Buchanan and Tullock [1962]. A more accurate phrase would be "behind the veil of uncertainty," because the effective decision maker is assumed to be knowledgeable about all conditions other than his or her own status in the postconstitutional stage.

7. There are good reasons why some social insurance may be approved at the constitutional stage. For the seminal analysis of these conditions, see Zeckhauser [1974]. For other conditions that would qualify this choice, see Buchanan [1985]. For a synthesis of this issue, see Niskanen [1986].

8. All of the data for these calculations are from the *Statistical Abstract of the United States.*

9. One referee observed that the several estimates of the c parameter are higher than the broad body of estimates of the elasticity of the supply of labor services. But taxes also affect the supply of output at other margins, most importantly the supply of savings and the allocation of labor and capital. One reality check on this parameter is the relation $R = 1 / (1 + c)$, where R is the revenue-maximizing average tax rate. If the c parameter is as low as the conventional estimates of the elasticity of supply of labor, the government could increase tax revenues to about 75 percent of GDP.

10. For an example of the voting and migration studies, see Niskanen (1992).

11. The respective *levels* of these variables are not comparable because they are based on different parameters. For a strict comparison of the fiscal rates, in addition, the rate of fixed costs in the fourth column should be increased to .078. For this case, this would reduce the rate of transfer payments to .067 without changing G, R, T, or Y.

12. These outcomes slightly overestimate the output and underestimate the tax rate of both democratic and optimal governments because the long-term fixed costs must increase to cover the interest costs of the short-term deficit.

13. Moreover, this model probably underestimates the cost of transfer payments because it assumes that such payments have no effect on total output independent of their effect on other government spending and the average tax rate.

14. See note 1.

17. A Vote for Perot Was a Vote for the Status Quo

In 1992 Ross Perot received more votes than any prior third-party candidate for president, and the vote for Perot in 1996 was only slightly smaller than that for George Wallace in 1968. There remains, however, substantial confusion about how to interpret the vote for Perot.

Four Hypotheses

Most political analysts seem to have concluded that most of the Perot voters would have otherwise voted for the Republican candidate, presumably based on the defeat of the Republican candidate in both elections and Perot's campaign focus on fiscal responsibility. Careful polls after the 1992 election, however, indicate that the composition of Perot voters was more like the total electorate than the composition of Republican voters—in terms of income, education, religion, and their vote in 1988—but with substantially more concern about current and future economic and fiscal conditions. And Perot's own anti-establishment campaign rhetoric seems unlikely to have appealed primarily to otherwise Republican voters.

An analysis of the popular vote for president in the 1992 and 1996 elections, I suggest, provides a better basis for estimating the effects of the Perot vote and the revealed concerns of the Perot voters. These two elections share two common conditions and two important different conditions: The common conditions were that the incumbent president was running for reelection, and Perot was the major third-party candidate in each election. The most important different conditions were that the incumbent president was a Republican in 1992 but a Democrat in 1996 and that economic conditions had

This article was first published in the *Cato Journal* 18, no. 1 (1998). My thanks to the *Cato Journal* for its permission to republish this article.

Table 17.1
SIGN OF THE PEROT VOTE EFFECT UNDER THE FOUR HYPOTHESES

	Election	
Hypothesis	1992	1996
1. Republican	−	+
2. Democratic	+	−
3. Protest	−	−
4. Status Quo	+	+

improved more substantially over the four years prior to the 1996 election.

These two elections provide a basis for sorting out among four alternative explanations of the Perot vote:

1. Most of the Perot voters would have otherwise voted for the Republican candidate.
2. Most of the Perot voters would have otherwise voted for the Democratic candidate.
3. Most of the Perot voters would have otherwise voted against the incumbent candidate of either party.
4. Most of the Perot voters would have otherwise voted for the incumbent candidate of either party.

An analysis of the effect of the Perot vote on the incumbent candidate's share of the total major party vote provides a sufficient basis for selecting among these four hypotheses, based only on the sign of this effect in the two elections. For example, if the Perot vote reduced the Bush share of the total major party vote in 1992 but increased the Clinton share in 1996, as is the conventional wisdom, this pair of signs is most consistent with the first hypothesis. Similarly, each of the other possible pairs of signs of the Perot vote effect is most consistent with one of the other hypotheses. (Table 17.1 lists the various possibilities.) Estimates of the sign and magnitude of the Perot vote effect in each of the two elections are presented following a discussion of the characteristics of Perot voters.

Who Were the Perot Voters?

First, it is useful to summarize the available information about the Perot voters. The most detailed information is from an exit poll of 15,232 voters after the 1992 election, a poll prepared for the networks by Public Opinion Strategies (1993). Table 17.2 presents the most relevant results from this poll.

The most striking observation from these data is that the composition of those who voted for Perot in 1992 is very similar to the composition of all voters. Other data from the same exit poll (not shown) also indicated no significant difference by religion. The largest differences in the demographics of the Perot voters were a somewhat smaller percent of minorities, those over 60, and those with postgraduate education.

More important, "The bottom line is that Perot voters are more identifiable by their attitudes rather than their demographics" (Public Opinion Strategies 1993: 1). A higher percent of the Perot voters, especially compared to the Bush voters, regarded their personal finances as worse and the prospects for the national economy as poor. Later polling by Public Opinion Strategies indicated that the Perot voters were the most pessimistic about the direction of the country and were much more focused on economic issues, especially the federal budget deficit.

The characteristic Perot voter, in summary, was an average voter with an attitude. For all that, it is not obvious how the Perot vote affected the 1992 and 1996 elections and how this group may vote in future elections when Perot is not a candidate.

What Were the Effects of the Perot Vote?

My analysis of the effects of the Perot vote is based on regression estimates of the following vote function in both the 1992 and 1996 elections:[1]

$$(V/(1-V)) = ec + bVL + cO + d\,(Y/YL), \text{ or}$$

$$1n(V/(1-V)) = C + bVL + cO + d(\ln(Y/YL)), \text{ where}$$

V = popular vote for the incumbent president as a share of the major party popular vote,
VL = popular vote for the winning candidate in the prior election as a share of the total popular vote,
O = popular vote for all minor party candidates as a share of the total popular vote,
Y = real per capita personal income, and
YL = Y in the prior election year.

Table 17.2
CHARACTERISTICS OF VOTERS IN 1992

Characteristics	Candidate All	Clinton	Bush	Perot
		(Percent of Voters)		
Sex				
Men	47	45	47	52
Women	53	55	53	48
Race				
White	87	79	94	94
Black	8	16	2	3
Other	4	5	4	4
Age				
18–29	21	21	19	24
30–44	36	34	36	39
45–59	23	22	24	23
60 +	20	23	21	13
Education				
No high school	7	9	5	7
High school graduate	25	25	25	27
Some college	29	27	29	32
College graduate	23	21	26	23
Postgraduate	16	18	15	11
Income				
Up to $15,000	14	19	9	13
$15–30,000	24	25	23	25
$30–50,000	30	28	23	32
$50–75,000	20	18	22	19
Over $75,000	12	10	16	10
Personal finances				
Better	24	13	40	18
Same	41	38	46	37
Worse	34	47	13	44
National economy				
Good	19	4	41	10
Not good	47	46	47	49
Poor	32	48	10	40
Party identification				
Democratic	38	68	10	26
Republican	34	8	67	31
Other	27	24	23	43
Vote in 1988				
Bush	53	25	84	56
Dukakis	27	51	4	17
Other	2	3	0	3
No vote	15	16	10	21

First, a word about the test equation: Statistical criteria suggest the use of the logit transformation $ln(V/(1-V))$ rather than V as the dependent variable; the logit form is unbounded, and the variance of the residuals is symmetric. The coefficients of a vote function with V as the dependent variable would be equal to $V(1-V)$, or about .25, times the estimated coefficients of the above test equation. The constant C, in this case, reflects the sum of two effects—the advantage of being the candidate of the incumbent party and the advantage of the specific candidate that is common to the whole sample. The variable O includes the votes for all minor party candidates but is only slightly larger than the Perot vote share. The sample for each regression is the 50 states plus the District of Columbia. All of the data are from the *Statistical Abstract of the United States* (1997). The two vote functions are estimated by a weighted least-squares regression, where the weight is the electoral college vote of each unit; this yields a near perfect fit for the largest states with a small increase in the residuals for the smallest states.

For this paper, the most important finding from the regression results summarized in Table 17.3 is that the Perot vote increased the incumbent president's share of the major party vote in both the 1992 and 1996 elections by drawing primarily from votes that would have otherwise gone to the opposition candidate. The Perot vote helped Clinton in 1996 more than it helped Bush in 1992 but was strongly significant in each case.

The other findings from these regressions are interesting but less important. Clinton's incumbent advantage in 1996 was somewhat higher than Bush's advantage in 1992, and the Clinton vote share in 1996 was slightly more dependent on his vote share in the prior election. The variance of the change in real per capita income among the states, however, was more important to the Bush share of the major party vote. The differences of these several effects between the two elections, however, are not statistically significant.

These two vote functions, plus the national averages of the independent variables, also make it possible to estimate how much of the popular vote for Bush in 1992 and for Clinton in 1996 was attributable to each of the several independent variables. These estimates are summarized in Table 17.4.

Again, for this paper, the most important issue is the effect of the Perot vote. In 1992, the minor party vote increased the Bush share

Table 17.3
WEIGHTED LEAST-SQUARES ESTIMATES OF THE VOTE FUNCTIONS

	Election	
	1992	1996
Independent Variables		
Incumbency	−2.631 (0.132)	−2.286 (0.207)
Prior vote	4.044 (0.218)	4.62 (0.366)
Minor party vote	1.343 (.296)	3.927 (1.016)
Income change	1.917 (0.247)	1.245 (0.787)
Weighted statistics		
Adjusted R-Squared	0.933	0.864
S.E. of Regression	0.092	0.155

NOTE: Numbers in parentheses are the standard errors of the coefficients.

Table 17.4
SOURCE OF THE POPULAR VOTE FOR BUSH AND CLINTON

	Election	
	1992	1996
Condition	(Percent of the Major Party Popular Vote)	
Incumbency	6.7	9.2
Prior vote	31.7	33.3
Minor party vote	6.4	9.8
Income change	0.9	2.1
Total	45.7	54.5

of the major party vote by a net 6.4 percentage points by drawing votes that would otherwise have gone to the Democratic candidate; most of the minor party vote, however, would not otherwise have voted. Bush would have lost by an even larger margin in 1992 if not for the minor party vote. In 1996, the minor party vote increased the Clinton share of the major party vote by a net 9.8 percentage points by drawing votes that would otherwise have gone to the Republican candidate; in this case, however, only a small share of the smaller minor party vote would not otherwise have voted. Clinton would apparently have lost the election in 1996 if not for the minor party vote.

In both cases, again, the minor party vote increased the incumbent president's share of the major party popular vote. Another finding is that conditions that were common to the whole sample favored Clinton by 2.5 percentage points more in 1996 than they helped Bush in 1992. In both cases, 60 to 70 percent of the variance among the states of the vote for the incumbent president was explained by the popular vote by state for the same candidate in the prior election. Economic conditions favored Clinton more in 1996 than Bush in 1992, but the variance of the change in real per capita income among the states explained only 2 to 4 percent of the vote for the incumbent president by state in these elections.

Conclusion

The characteristic Perot voter, in summary, was very similar to the average voter, except for a concern about his or her personal economic condition and an anxiety about future general economic conditions. One might think that this would lead to a vote for change, drawing largely from votes that would otherwise go to the candidate of the incumbent party. In both 1992 and 1996, however, the minor party vote, almost all of which was for Perot, increased the incumbent president's share of the major party vote, drawing from votes that would have otherwise have gone to the opposition candidate. Anxious voters, in these two elections, apparently voted against change. In this sense, the vote for Perot was a vote for the status quo.

References

Niskanen, W. (1979) "Economic and Fiscal Effects on the Popular Vote for the President." In *Public Policy and Public Choice*, ed. D. W. Rae and T. J. Eismeier, pp. 93–120. Beverly Hills, CA: Sage Publications.

Public Opinion Strategies. (1993) "Ross Perot/Perot Voters." A memorandum (recipient not identified), Arlington, VA, May 20.

Note

1. This vote function is similar to that which I tested with a time-series sample in Niskanen (1979).

18. On the Constitution of a Compound Republic

The Constitution of the United States established the basic structure of a compound republic, a federal structure in which there are two or more levels of government each of which has the primary if not sole authority for a specific set of collective decisions. The U.S. federal structure is characterized by a separation of powers within the federal government and between the federal and state governments but without any explicit provision for resolving constitutional disputes. Early in the U.S. history under the Constitution, however, in several important decisions by Chief Justice John Marshall, the Supreme Court asserted its authority to adjudicate these disputes, and this role has been accepted, albeit not without controversy, since that time.

This article makes the following major points:

1. The Constitution establishes no explicit provision for resolving constitutional disputes. Judicial review has not been sufficient to prevent a massive erosion of the limits on the powers of the federal government.
2. The primary effects of the changes in the effective constitution that weakened the separation of powers between the federal and state governments have been a substantial increase in the powers of the federal government and a somewhat larger increase in the total powers of the government.
3. The most promising means to sustain the constitution of a compound republic is to make the federal government the guarantor of individual rights against an abuse of power by the states and to make the state governments the guarantor of these rights against an abuse of power by the federal government.

This article was first published in *Constitutional Political Economy* 10, no. 2 (1999). My thanks to *Constitutional Political Economy* for its permission to republish this article.

4. For the United States, the necessary change to make the federal government an effective guarantor of individual rights is to restore the federal protection of the privileges and immunities of all citizens, a protection formally guaranteed by the Fourteenth Amendment but eroded by later court decisions.
5. For the United States, the necessary changes to make the state governments an effective guarantor of individual rights are to provide formal constitutional authority for (a) a specified *group* of states to nullify an action by the federal government, primarily to force a determination whether the action would meet the Article V tests for a constitutional amendment, and *maybe* (b) for an individual state to secede from the federal union, preferably by two successive votes over some interval and subject to some agreed rule for the allocation of the assets and liabilities of the federal government.

These points reflect my still tentative judgments and are intended to provoke controversy, in the hope that both you and I will learn from this controversy.

Sustaining a Constitutional Contract

As I noted in a prior article (Niskanen 1990), we have only the most primitive understanding about what sustains a constitutional contract. The conventional American civics textbook explains that the Supreme Court is the guardian of the Constitution, but there are at least three problems with this explanation:

1. There is no explicit constitutional authority for judicial review of constitutional disputes. Alexander Hamilton (1788), among the Framers the strongest supporter of the role of the courts under the new Constitution, acknowledged (in *Federalist* No. 81) that

> ... there is not a syllable in the plan under consideration which directly empowers the national courts to construe the laws according to the spirit of the Constitution ... the Constitution ought to be the standard of construction for the laws, and that wherever there is an evident opposition, the laws ought to give place to the Constitution. But this doctrine is not deducible from any circumstance peculiar to the plan of convention, but from the general theory of a limited Constitution.

Hamilton had previously developed an argument (in *Federalist* No. 78) that

> The complete independence of the courts of justice is peculiarly essential in a limited Constitution, . . . [that such limitations] can be preserved in practice no other way than through the medium of the courts of justice, whose duty it must be to declare all acts contrary to the manifest tenor of the Constitution void. Without this, all the reservations of particular rights or privileges would amount to nothing . . . where the will of the legislature, declared in its statutes, stands in opposition to that of the people, declared in the Constitution, the judges ought to be governed by the latter rather than the former.

Chief Justice John Marshall relied primarily on the above argument by Hamilton, that the power of judicial review is inherent in or implied by a limited constitution, when he asserted this power in *Marbury v. Madison* (1803). Marshall's decision was understandable, albeit then controversial. The Constitution is strangely silent on this issue, and political power rushes to fill a vacuum. In any case, judicial review has become part of the effective constitution and has been the primary process by which constitutional disputes are resolved.

2. Judicial review, of course, cannot provide a sufficient defense against changes in the effective constitution either initiated or ratified by the judiciary. Hamilton was not concerned that the judiciary might abuse this power, describing the judiciary (in *Federalist* No. 78) as the "least dangerous to the political rights of the Constitution . . . [as it] has no influence over either the sword or the purse." At the same time, however, he recognized that ". . . it would require an uncommon portion of fortitude in the judges to do their duty as guardians of the Constitution, where legislative invasions of it had been instigated by the major voice of the community."

As it has turned out, the structural and procedural provisions of the Constitution have proved to be remarkably stable, but the substantive provisions have been changed in major ways by both judicial initiative and by judicial acquiescence to pressure from Congress and the president. (Niskanen 1988) For the moment, my argument is not that these changes in the effective constitution were necessarily wrong but that these changes were made without the test of broad consensus required by the Article V procedures for amending the Constitution. Most of these changes in the effective constitution were made during the New Deal, a period that law professor Bruce Ackerman (1991) correctly describes as the third constitutional revolution. At the birth of the U.S. welfare state—when proposed legislation that would establish social security, aid to dependent children, and unemployment insurance was before the House—President Franklin Roosevelt wrote a member of the Ways and Means Committee in July 1935 that "I hope that your committee will not permit doubts as to constitutionality, however reasonable, to block the suggested legislation." Congress approved the Social Security Act in August 1935, and the Supreme Court indirectly validated this act in January 1936, ruling (in *United States v. Butler*, 1936) the "the power of Congress to authorize appropriations of public money for public purposes is not limited by the direct grants of legislative power found in the Constitution." This first major accommodation to the New Deal saved the Court from Roosevelt's later threat to pack it with more acquiescent justices, but it effectively destroyed the fiscal constitution. In effect, each Congress may now write its own fiscal constitution, subject only to the restraint that the appropriations must serve some vague concept of public purpose. Hamilton's fear that the Court could not defend the Constitution against "the major voice of the community" proved to be correct. Even with "an uncommon portion of fortitude," no group that could all be put in one paddy wagon can stop a parade.

3. The third problem of the conventional explanation is that it is specific to the United States and a few other nations. In most other nations, the highest court has no constitutional role. Even if the conventional explanation fit the U.S. experience, it fails to provide a general theory of constitutional maintenance.

A Compound Republic without a Separation of Powers

Conventional public finance suggests that the size of government in a federal system would be smaller than in an economy with a unitary government, because regional governments are more constrained by the potential mobility of labor and capital. That advantage of a federal system, however, is dependent on an effective separation of powers between the national government and the regional governments. For the most part, that was the case through the 1920s. In 1929, the last cyclical peak before the Great Depression, current expenditures by the U.S. federal government were 2.6 percent of GDP, most of which was for the military and the deferred costs of prior wars, and total U.S. government expenditures were 9.9 percent of GDP. Since that time, however, real government spending has increased at about the same rate in both federal and unitary governments. (Grossman and West 1994) As of 1997, current expenditures by the U.S. federal government were 21.5 percent of GDP, most of which was for programs for which there is no explicit constitutional authority, and total U.S. government expenditures were 30.5 percent of GDP.

Why did this happen? Most important, the constitutional limits on the fiscal and regulatory powers of the federal government have been almost completely eroded since the 1920s. Second, with no constitutional wall between the powers of the federal and state governments, both federal and state politicians have an incentive to compete to provide the same services in a given state. As explained in an important recent article by Jean-Luc Migue (1997), this has much the same effects as two parties pumping oil or water from a common pool—oversupply of the service and, in the limit, the dissipation of any rents to both parties. Moreover, federal interventions are likely to expand most, because the federal government is less constrained by the potential mobility of labor and capital. This explanation is wholly consistent with the U.S. record on government expenditures, regulation, and even the criminal law but may not be the best or most general explanation. Competing explanations of these same developments are welcome.

Using a Compound Republic to Enforce the Constitution

The unique potential strength of a compound republic is the opportunity to use each level of government to protect individuals against abuses of constitutional authority by the other level. Only power can check power. In a prior age, only the king could protect individuals against the barons, and only the barons could protect individuals against the king. In our age, both the federal government and the state governments must be sufficiently strong so that neither party easily dominates the other, and the interests of the leaders of the two levels of government must be sufficiently different to assure that they would not collude to exploit the general population. This concept of a compound republic was broadly shared among the Framers of the U.S. Constitution. In *Federalist* No. 28, Hamilton stated that is was an "axiom" of the American system of government "that the state governments will in all possible contingencies afford complete security against invasions of the public liberty by the national authority." Should the national government prove to be a danger, Hamilton expected the states to

> at once adopt a regular plan of opposition, in which they can combine all the resources of the community. They can readily communicate with each other in the different states; and unite their common forces for the protection of their common liberty.

And James Madison, in *Federalist* No. 51, described how the federal government and the states "will controul each other; at the same time each will be controulled by itself." In the limit, an abuse of constitutional authority by either level of government can only be constrained by actions that risk civil war. This is a disturbing conclusion, but the only alternative seems to be a unitary government that is dominant enough to define its own powers; I would welcome to be proved wrong on this issue.

Federal Protection of our Privileges and Immunities

The necessary constitutional authority for the federal government to protect individuals against an abuse of authority by the states is already in place: the Privileges or Immunities Clause of the Fourteenth Amendment. Although this clause, for lack of use, now seems as quaint as knee breeches and powdered wigs, it was part of common Anglo-American legal parlance through the 1860s. And it had a distinguished lineage—included in Article IV of the Constitution, the Articles of Confederation, Blackstone's *Commentaries*, and the founding documents of the American colonies dating back to the Charter of Virginia in 1606. Hamilton (in *Federalist* No. 80) described the Article IV clause as "fundamental . . . the basis of the Union."

What does this clause mean? How did a protection so fundamental to American constitutions become ineffective? Why is it important to revive this protection?

First, this clause is rooted in natural law, a concept broadly shared among the American Founders and integral to the Declaration of Independence. As expressed by two modern lawyers (paraphrasing Blackstone), "immunities are. . . the natural rights we retain when we enter into civil society, . . . privileges (are what) we gain at that time in exchange for surrendering certain of our natural liberties" (Shankman and Pilon 1998).

From the beginning, the Constitution guaranteed that "The Citizens of each State shall be entitled to all Privileges and Immunities of Citizens in the several States." But that federal guarantee was limited to citizens, and the definition of citizenship was left to each state. In 1868, the Fourteenth Amendment extended citizenship to "All persons born or naturalized in the United States" and thus extended the federal guarantee of privileges and immunities to all such persons. Although initially targeted against the "black codes" that were emerging in the postwar South, the amendment was written broadly to protect all Americans against an abridgement of these rights by the states. Five years later, however, in the tragically misreasoned *Slaughterhouse Cases* (1873), the Court stripped the Fourteenth Amendment of these substantive protections, thus limiting the federal guarantees to due process and equal protection. These procedural guarantees, unfortunately, did not prove to be sufficient to protect blacks against the legal discrimination that lasted for a century after the Civil War or business firms against the substantial increase in state regulation. A reflection on this history led the two lawyers mentioned above to conclude that "Had the *Slaughterhouse* Court properly read and applied the Privileges or Immunities Clause, we would doubtless have today a very different body of constitutional law than we have—and a very different nation, not least in the area of race relations, but not there alone" (Shankman and Pilon 1998).

At great cost, the Civil War demonstrated the power of the federal government to protect individuals against an abuse of their rights by the states. The Fourteenth Amendment provided the clear authority. And the federal role to defend civil rights proved the importance of an occasional, forceful intervention to reassert this authority. The legitimate concern about a broader abuse of authority by the federal government should not weaken this important federal role in a compound republic. For this role to be fully effective, moreover, the federal government should reassert its authority to protect the privileges and immunities of individuals against unjust state action, so that the rights of individuals are not dependent on the weaker procedural guarantees of due process and equal protection.

State Protections against an Abuse of Federal Power

Sustaining a compound republic, however, also requires a countervailing power to protect against an unconstitutional assertion of powers by the national government. In the American system, the state governments are the logical and possibly the only group with a sufficient potential to serve this role. My position on this issue, however, differs strongly from the misleading and divisive concept of "states' rights." First, governments have authorized powers, not rights; only individuals have rights. In the American system, moreover, the state governments are limited to those residual powers not delegated to the federal government by the Constitution nor prohibited by it to the states. And these state powers do not include the authority to limit those rights that are common to all citizens of the United States. For the United States to maintain a compound republic, state governments must have sufficient authority to check an abuse of power by the federal government but not enough to abuse the rights of people or organizations in these states. The history of the United States suggests that this may be a difficult, but hopefully not impossible, challenge to constitutional design.

Nullification

The U.S. Constitution, in brief, does not establish an adequate procedure for forcing a constitutional test of the assertion of undelegated powers by the federal government (Niskanen 1980). Article V provides an adequate procedure for testing the consensus on any formal amendment proposed by Congress or a convention, but there is no procedure for forcing a constitutional test on issues for which the Supreme Court is unwilling or unable to enjoin the actions of Congress or the presidency or of a decision by the Court itself. In that sense, the U.S. Constitution is asymmetric: a vote by more than one-fourth of the states can block a formal amendment, but there is no corresponding procedure for even a majority of states to force a constitutional test by enjoining a change in the effective constitution.

The procedural solution to this asymmetry is as old as the Magna Carta and has been circulating in the backwater of American political theory since the beginning of our republic: some proportion of the parties to the constitutional contract must be able to enjoin the actions of the government established by that contract in order to force a formal constitutional test of a unilateral assertion of powers by the larger government. Clause 61 of the Magna Carta established a group of 25 "guardians of the charter," any four of which could notify the king of violations of the charter and, if not resolved within 40 days, bring the matter to the other guardians. This famous clause, probably the contribution of Stephen Langton, then Archbishop of Canterbury, was subject to continuous attack by defenders of the royal prerogatives and was omitted from later versions of the charter when the king regained power.

The Kentucky and Virginia resolutions, written respectively by Jefferson and Madison, tried to establish a similar procedure in the new American republic in 1798. These resolutions articulated the concept that the exercise of undelegated power had no force of law, but proposed nothing more than a common appeal of the states to Congress to repeal the Alien and Sedition laws. The election of Jefferson and a Republican Congress in 1800 led to early repeal of these laws but deferred consideration of the basic constitutional issue.

John Calhoun raised this issue again in 1832 in the South Carolina Ordinance of Nullification, declaring that the 1828 "tariff of abominations" was unconstitutional and would not be enforced in that state. This issue was resolved by Congress in the compromise tariff legislation of 1833. Calhoun, unfortunately, confused the case for a collective responsibility of the states to enjoin a breech of the Constitution by the federal government with a nonviable concept of "states' rights," asserting that individual states are "free, independent, and sovereign communities." The State of Wisconsin next raised this issue in 1859 to force a constitutional test of the Fugitive Slave Law; this confrontation was resolved only when a newspaper editor who had been arrested was pardoned a few days before the start of the Civil War.

The doctrines of nullification and interposition have been criticized or dismissed by later political theorists, primarily because they were used to defend slavery and the continued denial of civil rights to blacks. Americans have an unfortunate habit, however, of evaluating a legal concept by the motivations of its advocates. Most contemporary Americans probably regard the Alien and Sedition laws, discriminatory tariffs, and slavery as repugnant. The doctrine of nullification, however, should not be evaluated by the fact that it was first used to attack bad law and later used to defend other bad law, but rather whether it would, in general, promote law that reflects the broad consensus of the population. The Civil War was the first major tragic failure to correct the constitutional flaw to which this doctrine was addressed. The constitutional anarchy of our time, I suggest, is the result of the same problem. My reading of this history leads me to conclude that there is a fundamental flaw in the Constitution, a flaw that has led to occasional problems that were resolved in an ad hoc manner that deferred a more general recognition and correction of this flaw.

The prospect for liberal democracy, I contend, will depend on some constitutional reform that would enforce a constitutional process of constitutional change. This reform should build on Madison's concept of a compound republic. The federal government is now a more effective guardian of individual rights against an abuse of power by the states. The state governments, correspondingly, should be the "guardians of the charter" of the federal government. Andrew Jackson's response to Calhoun was correct in asserting that the federal union could not survive if each state could nullify federal law. It is also important to recognize that a constitutional democracy cannot survive the subjugation of any substantial minority. The general nature of the constitutional reform that derives from this analysis would be to authorize some specified number of states to enjoin any federal law, regulation, or court ruling within some specified period. A specific amendment to the Constitution consistent with these principles would provide for the nullification of any federal action by the vote of more than, say, one-third of the state legislatures within one year after the date of the last vote. Such an amendment would be designed to force a constitutional test of any action and would be nearly symmetric with the present provision for approving constitutional amendments. This amendment would provide a considerable period for both reasoned evaluation of the federal action and continued federal abuse of its constitutional powers, but it should protect the nation against both ephemeral whim and an indefinite extension of federal power. (William Watkins (1999) has recently proposed a much-too-complicated amendment that would provide formal authority for such a nullification process.) The primary expected effect of such an amendment would be to force a compromise that would avoid exercise of the nullification authority on most issues.

Secession

One other asymmetry in the U.S. Constitution, of course, is that it provides specific rules for admitting or forming a new state but no rule for a secession. (In that sense, the Constitution is like a roach motel; you can get in, but you can't get out.) This is a sensitive issue for Americans, because the Civil War, at great cost, seems to have foreclosed the opportunity for secession. Almost all American politicians and political commentators, until days before the Civil War, supported the authority of a state to secede, even when, as was usual, they questioned its wisdom (DiLorenzo 1998). Those public choice scholars who have addressed this issue, moreover, all conclude that a secession clause is desirable if there is any threat of a geographically based permanent coalition. (Buchanan and Faith 1987; Lowenberg and Yu 1992; and Mueller 1996) Most recently, for example, Dennis Mueller (1996) writes

> that the danger always exists that some permanent coalition forms and tyrannizes over a permanent minority. By allowing the people in a contiguous area to secede, under some conditions, the constitution could protect against such future tyranny. Thus, a secession clause might be an optimal part of any constitution, (and) it seems more likely to be valuable in constitutions that join states than in those that join citizens.

And Mueller concludes that

> If there is one simple lesson to learn from the unfortunate experience of the United States regarding secession, it is that any autonomous nation joining in a constitutional contract with other nations should, if it has any reason to fear that this contract may at some point prove to be to its disadvantage, require the precise stipulation in the contract of the conditions under which secession is possible.

This line of reasoning, which I share, invites questions about the desirable terms of a secession clause. First, secession should not be based on a casual or ephemeral decision. For that reason, I suggest, secession might be conditional on the approval by two successive votes in the affected region, separated by, say, two years. Second, the secession clause should include clear provisions affecting the disposition of the local assets and the general liabilities of the larger government. Subject to these terms, secession should not depend on the approval by the larger government.

My judgment, in summary, is that the authority of a regional government to secede from the national government is a logical part of the constitution of a compound republic. Adding a secession clause to the U.S. Constitution, however, does not seem to be worth the effort. The major potential fault lines in American politics—economics, ethnicity, religion, language, and culture—are no longer very correlated with geography. One ironic effect of maintaining the Union seems to have been a reduction of just those types of regional tensions that led to the Civil War. As a consequence, the authority of a state to secede from the United States would no longer provide much protection against a dominant coalition, such as those who receive net benefits from the federal government, that reflects roughly equal representation among the states. For that reason, a secession clause in the U.S. Constitution would be an insurance policy against a dominant coalition that is geographically based but one that is unlikely to be very valuable in the foreseeable future.

Conclusion

The effective constitution of the United States has changed enormously from that which the Framers designed, for the most part without a formal amendment. The most important challenge is broader than the issues addressed in this paper, to restore the idea of a constitution as a set of rules that the government itself may not change. Only then do the distinctive benefits and features of the constitution of a compound republic become important. One step at a time.

References

Ackerman, B. (1991) *We The People: Foundations*. Cambridge: Harvard University Press.

Buchanan, J. M., and Faith, R. L. (1987) "Secession and the Limits of Taxation: Towards a Theory of Internal Exit." *American Economic Review* (December) 77: 1023–31.

DiLorenzo, T. J. (1998) "The Great Centralizer: Abraham Lincoln and the War between the States." *The Independent Review* III (2): 243–72.

Grossman, P. J., and West, E. G. (1994) "Federalism and the Growth of Government Revisited," *Public Choice* 79: 19–32.

Hamilton, A., Madison, J. and Jay, J. [1961 (1788)] *The Federalist Papers*. New York: The New American Library, Inc.

Lowenberg, A. D., and Yu, B. T. (1992) "Efficient Constitution Formation and Maintenance: The Role of Exit." *Constitutional Political Economy* 3: 51–72.

Migue, J. L. (1997) "Public Choice in a Federal System." *Public Choice* 90 (1–4): 235–54.

Mueller, D. C. (1996) *Constitutional Democracy*, pp. 330–34. New York: Oxford University Press.

Niskanen, W. A. (1980) "The Prospect for Liberal Democracy." In *Fiscal Responsibility in Constitutional Democracy*, ed. J. M. Buchanan and R. E. Wagner, pp. 157–80. Dordrecht, Netherlands: Kluwer Academic Publishing.

______. (1988) "The Erosion of the Economic Constitution." In *Public Choice and Constitutional Economics*, ed. J. D. Gwartney and R. E. Wagner, pp. xi–xiii. Greenwich, Connecticut: JAI Press, Inc.

______. (1990) "Conditions Affecting the Survival of Constitutional Rules." *Constitutional Political Economy* 1 (2): 53–62.

Shankman, K. C., and Pilon, R. (1998) "Reviving the Privileges or Immunities Clause to Redress the Balance among States, Individuals, and the Federal Government." Cato Institute Policy Analysis No. 326.

Watkins, W. J. (1999) "The Kentucky and Virginia Resolutions: Guideposts of Limited Government." *The Independent Review* 3 (3): 385–411.

19. Bureaucracy: A Final Perspective

Most government services are supplied by bureaus, so any comprehensive theory of government must include a theory about the behavior of bureaus in the broader political environment. This chapter summarizes the development of the economic theory of bureaucracy. As I made a major early contribution to this theory (Niskanen 1971), my review of this literature reflects a continuing interest but, possibly, some personal bias. This review also borrows broadly from my two prior reassessments of this literature (Niskanen 1991, 1994), since my perspective on this topic has changed little in recent years. For other recent reviews of this literature, see the fine articles by Ronald Wintrobe (1997) and Terry Moe (1997).

Building Blocks

Contributions from Other Traditions

The study of bureaucracy, like the broader study of politics, was the almost exclusive domain of sociology and political science until several decades ago; as of 1968, for example, the article on "Bureaucracy" in the *International Encyclopedia of the Social Sciences* did not cite one study of bureaucracy by an economist. At that time, the modern scholarly literature on bureaucracy was dominated by the writings of Max Weber, a German sociologist. Weber recognized bureaucracy as the characteristic form of public administration for a state with extended territorial sovereignty, using the term "bureaucracy" largely as a synonym for a system of relations based on rational-legal authority. The modern literature on public administration was also strongly influenced by Weber's writings, with occasional infusions of Confucian and Platonist guidance on how a good

This article was first published in *The Elgar Companion of Public Choice*, ed. William A. Shughart and Laura Razzolini (Cheltenham, U.K.: Edward Elgar, 2001). My thanks to Edward Elgar for its permission to republish this article.

bureaucrat, now civil servant, ought to behave. An important contribution by James Q. Wilson, *Bureaucracy* (1989), is the best recent book in this general tradition.

Although the scholarly literature usually represented bureaucracy as desirable, or at least necessary, form of public administration, popular attitudes reflecting personal experience are often critical of the methods and performance of bureaucracy. These popular attitudes are probably best reflected in the irreverent and sometimes caustic form of literary satire, ranging from Honoré de Balzac's observations on the mentality and behavior of bureaucrats to Cyril Northcote Parkinson's mock-scientific observations on the behavior and performance of bureaus. The late Joseph Heller's *Catch-22* will probably become the modern classic in this tradition.

The Distinctive Nature of Economic Theory

As has since become clear, economics offers a valuable new perspective on bureaucracy—one based on the distinctive nature of economic theory. The compositive method of economics develops hypotheses about social behavior from models of purposive behavior by individuals. The individual consumer, entrepreneur or, in this case, bureaucrat is the central figure in the distinctive method of economics. He is assumed to face a set of possible actions and to choose that action within the possible set that he most prefers. The larger environment influences the behavior of the individual by constraining the set of possible actions, by changing the relations between actions and outcomes and, to some extent, by influencing his personal preferences. The economist develops models based on the purposive behavior of individuals, not to explain the behavior of individuals but to generate hypotheses about the aggregative consequences of the interaction among individuals in specific institutional arrangements.

The central insight of conventional economics is that the provision of private goods and services is an incidental effect of the incentives and constraints of consumers, entrepreneurs and employees. In other words, the provision of private goods and services is an effect, but is not the primary objective, of any participant in the private economy. Similarly, the central insight of the literature now described as public choice is that the provision of government services is an incidental effect of the incentives and constraints of voters, politicians, and bureaucrats. Although this perspective on government services is now more broadly shared, one should recognize how radical this perspective was first regarded and how radical it still seems among some groups.

Early Contributions by Economists

As of the late 1960s, only a few venturesome economists had taken on the bureaucracy as a subject for scholarship. Ludwig von Mises's book, *Bureaucracy* (1944), was more a forceful polemic against socialism than an analysis of bureaucracy, but it provided some of the first critical insights for a theory of bureaucracy. Specifically, Mises recognized that bureaus specialize in the supply of those services that are not sold at per-unit prices. He concludes, however, that the problems often attributed to bureaucracy are inherent in the scope and scale of government. One of Gordon Tullock's first sorties into the poorly defended province of political science was his *The Politics of Bureaucracy* (1965). Based on his own experience in the U.S. Department of State, Tullock focused on the information flows and advancement procedures within bureaus, providing an entertaining guide to the maximizing bureaucrat. I especially liked his comparison of a bureau to a gaseous diffusion plant. Similarly, Anthony Downs's book, *Inside Bureaucracy* (1967), focused primarily on the behavior within and among bureaus. Downs builds on the insight by von Mises that bureaus do not receive most of their revenues from the per-unit sale of output, but his typology of bureaucrats leads to the awkward conclusion that the behavior of a bureau is dependent on the motivation of the specific person who heads the bureau. One interesting characteristic of these early contributions, as well as my own, is that they were each written by an economist working outside the academy.

The Distinguishing Characteristics of Bureaus

From Weber to Downs, each of the major writers on bureaucracy developed his own list of the characteristics of bureaus and the bureaucracy. Paring down these lists to the smallest common set, one is left with a definition of bureaus as those organizations that have the following characteristics:

1. The owners and employees of these organizations do not appropriate any part of the net revenues as personal income.

2. A major part of the recurring revenues of the organization derive from other than the sale of output at per-unit prices.
3. In a single sentence: bureaus are nonprofit organizations that are financed primarily by a periodic appropriation or grant.

The first characteristic includes all government agencies, most government enterprises, most educational institutions and hospitals, and the many forms of social, charitable, and religious organizations. This characteristic clearly excludes corporate businesses, partnerships and sole proprietorships. Many staff units in profit-seeking organizations, however, have both of the critical characteristics of bureaus. The more difficult it is to identify a unit's or a division's contribution to a firm's profits, the more likely that the unit will behave like a bureau. The first characteristic also excludes mutual financial organizations, cooperatives and families; although these organizations are normally classified as nonprofit organizations, the identity of owners and consumers permits the appropriation of residual revenues either in the form of personal income or in lower prices for certain goods and services.

The second characteristic includes most nonprofit organizations. Some government enterprises (such as electric power, bridge and toll-road authorities) and some private nonprofit organizations are excluded by this characteristic, as their recurrent operations are financed entirely by the sale of output at a per-unit rate, even though these organizations may have been established initially by an appropriation or grant.

The appropriate definition of a bureaucrat or a bureaucracy follows directly from the above definition of a bureau. A bureaucrat is best defined as the head of a bureau with a separate budget. And a bureaucracy is some set of bureaus with a similar role or other common feature. None of these terms, of course, has any inherent normative connotation.

The Contemporary Economic Role of Bureaus

Given the above definition of bureaus, what is the economic role of bureaus in the United States and how has it changed? No one indicator, unfortunately, adequately reflects the scope and scale of the activities of bureaus. The three indicators presented in Table 19.1, however, provide rough estimates of the relative magnitude of the economic activities of bureaus.

Table 19.1
RELATIVE SIZE OF ECONOMIC ACTIVITY BY BUREAUS
(PERCENT OF U.S. GDP)

	1929	1949	1969	1989
Factor payments				
Nonprofit	1.1	1.4	2.5	3.8
Government	4.3	7.8	13.2	12.1
Government purchases	8.6	19.9	22.8	20.1
Government expenditures	10.0	23.2	31.4	33.9

The top two rows of numbers indicate the payment for factors employed by nonprofit institutions and general government (primarily the compensation of employees) as a percentage of the gross domestic product. This aggregation includes some nonprofit institutions and government enterprises financed entirely by the sale of services but, of course, excludes the bureaucratic components of profit-seeking firms. By this measure, assuming the value of the services supplied by bureaus is equal to their cost, the share of GDP originating in bureaus increased rapidly through 1969 and has since been a relatively stable 16 percent.

The third row indicates the total purchases by government, the sum of factor payments plus purchases from private firms. This is the broadest measure of the cost of services supplied by the government. By this measure, the relative size of government bureaus increased rapidly through 1949 and since then, except during wars, has been a relatively stable 20 percent of GDP.

The fourth row indicates the total expenditures by government—the sum of government purchases, transfer payments, interest payments, and subsidies. All of these expenditures pass through government bureaus, but the final expenditures financed by these transfer and other payments are largely determined by the recipients. By this measure, the relative size of expenditures made by or through government bureaus increased rapidly through 1969 and since then has been a relatively stable 33 percent of GDP. More interesting, perhaps, the increase in transfer payments accounts for almost all of the increase in the relative size of government in the United States since 1949.

One other dimension of the role of bureaus is not reflected in Table 19.1. Government regulatory bureaus also impose substantial costs on the private sector—an amount, including paperwork costs, which may be 5 to 10 percent of GDP. Although the costs of the older forms of price and entry regulation have declined since the late 1970s, this has been more than offset by the rapid increase in the regulation of health, safety, and the environment.

The Budget-Maximizing Bureaucrat

A Personal Note

At the time I began writing *Bureaucracy and Representative Government* (Niskanen 1971), I had worked a dozen years as a defense analyst at the RAND Corporation, the Pentagon, and the Institute for Defense Analyses. That experience shaped my perspective on bureaucracy in several ways that I was slow to understand. Most important, it was a frustrating but maturing experience, the transformation of a technocrat into a political economist. Gordon Tullock, when working briefly at IDA in 1966, helped shape my still inchoate views on bureaucracy and urged me to distill them in a professional article. And since the opportunities for career advancement in the military are almost exclusively limited to one's own service, I carelessly assumed that was also the case in other bureaus. The book that developed from this perspective provided the first formal economic analysis of the supply of government services, a framework that proved to be important but conspicuously flawed.

The Core Elements of the Initial Framework

Any theory of the behavior of bureaus must be based on the relationship between bureaus and their sponsors, usually some group of politicians. This relationship, in turn, is shaped by the distinctive incentives and constraints faced by bureaucrats and politicians. The primary elements of my initial framework that have survived subsequent analysis and comment are the following:

1. Bureaucrats are much like officials in other organizations. Their behavior will differ, not because of different personal characteristics but because of the incentives and constraints that are specific to bureaus.

2. Most bureaus have a monopoly buyer for their service. The effective demand for the output of the bureaus comes from this sponsor, rather than from the ultimate consumers of the service.
3. Most bureaus are monopoly suppliers of their service. More specifically, most bureaus face a downward-sloping effective demand function, even if there are alternative actual or potential suppliers of the same or similar service.
4. The bilateral monopoly relation between a bureau and its sponsor involves the exchange of a promised output for a budget, rather than the sale of output at a per-unit rate.
5. As in any bilateral monopoly, there is no unique budget-output equilibrium between the preferences of the sponsor and those of the bureau. The sponsor's primary advantages in this bargaining are its authority to monitor the bureau, to approve the bureau's budget, and to replace the senior bureaucrats. The bureau's primary advantage is that it has much better information about the costs of supplying the service than does the sponsor.
6. Finally, neither the members of the sponsor group nor the senior bureaucrats have a pecuniary stake in the outcome of this bargain. The effect is that the outcome will serve the interests of the sponsor and the bureaucrats in different ways, but not as direct compensation.

My initial framework, in addition, included three assumptions about the behavior of bureaucrats and their political sponsors that proved to be the focus of most subsequent criticism. Specifically, bureaucrats were assumed to act to maximize the expected budget of their bureau. Second, the sponsors were assumed to be "passive" in accepting or rejecting the bureau's budget output proposal without any careful monitoring or evaluation of alternatives. A third implicit assumption that I did not recognize at that time was that bureaucrats and their sponsors bargain over the full range of the possible combinations of budget and output.

The Implications of the Initial Framework

The primary implication of the initial framework is that both the budget and output of a bureau are larger than optimal; more precisely, the marginal value of the bureau's service to the constituents of the median voter in the legislature is lower than the marginal cost, the bureau appropriating the potential surplus to this group by expanding output beyond the optimal level. This outcome also generates a larger surplus to any labor or capital resources that are specific to the production of the service.

This framework also led to an awkward two-region solution to the budget output outcomes. In the "budget-constrained" region, the budget is equal to the minimum total cost of producing the output promised to the sponsor; here the service is produced efficiently but at a higher-than-optimal level of output. At a sufficiently high level of demand, however, the resulting budget-output outcome is in a "demand-constrained" region. In this region, the marginal value of output is zero, and the budget is larger than the minimum total cost of producing the promised output. In this region, the waste due to bureaucratic supply is some combination of both allocative and productive inefficiency.

At the time that I developed this framework, I recognized that it was incomplete. Specifically, the framework did not develop the other side of this market—the behavior of the sponsors in monitoring the bureau and bargaining over the budget. Over time, I also came to recognize that the several behavioral assumptions in my initial framework led to conclusions that are both theoretically inelegant and inconsistent with the available evidence.

The Major Criticisms of this Framework

What Do Bureaucrats Maximize?

Fortunately, the most important early comment on my book, by Jean-Luc Migue and Gerard Belanger (1974), suggested an approach that both generalized and simplified my initial framework. They made an assumption, more consistent with that of a profit-maximizing firm, that bureaucrats act to maximize the bureau's discretionary budget, defined as the difference between the total budget and the minimum cost of producing the output expected by the bureau's sponsor. This assumption leads to somewhat different conclusions: the budget of a bureau is too large, the output (again in terms of the demand revealed by the sponsor) is generally too small and that inefficiency in production is the normal condition. My 1975 article, "Bureaucrats and Politicians," incorporated this important modification.

The superiority of a slack-maximizing model was reinforced by several other considerations. In their 1975 article, Albert Breton and Ronald Wintrobe observed that the incentive for budget maximizing is likely to be limited to those bureaus, such as the military, in which the opportunities for promotion are limited to that bureau. Subsequent empirical work by Ronald Johnson and Gary Libecap (1989) and by Robert Young (1991) also indicated that the salaries of bureaucrats are only weakly related to the level and growth of their bureau's budget. And the accumulation of empirical studies indicates that inefficiency in production is a more general condition than suggested by my initial model.

The Behavior of Sponsors

A bureau's sponsor, of course, is not passive. I knew that, having served as a policy and budget review official in the Pentagon and later in two other federal review positions.

The first review of my book, by Earl Thompson (1973), correctly observed that a sponsor has both the authority and the opportunity to monitor a bureau by means that would reduce the inefficiency of bureaucratic supply. In 1975, Breton and Wintrobe expanded on this point with a simple model of the review process that determines the optimal amount of control devices and the consequent effects on the budget. The behavior of the sponsor was further developed in the political science literature by Gary Miller and Terry Moe in 1983 and by Jonathan Bendor and others (1985 and 1987).

I acknowledged the early contributions by Thompson and by Breton and Wintrobe in my 1975 article, but pointed out that their model did not reflect the specific institutions of the review process or the incentives of the legislators. In the United States, for example, legislative review is mostly conducted by specialized legislative committees that are largely self-selected. This introduces two powerful biases in the review process: most of the costs of effective review are borne by members of the committee, but almost all of the benefits accrue to a broader population; this creates a substantial free-rider problem internal to the legislature and the expectation that monitoring activities will be undersupplied. The 1976 study by Morris Ogul confirmed the general perception that members of Congress engage in very little oversight. Second, self-selection for committee assignment leads to committees that have a higher relative demand for the services of the bureaus subject to their oversight than the demand of the broader legislature. A high-demand committee, thus, is less likely to monitor oversupply by the bureau than would a randomly selected committee.

Several recent articles explore the institutions of the review process in more detail. In 1998 Glenn Parker and Suzanne Parker, for example, conclude that party leaders in Congress are more effective in influencing floor votes than committee decisions, but that obligations to interest groups will be more immune to leadership influence because of the incentives for committee members to adhere to their bargains. Hirofumi Shibata (1998) develops the implications of the budget-review process in the government of Japan and other parliamentary systems.

What Is the Range of Budget Bargaining?

One implicit assumption of my initial framework is that a bureau and its sponsor bargain over the whole range from a zero budget to the bureau's proposed budget. As I had previously served as a budget review official, this was a mistake for which I had no excuse. An important article by Thomas Romer and Howard Rosenthal (1978b) fortunately provided a better framework for analyzing each step in this process. They define the reversion level of the budget in a specific year as the level that will be maintained if there is no agreement on a new budget. If the sponsor's preferred budget is higher than the reversion level, a bureau has an incentive to propose an even larger budget that the sponsor values only slightly more than the reversion level. This framework leads to a conclusion that the excess budget will be roughly equal to the difference between the sponsor's preferred budget and a lower reversion level.

The rule for defining and changing the reversion level is thus very important. In many cases, for example, the reversion level in the annual budget review is the prior year's budget for that bureau. Sometimes, the reversion level is the budget for which the benefits to the sponsor are so low that it leads the sponsor to replace the managers of the bureau. Romer and Rosenthal estimated the results of school budget referenda in which the school board was the agenda setter and the reversion level was the budget at which the schools would have to be closed. The more general practice of setting the reversion level at the prior year's budget may seem to minimize the excess budget that year, but that may be misleading because the accumulation of the excess budgets in prior years is included in this year's reversion level. I have not worked out the long-term implications of a series of such annual budget reviews, however; nor, to my knowledge, has anyone else.

What Group Is the Effective Agenda Setter?

My initial framework, in which the bureau is assumed to act strategically and the sponsor is passive, provoked a productive reaction among political scientists, initially led by Barry Weingast and his colleagues. Weingast and Mark Moran (1983) and Weingast (1984) assert that congressional committees have as much control over bureaus as they desire—by use of their legislative and appointment powers and by shifting the burden of monitoring to constituency groups. This position, in turn, was challenged by Terry Moe (1989) and Murray Horn (1995), who emphasized the incentives of the current effective coalition to bind a subsequent legislature from breaking promises that the current coalition has made to their favored constituents. Reflecting on this controversy, Moe (1997, p. 466) concludes that "the theme of this literature ought to be that Congress has a difficult time controlling the bureaucracy, and that the latter has much autonomy. This is precisely what mainstream work by political scientists has long maintained."

Back to square one. What group or groups are most effective in setting the budget agenda? On this issue, I also agree with Moe (p. 472) that "attention to institutional context . . . should be central to any theory of bureaucracy." In the American political system, I suggest, the bureau and the specialized committee effectively collude to set the budget agenda, with the executive and the body of the legislature as the nearly passive sponsors. The bureau and the committee agree on the budget and program to be submitted to the whole legislature. The reversion level is the budget for which the benefits to the decisive voter in the legislature are so low that the legislature will discipline the committee (by changing its leadership or by removing some authority from the committee) or the executive will similarly discipline the bureau. The committee will submit the largest budget that the legislature will approve and not be vetoed by the executive, a budget that the legislature prefers only slightly to the reversion level. Again, the lower the reversion level, the larger the excess budget. Members of the legislature tolerate the agenda-setting powers of the committees because of the costs of monitoring, the necessity of a division of labor, and to prevent their own committee from being similarly disciplined. Most of the bargaining between the bureau and the committee is specific to the division of the excess budget between activities that serve the interests of the bureau and those that serve the interests of the committee. The committee is likely to threaten or initiate monitoring only when the bureau breaks its promise concerning the division of the spoils.

Barry Weingast was correct to assert the dominance of the legislature in the American political system, but the committees, in effective collusion with the bureaus, are the groups that exercise this power. And, as Terry Moe suggests, the powers of the bureaucracy are likely to be different in a different political system. Future scholarship on the supply of government services, I suggest, should focus on the relation between a committee and the legislature in the American political system and on the characteristic institutions of the budget review process in other political systems.

The Current State of the Economics of Bureaucracy

Empirical Evidence

My initial framework and the major criticisms of this framework provoked a wealth of empirical studies that bear on the hypotheses derived from the developing economic theory of bureaucracy. An article by Roderick Kiewiet (1991) provides the broadest recent summary of these empirical studies. A range of indirect, but not very discriminating, tests of the oversupply hypothesis provides little evidence in support of this hypothesis. On the other hand, there are now dozens of studies that support the inefficiency hypothesis. Almost all such studies find that the production cost of private firms is significantly lower than that for bureaus supplying the same or a similar service. A part of the problem may be due to the poor information on the cost of government services that is available to the political sponsor. In a recent letter to Congress summarizing an audit of the first consolidated financial statements for the federal government, for example, the acting controller general of the General Accounting Office reported that, "significant financial systems weaknesses, problems with fundamental record-keeping, incomplete documentation, and weak internal controls, including computer controls, prevent the government from accurately reporting a large portion of its assets, liabilities, and costs" (Hinchman 1988). The fact that most federal services have yet to be privatized, however, suggests that some amount of "waste, fraud, and abuse" may be just what Congress ordered.

A growing body of studies also supports the hypothesis that competition among bureaus, both within and among jurisdictions, reduces production inefficiency. The earlier studies in this group were unfortunately subject to an alternative interpretation that the lower local government expenditures in a multijurisdictional metropolitan area result from the intercity competition for tax base rather than from bureaucratic competition. Later studies were more careful to focus on inefficiency rather than expenditures and to control for a variety of socioeconomic characteristics. A recent study of school districts in New York State (Duncombe et al. 1997, p. 15), for example, concludes that "efficiency is negatively related to school district size, percent tenured teachers, district wealth, nonresidential property values and labor intensity and positively related to the percent of adults who are college educated." A recent study of Illinois cities (Hayes et al. 1998, p. i) yields similar results, concluding that "inefficient behavior is associated with richer communities, lower education levels and a lack of competition for residents among municipalities."

Several types of studies also confirm the hypothesis that government expenditures are higher than preferred by the median voter. My own study of presidential elections (Niskanen 1979) finds that the popular vote for the candidate of the incumbent party is a negative function of the increase in real per-capita federal expenditures since the prior election. The classic studies of school district referenda by Romer and Rosenthal (1979, 1982), the numerous studies of the "flypaper effect" (such as by Courant et al. 1979 and Wyckoff 1988) and the occasional popular vote for a supermajority rule on major fiscal decisions (Olmsted et al. 1988) all confirm the general hypotheses of the agenda-setter model.

Reflecting on the empirical studies of bureaucracy, Kiewiet (1991, p. 161) observes that "Niskanen's model is more one of legislative failure than of bureaucracy chicanery," and he concludes (p. 166) that this model "has fared at least as well as any other model in political economy of comparable generality."

Figure 19.1
SLACK AND BUDGET-MAXIMIZING MODELS

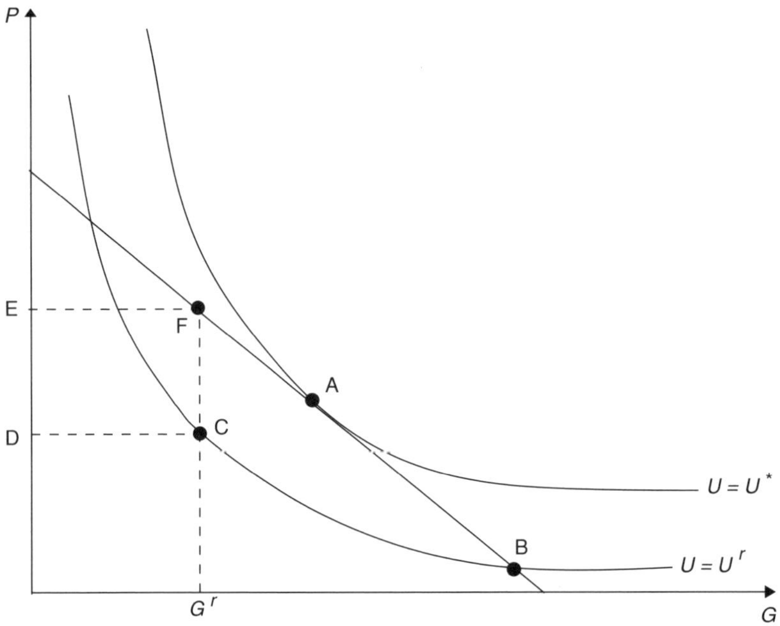

Theory

Sorting out the major criticisms of my initial framework and the developing empirical literature has led to a broad consensus for two major changes to this framework:

1. Maximizing the discretionary budget is a better description of bureaucratic behavior than budget (or output) maximizing.
2. The reversion-level budget is very dependent on the institutions of the budget review process but, in general, is not zero. In the limiting case, the reversion level is that for which the benefits to the sponsor are so low that the sponsor exercises its authority to replace or otherwise discipline the bureau.

The implications of this modified framework are summarized efficiently in an article by Paul Wyckoff (1990), from which Figure 19.1 is drawn. On this figure, the vertical axis is the level of private goods and services (*P*), and the horizontal axis is the level of government services (*G*). The point *A* is the optimal combination of *P* and *G* for the decisive voter in the sponsor group, given the budget constraint, yielding the utility level U^*. Wyckoff posits that the reversion utility level for the decisive voter is U^r, below which he or she will vote against the public official or leave the community. For these conditions, the budget- (or output-) maximizing bureaucrat will propose an output indicated by the point *B*, an output that is too large but is produced efficiently. For these same conditions, the discretionary-budget-maximizing bureaucrat will propose an output indicated by the point *C*, an output that is generally too low and yields an excess budget ("slack") of *CDEF*. Figure 19.1 also illustrates that a bureau's output will be higher and the excess budget will be lower, the higher is the reversion utility level. Since the consequences for the bureau of underestimating the reversion level can be quite severe, a risk-averse bureaucrat is likely to opt for a higher output and a lower excess budget.

There is less agreement on two other major issues, in part because these issues are very dependent on the institutional details of the political system. Most important, and peculiar to the U.S. political system, do the specialized review committees act as agents of the broader legislative membership or are they in effective collusion with the bureaus? As noted above, my judgment is that the review committees are the effective agenda setters, and their interests are largely in common with the bureaus except for the division of the excess budget. In this case, the body of the legislature should be considered to be the sponsor, and my initial assumption that the sponsor is passive may not be far off the mark. I encourage other scholars to weigh in on this issue, including how to test this hypothesis. Second, how much of a difference from the budget-output combination preferred by the decisive voter in the legislature is necessary to trigger special investigative hearings and possible disciplining of the normal review committee or the bureau? It is important to identify the conditions that determine the reversion level and how much the reversion level may be increased by changes in voting rules, committee organization and monitoring by the broader sponsor group.

In summary, those of us who have worked to formulate and refine the economic theory of bureaucracy have made major progress, but there is still a lot of productive work to do.

References

Bendor, Jonathan, Serge Taylor, and Roland van Gaalen. (1985) "Bureaucratic Expertise vs. Legislative Authority: A Model of Deception and Monitoring in Budgeting," *American Political Science Review* 79: 1041–60.

______. (1987) "Politicians, Bureaucrats, and Asymmetric Information." *American Journal of Political Science* 31: 796–828.

Breton, Albert, and Ronald Wintrobe. (1975) "The Equilibrium Size of a Budget-Maximizing Bureau: A Note on Niskanen's Theory of Bureaucracy." *Journal of Political Economy* 82: 195–207.

Courant, Paul, Edward Gramlich, and Daniel Rubinfeld. (1979) "The Stimulative Effects of Intergovernmental Grants: Or Why Money Sticks Where It Hits." In *Fiscal Federalism and Grants in Aid*, ed. Peter Miezkowski and William Oakland, pp. 5–21. Washington, DC: Urban Institute.

Downs, Anthony. (1967) *Inside Bureaucracy*. Boston: Little, Brown.

Duncombe, William, Jerry Miner, and John Ruggiero. (1997) "Empirical Evaluation of Bureaucratic Models of Inefficiency." *Public Choice* 93: 1–18.

Hayes, Kathy J., Laura Razzolini, and Leola B. Ross. (1998) "Bureaucratic Choice and Nonoptimal Provision of Public Goods: Theory and Evidence." *Public Choice* 94: 1–20.

Hinchman, James F. (1988) "Letter to Congress from the Acting Comptroller General of the General Accounting Office." March 31.

Horn, Murray J. (1995) *The Political Economy of Public Administration*. Cambridge: Cambridge University Press.

Johnson, Ronald N., and Gary D. Libecap. (1989) "Agency Growth, Salaries, and the Protected Bureaucrat." *Economic Inquiry* 27: 431–51.

Kiewiet, D. Roderick. (1991) "Bureaucrats and Budgetary Outcomes: Quantitative Analysis." In *The Budget-Maximizing Bureaucrat*, ed. André Blais and Stéphane Dion, pp. 143–73. Pittsburgh: University of Pittsburgh Press.

Migué, Jean-Luc, and Gerard Bélanger. (1974) "Toward a General Theory of Managerial Discretion." *Public Choice* 17: 27–43.

Miller, Gary, and Terry Moe. (1983) "Bureaucrats, Legislatures, and the Size of Government." *American Political Science Review* 77: 297–322.

Mises, Ludwig von. (1944) *Bureaucracy*. New Haven, CT: Yale University Press.

Moe, Terry. (1989) "The Politics of Bureaucratic Structure." In *Can the Government Govern?* ed. John E. Chubb and Paul Peterson, pp. 267–329. Washington: Brookings Institution.

______. (1997) "The Positive Theory of Public Bureaucracy." In *Perspectives on Public Choice: A Handbook*, ed. Dennis C. Mueller, pp. 455–80. Cambridge: Cambridge Unviersity Press.

Niskanen, William A. (1971) *Bureaucracy and Representative Government*. Chicago: Aldine-Atherton.

______. (1975) "Bureaucrats and Politicians." *Journal of Law and Economics* 18: 617–44.

———. (1979) "Economic and Fiscal Effects on the Popular Vote for the President." In *Public Policy and Public Choice*, ed. Douglas W. Rae and Theodore J. Eismeier, pp. 93–120. Beverly Hills: Sage.

———. (1991) "A Refelection on Bureaucracy and Representative Government." In *The Budget-Maximizing Bureaucrat*, ed. André Blais and Stéphane Dion, pp. 13–32. Pittsburgh: University of Pittsburgh Press.

———. (1994) "A Reassessment." In *Bureaucracy and Public Economics*, ed. William A. Niskanen, pp. 269–83. Aldershot, UK, and Bookfield, VT: Edward Elgar.

Ogul, Morris. (1976) *Congress Oversees the Bureaucracy.* Pittsburgh: University of Pittsburgh Press.

Olmstead, George, Judith Roberts, and Arthur Denzau. (1988) "We Voted for This? Institutions and Educational Spending." Political Economy Working Paper 128, Washington University.

Parker, Glenn, and Suzanne Parker. (1998) "The Economic Organization of Legislatures and How It Affects Congressional Voting." *Public Choice* 95: 117–29.

Romer, Thomas, and Howard Rosenthal. (1978) "Political Resource Allocation, Controlled Agendas, and the Status Quo." *Public Choice* 33: 27–43.

———. (1979) "Bureaucrats vs Voters: On the Political Economy of Resource Allocation by Direct Democracty." *Quarterly Journal of Economics* 93: 563–87.

———. (1982) "Median Voters or Budget Maximizers: Evidence from School Expenditure Referenda." *Economic Enquiry* 20: 556–78.

Shibata, Hirofumi. (1998) "The Budget Minimizing Bureaucrat: Working of the Invisible Hand in the Public Sector." Unpublished manuscript, presented at the 1998 annual meeting of the Public Choice Society.

Thompson, Earl A. (1973) "Bureaucracy and Representative Government." (book review) *Journal of Economic Literature* 11: 950–53.

Tullock, Gordon. (1965) *The Politics of Bureaucracy.* Washington: Public Affairs Press.

Weingast, Barry R. (1984) "The Congressional-Bureaucratic System: A Principal Agent Perspective (with Applications to the SEC)." *Public Choice* 44: 147–91.

Weingast, Barry R., and Mark J. Moran. (1983) "Bureaucratic Discretion or Congressional Control? Regulatory Policy-Making by the Federal Trade Commission." *Journal of Political Economy* 91: 765–800.

Wilson, James Q. (1989) *Bureaucracy: What Government Agencies Do and Why They Do It.* New York: Basic Books.

Wintrobe, Ronald. (1997) "Modern Bureaucratic Theory." In *Perspectives on Public Choice: A Handbook*, ed. Dennis C. Mueller, pp. 429–54. Cambridge: Cambridge University Press.

Wyckoff, Paul G. (1988) "A Bureaucratic Theory of Flypaper Effects." *Journal of Urban Economics* 23: 115–29.

———. (1990) "The Simple Analytics of Slack-Maximizing Bureaucracy." *Public Choice* 67: 35–47.

Young, Robert A. (1991) "Budget Size and Bureaucratic Careers." In *The Budget-Maximizing Bureaucrat*, ed. André Blais and Stéphane Dion, pp. 33–58. Pittsburgh: University of Pittsburgh Press.

20. Bringing Power to Knowledge: Choosing Policies to Use *Decentralized* Knowledge

Information Overload

For most of my adult life, I have worked as a policy analyst, to advise the prince, to bring knowledge to power. That has often been a frustrating and morally challenging profession. That can also be a valuable and honorable profession. Most of this conference is focused on the challenge of improving the knowledge available to and used by our political leaders. That was also the focus of a similarly distinguished group of scholars and senior politicians at a symposium organized by the Library of Congress 10 summers ago.

For this hour, however, I want to turn this topic on its head—to challenge you to understand the reasons and the means to bring power to knowledge, to empower individuals to use knowledge that can be centralized only at great cost, usually the loss of information. This challenge is compounded by recognizing that some policies can be decentralized only at great cost, usually the loss of effectiveness.

One reason to pay more attention to policies that use decentralized knowledge is that our political leaders are already subject to information overload, a condition that will almost surely increase. The massive information available to our political system does not become knowledge unless our political leaders have the capacity and the incentive to understand this information. Two senior politicians at the Library of Congress symposium expressed this point forcefully: Claiborne Pell, then a senior senator, observed that "In theory, the

This article was presented on July 4, 1998, at a conference in Turin organized by the Fondazione Rosselli and was first published in *Knowledge and Politics*, ed. Ricardo Viale (Heidelberg, Germany: Physica-Verlag, 2001). My thanks to Physica-Verlag for its permission to republish this article.

more accurate the knowledge available to governments, the more wisely they will wield power. The reality is often quite different. At times knowledge is not absorbed or perceived promptly; is garbled in transmission; or it is simply not believed. Knowledge is often rejected because it clashes with the political or intellectual fads of the moment."[1] Thomas Foley, then the majority leader in the House of Representatives, similarly observed that "What Members (of Congress) miss most is the opportunity to utilize the extraordinary amount of information available. The country has not yet devised a congressional way of life that allows all but a few unusually efficient legislators to draw on their new resources."[2]

Daniel Boorstin, a distinguished historian, expressed a related concern:

> A continuing and historic fusion in the twentieth century of the realm of the discoverer and the realm of the inventor has helped make possible the world-transforming scientific advances with which the holders of political power are struggling to cope . . . the explosion of knowledge that they have produced seems to be on a collision course with the growth of liberal political institutions. The technological instruments and discoveries that shape the community's fate are increasingly mysterious to its members.[3]

The new technology, in brief, increases the amount of information available but not the capacity of our political leaders to absorb and understand this information.

The more types of services that a government supplies, the lower is any politician's average knowledge about a specific service. This leads to an increasing delegation of decisions, even rule-making, to committees of legislators or ministers and from both to their specialized staffs, a delegation that reduces both the control and the accountability of the political authorities. These problems are more a function of the scope than of the scale of government. As a consequence, all governments of a similar scope have a roughly similar problem of transforming information into knowledge, even if there are huge differences in the scale of these governments.

The Nature of Decentralized Knowledge

A more important reason to choose policies that make use of decentralized knowledge is that most of us value both freedom and efficiency, for individual decisionmaking based on those types of knowledge that are only available to the individual.

Unconscious Knowledge

One type of knowledge that cannot be centralized is the vast scope of unconscious knowledge by which we conduct most of our daily lives. Some of this knowledge may be genetically programmed, some of it may be learned; in any case, this type of knowledge is hard-wired and cannot be articulated. Writing about the challenge of designing intelligent robots, the eminent physicist and futurist Michio Kaku observes that

> common sense is so embedded in our brains at such an unconscious level that we don't even ponder how we use it in our daily lives. Only the tiniest fraction of our thinking is devoted to conscious thought. Most of our thinking is actually unconscious thought, including common sense.[4]

(Another eminent physicist who is studying the architecture of the human brain, by the way, is Miguel Virasoro of Trieste.) The history of robot design illustrates the importance of making use of such decentralized common preprogramming, and little learning ability; these robots proved to be clumsy and unadaptive to any unanticipated change in its environment. The most successful mobile robots, however, like the rover on the recent mission to Mars, have much less computing power but the ability to learn and improvise, like a baby, by interacting with the immediate environment. Similarly, people with common sense make much better decisions over a range of issues than those that operate by preprogrammed instructions.

Values

Only an individual knows his or her own values. They may be able to articulate these values, but any process of aggregating these values loses information and may distort the underlying preference order. Voting and opinion polling, the two processes for determining values on which our political system is dependent, are conspicuously flawed. Neither of these processes adequately reflects differences in the intensity of preferences or assures that the revealed preference order is consistent with the underlying order. A policy that permits each individual to express his or her preferences will lead to a greater diversity of outcomes without the problems specific to these processes.

Knowledge Specific to Person, Time, and Place

All of us have information that is available only to us and is specific to time and place. Such information could conceivably be centralized but, in general, it is more efficient for each individual to act on this information. As on so many issues, Friedrich Hayek said it best:

> . . . practically every individual has some advantage over all others because he possesses unique information of which beneficial use might be made, but of which use can be made only if the decision depending on it are left to him or are made with his active co-operation. We need to remember only how much we have to learn in any occupation after we have completed our theoretical training, how big a part of our working life we spend learning particular jobs, and how valuable an asset in all walks of life is knowledge of people, of local conditions, and of special circumstances. To know of and put to use a machine not fully employed, or somebody's skill which could be better utilized, or to be aware of a surplus stock which can be drawn upon during an interruption of supplies, is socially quite as useful as the knowledge of better alternative techniques. The shipper who earns his living from using otherwise empty or half-filled journeys of tramp-steamers, or the estate agent whose whole knowledge is almost exclusively one of temporary opportunities, or the arbitrageur who gains from local differences of commodity prices—are all performing eminently useful functions based on special knowledge of circumstances of the fleeting moment not known to others."[5]

On the Possibility of Socialist Calculation

In the extended debate on the possibility of socialist calculation, several writers claimed that Vilfredo Pareto and Enrico Barone had solved this problem long ago. Given the enormous computational power of modern computers, it is especially important to understand that Pareto himself denied this possibility, making the following argument:

> Let us make the most favourable assumption for such a calculation, let us assume that we have triumphed over all the difficulties of finding the data of the problem and that

> we know the *ophélimités* (value) of all the different commodities for each individual, and all the conditions of production of all the commodities, etc. This is already an absurd hypothesis to make [. . .] [Given the number of necessary equations], it would not be mathematics which would assist political economy, but political economy which would assist mathematics. In other words, if one really could know all these equations, the only means to solve them which is available to human powers is to observe the practical solution given by the market."[6]

There is no reason to continue the debate on the possibility of socialist calculation. Hayek was correct to describe socialism as "the fatal conceit." The lessons from the division of Europe and Asia between market and socialist economies after World War II are, or should be, obvious. Both our freedom and our economic well-being are best served, wherever possible, by policies that use the decentralized information available only to individuals—some of which is unconscious and cannot be articulated, some of which are individual values that cannot be adequately aggregated, some of which is specific to time and place and cannot be efficiently centralized.

Some General Guidance for the Choice of Policies

So far, I have made the case that our political leaders are already subject to information overload and that individuals have a lot of information and knowledge that cannot easily be centralized. If so, where do we go from here? What types of policies are most likely to fail? And what types of policies are likely to be most successful?

Fortunately, there is a profound new book, *Seeing Like a State*, that suggests some general answers to these questions: the author is James C. Scott, a Yale University political scientist and anthropologist.[7] Scott documents some of the more tragic modern examples of social engineering in fascinating detail and then suggests the common characteristics of policies that are most likely to fail and, more tentatively, those more likely to succeed. The major case studies focus on scientific forestry, urban planning, the Bolshevik revolution, collective farms, and the compulsory resettlement projects in Tanzania and Ethiopia, in each case in the context of informed commentary about a wide range of similar historical and contemporary examples.

Scott attributes these tragic episodes to the pernicious combination of four conditions:

1. A society must be sufficiently "legible" to the State to permit the desired intervention. The more detailed the desired intervention, the more detailed the necessary information. Scott is perceptive to recognize that the types of modern information systems that serve the tax, regulation, and police interests of the State also serve the interests of research, commerce, and travel, at least in the short run—the standardization of weights, measures, time, money, business accounts, and language; the availability of good maps and a good census, the general use of surnames, etc. Indeed, such information systems are requisite to a modern political economy.

   Scott is also careful, however, to recognize that this same information may also be used for malign interventions, his most dramatic example of a 1941 map of the distribution of Jews in Amsterdam. Over time, moreover, the accuracy of the information is likely to be a function of the way it is used, with individuals and firms suppressing or distorting information that may trigger a malign intervention. Since much of this information serves both public and private interests, however, it is usually better to limit its use rather than to suppress it. In another important insight, Scott recognizes that the nature of the information available to the State is necessarily focused and aggregated, at the loss of peripheral and distributional detail. A State, in effect, "sees" a community or society as if from an airplane, gaining a broader perspective in some dimension but losing the detailed perspective of the man on the street. Many of the tragic episodes that he documents, in turn, are a consequence of some planner's assumption that his "bird's eye view" is a sufficient information base for a successful social policy.
2. The second, more distinctive, characteristic of the failed social experiments is what Scott calls "a high-modernist ideology," one based on a strongly held scientific or political theory or sometimes no more than a compulsive sense of social order. Scott identifies its primary advocates and practitioners as "the avant-garde among engineers, planners, technocrats, high-level administrators, architects, scientists, and visionaries."[8] Among the leading high modernists, Scott includes "Saint-Simon, Le Corbusier, Walther Rathenau, Robert McNamara, Robert Moses, Jean Monnet, the Shah of Iran, David Lilienthal, Vladimir Lenin, Leon Trotsky, and Julius Nyerere [. . .] [men who]

envisioned a sweeping, rational engineering of all aspects of social life in order to improve the human condition."[9]

3. The third necessary condition is an authoritarian State that is willing and able to use its powers to implement the grand high-modernist designs.
4. And the fourth condition is "a prostrate civil society that lacks the capacity to resist these plans,"[10]

"In sum," Scott concludes,

> the legibility of a society provides the capacity for large-scale social engineering, high-modernist ideology provides the desire, the authoritarian State provides the determination to act on that desire, and an incapacitated civil society provides the leveled social terrain on which to build.[11]

These four conditions provide a valuable framework for understanding the most tragic modern social experiments and insights about the failure of other social policies, such as the recurrent American attempts to restrict the consumption of alcohol, drugs, and tobacco. Scott is careful, moreover, to acknowledge that

> centralized high-modernist solutions can be the most efficient, equitable, and satisfactory for many tasks. Space exploration, the planning of transportation networks, flood control, airplane manufacturing, and other endeavors may require huge organizations minutely coordinated by a few experts. . . . On the other hand [he observes], these methods seem singularly maladroit at such tasks as putting a real good meal on the table or performing surgery.[12]

For me, Scott's most important insights are how to resist the temptations of authoritarian high modernism:

> Three factors seem decisive. The first is the existence and belief in a private sphere of activity in which the State and its agencies may not legitimately interfere. . . . The second, closely related factor is the private sector in liberal political economy . . . [one that is] far too complex for it ever to be managed in detail by a hierarchical administration. The third and by far most important barrier to thoroughgoing high-modernist schemes has been the existence of working, representative institutions through which a resistant society could make its influence felt.[13]

Scott is more tentative in identifying the characteristics of the institutions and policies that are most likely to be successful. As an anthropologist, he recognizes, like Hayek, that individuals have a lot of practical knowledge by which they live their daily lives. Scott uses the Greek word "*metis*" to distinguish practical knowledge that is specific to person, time, and place from epistemic or universal knowledge. And he suggests, I believe correctly, that successful institutions and policies must use both types of knowledge. He concludes with a case for *metis*-friendly institutions, observing that

> A good many institutions in liberal democracies already take such form and may serve as exemplars for fashioning new ones. One could say that democracy itself is based on the assumption that the metis of its citizenry should, in mediated form, continually modify the laws and policies of the land. Common law, as an institution, owes its longevity to the fact that it is not a final codification of legal rules, but rather a set of procedures for continually adapting some broad principles to novel circumstances. Finally, that most characteristic of human institutions, language, is the best model: a structure of meaning and continuity that is never still and ever open to the improvisations of all its speakers."[14]

As an economist, I would add the market to Scott's list of the most important *metis*-friendly institutions: Scott would probably agree, although he is ambivalent about modern global capitalism. As a policy analyst, Scott's suggested rule of thumb for the design of policies seem more tentative but are also very appealing:

> Take small steps. In an experimental approach to social change, presume that we cannot know the consequences of our interventions in advance. Favor reversibility. Prefer interventions that can easily be undone if they turn out to be mistakes.
>
> Plan on surprises. Choose plans that allow the largest accommodation to the unforeseen.
>
> Plan on human inventiveness. Always plan under the assumption that those who become involved in the project later will have or will develop the experience and insight to improve on the design."[15]

Some Specific Suggestions for the Choice of Policies

So far, so good. But the important insights of Hayek and Scott stop short of suggesting how the major policies of contemporary democratic States should changed to make better use of individual decisions based on decentralized knowledge. So I will conclude this paper with my personal suggestions for the general direction of the implied change in policies.

Devolution

The one most important change would be to devolve many government powers now exercised at a national or regional level to some lower level of government. In general, such powers should be devolved to the lowest level of government at which there are no significant economies of scale or external effects on the population in other jurisdictions. For many government services, the empirical studies suggest that most of the economies of scale and the internalization of external effects are realized at the level of quite small jurisdictions. For these services, devolution would serve three objectives:

1. Local officials are likely to have better knowledge of local conditions.
2. The local political process is more likely to be responsive to the values of the marginal voter in that jurisdiction.
3. The increased diversity of tax-service combinations increases the knowledge base for public decisions and increases the opportunity of both individuals and firms to choose a preferred policy combination by moving.

Of course, there would continue to be important roles for a national government. Some public objectives—such as military security, basic research, and some environmental objectives—are best served by the exercise of government powers at the national, or even international, level. As important, perhaps, a democracy is best structured as a *compound* republic in which the national government protects individuals against an abuse of power by the regional and local governments and the regional governments serve as a constraint on an abuse of constitutional authority by the national government. Although there is no common optimal distribution of powers by level of government, most national governments have assumed more powers than is consistent with either freedom or efficiency.

Debureaucratization

None of the broadly shared reasons for tax financing of some services imply a preference for the supply of these services by government bureaus. Many services or the inputs to these services now supplied by government could be supplied by private firms either under contract to the government or in response to tax-financed vouchers to individuals. And an accumulation of empirical studies now provides ample documentation that private firms can provide many such services with higher quality or lower cost. For such services that are inherently provided to all affected parties in a specific area, opening the service to the supply by firms operating under contract can serve several objectives:

1. Drafting a performance contract forces the political officials to think carefully about the value of the several dimensions of a service, something that is all too casual in the usual relations between politicians and a bureau.
2. Firms are likely to have a broader ranger of ideas about how to produce a service to the specifications in the contract.
3. Competition for the contract among firms and the bureaus is likely to improve the performance of both groups.

Nor is there any reason to preclude contracting for the inputs to a service, even when the final service is supplied by a bureau. For such services as military security, for example, most equipment and many support activities are most efficiently supplied under contract.

For those services supplied directly to individuals—such as schooling, food support, and health care—tax-financed vouchers are more efficient than the supply by either bureaus or firms under contract. The value of the voucher should be based on the value to other people of some minimum level of consumption of a service by the voucher recipients, and the vouchers may be limited to those who would not otherwise purchase this level of service. Such vouchers should permit each individual to purchase a higher level of service from their own income and to purchase the service from any authorized supplier. Since the voucher recipients have a higher incentive to monitor suppliers than if the service were supplied by a bureau or under contract, this also reduces the necessary government monitoring of suppliers. There may be some political reason to maintain some government schools, food distribution centers, hospitals and medical clinics, etc., but there should be no presumption that this is the only or the best form of organization to supply such tax-financed services, that they have any inherent claim to the tax revenues for these services or the recipients of these services.

Deregulation

Finally, many types of regulation should be changed or eliminated. Most of the costs of regulation are not included in government budgets, but they are probably 5–10 percent of GDP in many nations.

The most offensive types of regulation reflect the paternalism of the contemporary State, the assumption that the State knows what is better for adults than they do. Most of the modern regulation of health and safety is based on this premise. In some cases, the State may have specialized information about the costs, benefits, and risks of some activities; in these cases, however, the appropriate State role is to inform adults rather than to regulate their behavior. This may be a special problem only in the United States, but somehow I think not. State nagging about these activities is only slightly less offensive; Big Momma is as irritating as Big Daddy if only somewhat less threatening. A respect for the values of individual adults should lead to the elimination of all paternalistic regulation in exchange, where possible, for succinct, accurate, and timely information.

A more broadly shared rationale for regulation is that some activities by individuals or organizations impose benefits or costs on other parties. In this case, the form of the regulation is important. All too often, the left is inclined to make a requirement of every virtue, the right to make a crime of every sin. In the limit, this would make every human activity either required or prohibited, eliminating any remaining individual freedom. As a substitute, the government should subsidize those activities that benefit other parties at a rate equal to the marginal benefit to other parties. Similarly, the government should tax those activities that impose costs on other parties at a rate equal to the marginal cost to other parties. This would permit individuals and organizations to adjust their own activities in response to *both* their own values and those of others. In this case, my preferred rules would require more discriminating information about the level of marginal benefits and costs to other parties than a vague general sense that some types of activities are either good or bad. I do not know or much care whether these two rules would increase government expenditures more or less than tax revenues; they would surely increase the net benefits to individuals relative to a proliferation of requirements and prohibitions.

Moreover, neither regulation nor taxes may be the best policy to control some types of activities that impose costs on others. For the United States and other common-law countries until about 1970, the common law was the primary form of environmental control. This type of control proved quite effective in those cases for which the sources of pollution were known and concentrated. The required proof of harm disciplined the many frivolous cases that have plagued administrative law. And the court awards provided both the incentive for aggrieved parties to bring good cases to court and direct compensation for the victims of pollution, neither of which is provided by administrative law. The common law, of course, is less effective in those cases for which the sources of the pollution that caused a specific harm are uncertain, broadly diffused, or for which there is a long gestation period between the pollution and the harm. The common law, thus, is not a sufficient instrument of environmental control but it merits respect for its superior effectiveness in a broad class of cases. As both Hayek and Scott would surely agree, a common-law system is especially desirable because it is evolutionary by nature, addressing new circumstances by modifying broad principles without any sudden lurches in legal doctrine that create uncertainties for people that rely on the existing law.

Conclusion

The burden of this paper, in summary, is to make the case to bring power to knowledge, to change policies to make better use of the inherently decentralized knowledge of values and conditions. My dilemma, the Catch-22 of this argument, is that someone has to make this case to those who now have the centralized power or to the broader community to which they are responsive. I would value any suggestions you may have in this regard.

Notes

1. *Knowledge and Power: The Life of the Mind and the Conduct of Government*, Occasional Papers of the Council of Scholars no. 6, The Library of Congress, Washington, 1988, p. 21.
2. Ibid., p. 29.
3. Ibid., pp. 29, 30.

4. Michio Kaku, *Visions: How Science Will Revolutionize the 21st Century* (New York: Anchor Books, 1972), p. 63.
5. Friedrich A. von Hayek, "The Use of Knowledge in Society," *American Economic Review* 34, no. 4 (1945): 519–30.
6. Vilfredo Pareto, *Manual d'économie politique*, 2nd ed. (Paris: Lausanne, 1927), p. 233–34.
7. Scott, James C., *Seeing Like a State* (New Haven, CT: Yale University Press, 1988).
8. Ibid., p. 88.
9. Ibid., p. 88.
10. Ibid., p. 5.
11. Ibid., p. 5.
12. Ibid., p. 221.
13. Ibid., pp. 101–2.
14. Ibid., p. 357.
15. Ibid., p. 345.

21. On the Origin and Identification of Government Failures

Government failures are rooted in the same set of conditions as market failures: biased or insufficient information, principal-agent problems, insecure or incomplete property rights, monopoly, externalities, and so on. (My use of the term "government failures," rather than "non-market failures," is to make a distinction between the behavior of governments and that of the many types of institutions other than markets and governments.) The difference is that these conditions are pervasive and inherent in governments, whereas they are more often selective or temporary conditions in markets. Donald Wittman and others have made a valuable contribution by pointing out that the distinctive characteristics of democratic governments—such as elections, parties, pressure groups, legislatures, committees, vote trading, and so on—mitigate some of the problems that are rooted in these conditions, but they are a long way from convincing me and, at least, many other political economists that "democratic markets promote wealth-maximizing outcomes [and] work as well as economic markets" (Wittman 1989).

Conditions that Lead to Government Failures

Limited Information

The beginning of wisdom about democratic politics is that most voters have virtually no incentive to invest in information about candidate or policy choices. The value of such information is equal

---

This article was presented at a conference of the International Institute of Public Finance in Linz, Austria, in August 2001 and was first published in *Political Economy and Public Finance: The Role of Political Economy in the Theory and Practice of Public Economics*, ed. Stanley L. Winer and Hirofumi Shibata (Cheltenham U.K.: Edward Elgar, 2002). My thanks to Stanley Winer and Hirofumi Shibata for their permission to republish this article.

to the probability that a voter's decision will change the outcome times the difference in the net personal benefits of the leading alternatives, an expected value that is vanishingly small; moreover, the higher the probability of changing the outcome, the lower is the likely difference in the net benefits of that outcome. Most of the information on which voters make their decision is a by-product of work, social relations, and entertainment—information that is likely to be both biased and insufficient for an informed vote. Groups that have a larger stake in the difference in political outcomes, of course, have more of an incentive to invest in information but to promote the distribution of only that information that serves their interest. Some of these conditions also affect market behavior except that the outcome of each transaction is determined by only one buyer and one seller, increasing the incentive to invest information and the opportunity to learn from prior transactions and those by others.

Principal-Agent Relations

Most policy decisions in a democratic government are made by some *group* of representative agents, each of whom has the authority to address a *group* of policy issues and is elected by a *group* of voters. Very few voters, thus, are likely to be well represented on every policy issue, and the interests of many voters are likely to be poorly represented on many issues. One consequence of electing agents from single-member districts is a strong preference for district-specific net benefits; such "pork" is the inherent price of government services that provide more general benefits. Another consequence is that our agents have almost no incentive to invest in oversight that might lead to more general benefits. Good law is a public good; that is why we have so little of it. In normative public finance, the primary role of government is to provide public goods, but "politics without romance" provides such goods only at a substantial cost of the private goods that are necessary to motivate our agents.

A recent study of 17 U.S. federal agencies and departments, for example, identified about $220 billion of questionable spending, about 12 percent of the total budget and a higher share of the consumption expenditures of these agencies (U.S. General Accounting Office, 2001). Similar principal-agent problems in the market are much smaller because market participants use agents only for selective transactions, agents represent only one party in each transaction, and there is more competition among the agents.

Monopolies

Governments are generally monopoly suppliers of some services in a specific region. I am intrigued by the recent proposal by Bruno Frey for a system of Functional Overlapping Competitive Jurisdictions, or FOCJs, but this proposal needs both further study and a pronounceable acronym (Frey, 2001). For some services, one must either pay extra to a private supplier or move to another local government if one is dissatisfied with the services supplied in one's current jurisdiction. For other services, one must move to another nation to find an alternate supplier. And some regulations, such as on bank capital standards and the use of governments, have the power to prevent entry by a potential competitor. Such government monopolies have little potential to serve the diversity of demand within their jurisdiction and little incentive to be efficient. In contrast, monopoly power in the market is usually limited and temporary unless entry is limited by some government.

Externalities

In normative public finance, another important role of government is to correct for the external benefits and costs of private actions. The problem is that governments create pervasive and inherent externalities of a different kind. For many people, the marginal value of some government activity is higher than the marginal cost to them, and these people would benefit from an increase of this activity. For many people, the marginal value of some government activity is lower than the marginal cost to them, and these people would benefit from a reduction of this activity. Almost everyone would prefer either more or less of every activity of government. Given a diversity of demand for government activities, this would be the case even if the package of government activities were set at a level for which the net benefits were maximized. A government may be in a political equilibrium without clearing the market for any one activity, a consequence of charging the same tax price for all activities. Most market externalities, in contrast, are due to unclear or incomplete property rights, and the internalization of these market externalities is limited only by the cost of the available "fencing" technology.

Some Evidence of Government Failure

Don Wittman is "very skeptical about the research demonstrating government failure" (Wittman, 2001). In response, I will summarize some of the evidence that bears on this issue and let readers judge for themselves.

Economic Studies

A substantial number of studies have concluded that an increase in the relative size of government budgets reduces economic growth. (For a summary of these studies, see Holcombe, 2001.) Some of these studies are based on statistical analyses of the time series for a specific country. Edgar Peden (1991), for example, estimates that U.S. economic growth would be maximized by total government expenditures of about 20 percent of GDP. Gerald Scully (1994), with spurious precision, estimates that the growth-maximizing level of total government spending in the USA is from 21.5 to 22.9 percent of GDP. My own recent study (Niskanen, forthcoming) estimates that government spending of 9 to 12 percent of GDP plus the expenditures for national defense and net interest payments would maximize U.S. after-tax income. The most comprehensive recent study (by James Gwartney, Randall Holcombe and Robert Lawson, 1998), based on analysis of combined time-series cross-country samples, concludes that the growth-maximizing level of government expenditures is less than 15 percent of GDP. Democratic governments clearly do not promote wealth-maximizing outcomes, except possibly for the members of the effective control group.

Voting and Migration Studies

A broadly popular increase in the government budget should increase the popular vote for the candidate of the incumbent party in the next election. My own studies of U.S. presidential elections, however, estimate that a 10 percent increase in real per capita federal tax revenues since the prior election reduces the popular vote for the candidate of the incumbent party by 1.2 to 1.4 percent of the total major party vote (Niskanen, 1979 and 1992). A similar study by Sam Peltzman (1987) concludes that an increase in real per capita state tax revenues reduces the popular vote for the gubernatorial candidate of the incumbent party in the next election. The fiscal behavior of democratic governments, apparently, is not even consistent with vote maximizing.

A broadly popular fiscal program should also lead to net migration into the jurisdiction of that government. My own study of the net migration among the American states in the 1980s, however, estimates that a 10 percent higher level of state and local tax revenues per capita at the beginning of the decade *reduced* the net migration rate over the decade by 0.6 to 0.9 percent of the 1980 population (Niskanen, 1992). My preliminary estimates based on a sample of the states during the 1990s indicate that a relatively high level of state and local tax revenues per capita at the beginning of the decade reduced both the net migration rate and the growth of real personal income per capita over the decade.

Apparently, something is wrong with the fiscal rules that determine the level of government expenditures and tax revenues, at both the federal and the state levels. The economic growth, voting and migration studies suggest that government expenditures and tax revenues are higher than is consistent with either wealth maximization or vote maximization.

The Major Common Problem of Contemporary Democratic Governments

For all the evidence of government failure, the alternative may be worse. The magnitude of the several types of government failures is appropriate to consider when the issue at stake is whether the government should undertake some activity, but the net benefits of the activity, given the feasible alternatives, may still be positive. A defense budget, a highway program, or a research budget, for example, may include substantial pork and may not be the optimal scale, but may still be better than any feasible alternative. Any social process, however, should be judged by whether one agrees to the *rules* of this process, not whether one benefits from a specific outcome of this process. Some of the outcomes of the market, I suggest, are also unlovely; since I endorse the market rule that any transaction requires the unanimous consent of those with the relevant rights, however, I accept these outcomes. In the end, democratic government should also be judged—not by whether some amount of pork is the price of those public goods that we value; whether government spending, taxes and regulation reduce the growth of the economy; whether we regard the distribution of the benefits and costs as 'fair'—but whether the rules that lead to these outcomes are broadly supported by the affected population.

The awkward truth is that we do not know the answer to this critical question, because most democratic governments now act as if they have the authority to define their own powers. The U.S. federal budget in 1929, for example, was 2.6 percent of GDP, most of which was for the military and the deferred costs of prior wars. The federal budget is now over 18 percent of GDP, most of which is for programs for which there is no explicit constitutional authority. The massive expansion of federal spending, taxes and regulation in the United States in my lifetime has occurred without one amendment to the Constitution to authorize these additional powers. In effect, this expansion of federal authority represents a breach of contract, a change of the rules without our consent, a reduction of the clarity and security of property rights in the market and the authority of other levels of government.

The major common problem of contemporary democratic governments is that they now operate without effective constitutional limits on their powers. In the end, that is the most serious type of government failure. The first step toward correcting this failure must be to restore the idea of a constitution as a set of rules that the government itself may not change. The next step is to develop and promote rules to address this failure that would command a constitutional consensus. One step at a time.

References

Frey, Bruno S. (2001) "A Utopia? Government without Territorial Monopoly." *The Independent Review* 6 (1): 99–112.

Gwartney, James D., Randall G. Holcombe, and Robert A. Lawson. (1998) "The Scope of Government and the Wealth of Nations." *Cato Journal* 18: 163–90.

Holcombe, Randall G. (2001) "Public Choice and Economic Growth." In *The Elgar Companion to Public Choice.* Cheltenham, UK, and Northampton, MA: Edward Elgar.

Niskanen, William A. (1976) "Public Policy and the Political Process." In *Governmental Controls and the Free Market*, ed. Svetozar Pejovich, pp. 73–93. College Station, TX: Texas A&M Press.

______. (1979) "Economic and Fiscal Effects on the Popular Vote for the President." In *Public Policy and Public Choice.* ed. Douglas W. Rae and Theodore J. Eismeier, pp. 93–120. Beverly Hills, CA: Sage Publications.

______. (1992) "The Case for a New Fiscal Constitution." *Journal of Economic Perspectives* 6 (2): 13–24.

Niskanen, William. (forthcoming) *On Regimes: Fiscal Choices and Economic Outcomes.*

Peden, Edgar A. (1991) "Productivity in the United States and its Relationship to Government Activity: An Analysis of 57 Years, 1929–1986," *Public Choice* 69: 153–73.

Peltzman, Sam. (1987) "Economic Conditions and Gubernatorial Elections." *American Economic Review* 77 (2): 293–97.

Scully, Gerald W. (1994) *What Is the Optimal Size of Government in the United States?* Dallas, TX: National Center for Policy Analysis.

U.S. General Accounting Office. (2001) *Government at the Brink: Urgent Federal Government Management Problems Facing the Bush Administration.* Washington, GPO.

Wittman, Donald. (1989) "Why Democracies Produce Efficient Results." *Journal of Political Economy* 97: 1395–424.

Wittman, Donald. (2001) "Normative Public Finance without Guilt." In *Political Economy and Public Finance: The Role of Political Economy in the Theory and Practice of Public Economics*, ed. Stanley L. Winer and Hirofumi Shibata. Northampton, MA: Edward Elgar.

22. The Intellectual Case for a Free Market Economy

One is tempted to dismiss a discussion about the intellectual case for a free market economy by asking only the empirical question "What works?" And the evidence is very clear. Economic growth, income equality, and environmental conditions are all a positive function of the degree of economic freedom.[1] Moreover, almost all voluntary migration is from the more controlled economies to countries with greater economic freedom.

Some common language, culture, and religion may contribute to economic development but are clearly not sufficient to override the effects of major differences in political conditions. In the period since World War II, for example, there were numerous examples of strongly divergent economic development among peoples with a common language and national culture but with a different type of political regime. West Germany, for example, developed rapidly relative to East Germany, although eastern Germany was the dominantly Protestant region. South Korea developed rapidly relative to North Korea, South Vietnam relative to North Vietnam, the overseas Chinese relative to the mainland Chinese, and the overseas Indians relative to those who remained in India. In recent years, of course, economic growth has increased sharply in both China and India but only in response to a substantial reduction in state control of the economy. The end of the Cold War should have erased any illusions, except in the more sheltered groves of academe, that the combination

---

This article was presented on November 22, 2002, at a conference in Washington, D.C., and was first published in *The Changes in the North-East Asian Economic and Political Order and Korea's Preparations for the 21st Century*, ed. Dong-Se Cha and Yoon-Shik Park (Seoul: Graduate School of Pan-Pacific International Studies at Kyung Hee University, 2004). My thanks to Kyung Hee University for its permission to republish this article.

of autocratic government and state ownership of property serves the interests of anyone other than those in the control group.

The more complex question, about which there is less understanding and agreement, is why free market economies generate these superior outcomes. And that is the question to which I offer some tentative answers.

From the Beginning

All human institutions involve one or more of three types of relations: caring, exchange, and threat.

- In a caring relation, one party says to another, I will do what you want because I care for you.
- In an exchange relation, each party says to the other, I will do what you want if you do what I want.
- In a threat relation, one party says to another, I will do what you do not want unless you do what I want.

Simple observation leads one to conclude that caring relations are most important in families and among friends, exchange relations are most important in the market, and threat is most characteristic of the relations of the state to its subjects and to other states.

But only a little more careful observation is sufficient to recognize that almost all human institutions involve some amount of each type of relation. Any durable relation in families and among friends also involves a considerable amount of exchange and is enforced by an implied threat of breaking the relation. Repeated relations in the market often involve some amount of caring and are dependent on threat only to enforce the relevant rights and contracts. Political relations involve some genuine caring, a lot of phony caring reflected in the generosity with other people's money, and the implicit exchange of taxes for a package of government services. I am tempted to develop on the subtle combination of relations in each of these institutions, but the focus of today's discussion is on the intellectual case for a free market.

The Combination of Relations in the Market

The dominant relation in the market, of course, is exchange; for each exchange, both the buyer and seller must agree to the exchange of some amount of a good or service for a specific price. As Ronald Coase remarked in his 1991 Nobel lecture, however,

> It makes little sense for economists to discuss the process of exchange without specifying the institutional setting within which the trading takes place, since this affects the incentives to produce and the costs of transacting.[2]

Whether a potential exchange is realized, in turn, depends on the combination of caring or threat affecting the specific exchange. First, the buyer must expect that he cannot acquire the good or service by relying on the caring of some seller; children, for example, begin to understand the benefits of exchange only by testing the limits of the caring of each parent. More important, the buyer must realize that the cost of acquiring the good or service by exchange is lower than cost of acquiring it by extortion or theft. For this condition to hold, there must be a system of property rights that effectively protects the seller's property. And third, since the seller generally knows more about the quality of a good or service than the buyer, the buyer must have some recourse against sellers that misrepresent the quality of the good or service.

Second, the seller must not have sufficient caring for the buyer to make the good or service available without payment. More important, if the good or service is provided before full compensation, there must be some system of effective contracts to protect the seller against a buyer's failure to pay the agreed price.

Many of the potential problems of an individual exchange are substantially reduced by a mutual desire for continued exchanges, the single most important condition that distinguishes a modern market economy from an oriental bazaar. I learned this lesson late. As chief economist of the Ford Motor Company, I was surprised to learn that Ford made billions of dollars of purchases per year from regular suppliers over the telephone with only the skeleton of a contract and with few contract disputes. At any time that either party expected to end the relation or expected the other party to end the relation, moreover, the primary remaining discipline on the immediate transaction was the value of the firm's reputation with other parties, not the protection of the formal contract. Contract disputes were usually limited to those few cases in which one or both parties had no expectation or desire to deal with the other party again.

The cultural conditions that contribute to this "evolution of cooperation" are subtle but simple: a mutual commitment to exchange (rather than threat) as the primary means to coordinate economic activity, the self-restraint to leave something on the table for the other party in each transaction, and the use of the authority of the state only to discipline gross or repeated breaches of contract. The German liberal Wilhelm Röpke may have best expressed the importance of a specific set of cultural attitudes in writing that

> An intensive and extensive economic exchange cannot exist or last very long without a minimum of natural trust, confidence in the stability and reliability of the legal-institutional framework (including money), contractual loyalty, honesty, fair play, professional honor and that pride which makes us consider it unworthy of us to cheat, bribe, or to misuse the authority of the State for egoistic purposes.[3]

Fortunately, continued economic relations usually reinforces these attitudes. Most people, for example, develop some amount of caring for others with whom they have continued exchanges—enough, for example, to forgive the other party for some minor infrequent breaches of the expected exchange rather than to use the formal legal system to seek redress.

Some amount of implicit threat in a system of property rights and contracts is necessary for a market economy. Adam Smith and the other classical economists recognized that the value of property rights and contracts were dependent on the "powerful arm of the civil magistrate."[4] At the same time, it is important to recognize that the type of cultural attitudes, the business ethics and manners that Ropke described substantially reduce the reliance on the formal legal system. In that sense, there is a tradeoff between caring and threat as constraints on an exchange relation, a tradeoff illustrated by the breakdown in business ethics revealed by the recent collapse of several major corporations and the resulting increase in the political demands for business regulation.

There is an old saying that summarizes this condition: "Everything for a friend, nothing for an enemy, and the law for strangers." Property rights and contracts help extend the gains from trade from relations among friends to relations among strangers by ensuring payment, the expected quality of the good or service, and delivery.

The Economic Case for a Free Market Economy

An economic system based on exchange, property rights, and contracts is almost surely to be more prosperous than alternative systems for two primary reasons: information and incentives.

The market economizes on the necessary information flow, since prices convey most of the information necessary for a "spontaneous order." All of us have information available only to us and is specific to time and place. Some of this information could conceivably be centralized but, in general, it is more efficient for each individual to act on this information. In the extended debate on the possibility of socialist calculation first raised by Mises, several writers claimed that Vilfredo Pareto had solved this problem long ago. Given the enormous computational power of modern computers, it is especially important to understand that Pareto himself denied this possibility, making the following argument:

> Let us make the most favorable assumption for such a calculation, let us assume that we have triumphed over all the difficulties of finding the data of the problem and that we know the values of all the different commodities for each individual, and all the conditions of production of all the commodities, etc. This is already an absurd hypothesis to make. . . . Given the number of necessary equations, it would not be mathematics which would assist political economy, but political economy which would assist mathematics. In other words, if one really could know all these equations, the only means to solve them which is available to human powers is to observe the practical solution given by the market.[5]

There is no reason to continue the debate on the possibility of socialist calculation. Mises and Hayek won this debate. Both our freedom and our economic wellbeing are best served, wherever possible, by policies that use the decentralized information available only to individuals—some of which are unconscious and cannot be articulated, some of which are individual values that cannot be adequately aggregated, some of which are specific to time and place and cannot be efficiently centralized.[6]

The other major reason for the efficiency of a free market is that the necessary system of property rights provides much superior incentives to the market participants. Given clearly delineated and enforced property rights, it is generally more efficient to monitor and police trespass of these rights than to monitor and police the behavior of all those who might desire to use a specific property. Second, individual property rights substantially reduce the overuse that is characteristic of common property. And third, property rights that are both partitionable and alienable generally lead property to be reallocated to its highest value use. The combination of competition and property rights channels man's natural acquisitiveness (greed, if you will) into a socially productive process, in the same sense that competition and marriage domesticates lust.[7]

The Moral Case for a Free Market Economy

Finally, the case for any social system must ultimately be based on a moral argument. People should have the right, for example, to choose an economic system in which the dominant relation is either caring or threat, even at the expense of being poor, as long as they do not impose such a system on others. So the case for an economic system cannot be based entirely on economic arguments.

The primary moral case for a free market economy is that most economic decisions require the consent of all those with the affected rights. No one has the authority to dictate an outcome at the expense of another party, unless both parties have previously agreed to a contractual relation that grants this authority in specific cases. Freedom is an implicit moral value, because the concepts of good and evil have no moral meaning in the absence of choice. A free market economy, in summary, maximizes the conditions in which we are "free to choose."

The second moral case for a free market economy is that it is more consistent with our inherent moral nature, probably a consequence of our genetic heritage.[8] Most of us have a limited amount of caring, often specific to family and friends. Many of us are tempted to use threat to get our way unless the economic system sufficiently penalizes threat to make exchange the more rewarding relation. A free market economy minimizes the necessary use of threat and reduces our dependence on caring in routine economic relations.

Finally, an economy based on exchange and an effective system of property rights increases the prospects for peace in a community, because property rights permit people to protect their existing use of property and to acquire other property without conflict. A long time ago, Aristotle observed that ". . . those who own common property and share in its management are far more often at variance with another than those who have individual property rights."[9] In a contemporary phrase, "good fences make good neighbors."

Conclusion

Contrary to the critics of a market economy, in summary, an economic system based on exchange, property rights, and contracts contributes to both the peace and prosperity of a community.

Notes

1. For a representative of the large and growing empirical literature on this issue, see James Gwartney, Randall Holcombe, and Robert Lawson, "The Scope of Government and the Wealth of Nations," *Cato Journal* 18, no. 2 (1998): 163–90.
2. Ronald Coase, "The Institutional Structure of Production," *American Economic Review* 82, no. 4 (September 1992): 713–19.
3. Wilhelm Röpke, "Economic Order and International Law," *Recuil des Cours, Académie de Droit Internationale* 86, no. 2 (1954): 207–71.
4. Adam Smith, *The Wealth of Nations*, 1776.
5. Vilfredo Pareto, *Manuel d'économie politique*, 2nd ed. (Paris: Lausanne, 1927), pp. 233–34.
6. For a summary of the information advantages of the market, William Niskanen, "Bringing Power to Knowledge: Choosing Policies to Use Decentralized Knowledge," in *Knowledge and Politics*, ed. R. Viale (New York: Physica-Verlag Heidelberg, 2001), pp. 107–118.
7. Two good recent books, by noneconomists, on property rights are Richard Pipes, *Property and Freedom* (New York: Alfred A. Knopf, 1999); Tom Bethell, *The Noblest Triumph: Property and Prosperity Through the Ages* (New York: St. Martin's Press, 1998).
8. For a good recent introduction to the evolutionary origin of our values, see Paul Rubin, *Darwinian Politics: The Origin of Freedom* (Piscataway, NJ: Rutgers University Press, 2002).
9. Aristotle, *The Politics of Aristotle* (Oxford: Clarendon Press, 1263b).

23. U.S. Elections Are Increasingly Biased against *Moderates*

One important pattern in the 2002 congressional elections may have important implications for the 2004 elections and the future of American politics: the most vulnerable incumbents were *moderates* who had sometimes voted with the other party on an important issue.

I first suspected this pattern on reading the next-day newspaper reports of the election results. Sens. Jean Carnahan (D-Mo.) and Max Cleland (D-Ga.) lost, Sen. Mary Landrieu (D-La.) faced a December runoff election, and Sen. Tim Johnson (D-S. Dak.) faced a potential recount; all four, for example, had voted for the Bush tax cut and had campaigned as moderates. The only Senate Republican to lose was Tim Hutchinson of Arkansas, a conservative who had been involved in a personal scandal (there must be something in the water in Arkansas). The most visible House Republican to lose was Connie Morella of Maryland, who had made a career of being a moderate and had voted against the Iraq war resolution. Before making any statistical analysis, I reported this suspected pattern and the potential implications of this pattern in a November 20, 2002, op-ed in the *Investor's Business Daily*.

To my knowledge, the only other person to report this pattern was David Broder, a leading political commentator. In a January 2, 2003, column in the *Washington Post*, Broder observed that party

> caucuses on both sides of the Capitol have become more cohesive internally and further apart from each other philosophically . . . with almost every session, (there are) fewer moderates or progressives on the Republican side and fewer conservatives among the Democrats—especially when it comes to fundamental economic and social questions and the role of government in American life.

This article was first published in the *Cato Journal* 23, no. 3 (Winter 2004). My thanks to the *Cato Journal* for its permission to republish this article.

Table 23.1
WERE THE VULNERABLE INCUMBENTS MORE MODERATE THAN OTHER INCUMBENTS?

	Sample	Median	Score Mean	S.D.	*t*-ratio
Senate					
Vulnerable	6	30	24.00	13.13	
Nonvulnerable	21	10	12.19	9.90	
Difference		20	11.81	5.78	2.04
House					
Vulnerable	18	12	22.06	23.16	
Nonvulnerable	368	5	11.34	14.59	
Difference		7	10.72	5.51	1.9

This article first summarizes my statistical analysis of the 2002 congressional elections to test the hypothesis that the most vulnerable incumbents in this election were moderates. The implications of these findings for voting theory, the distribution of the ideological positions of the winning candidates, and the problems of governing are then considered.

A Statistical Analysis of the 2002 Congressional Elections

My null hypothesis, again, is that the most vulnerable incumbents in the 2002 congressional elections were moderates. My measure of the moderation of Republican incumbents is their Americans for Democratic Action rating during the first session of the 107th Congress. Similarly, my measure of the moderation of Democratic incumbents is their American Conservative Union rating in this same period. I test this hypothesis for both the Senate and the House by a difference-of-means test. Only three Senate incumbents and four House incumbents lost their bids for reelection. These samples of losing incumbents are too small for this test, so I have defined the vulnerable incumbents in both houses as those who won less than 55 percent of the popular vote in their states or districts in this election. Even by this measure, the samples of vulnerable incumbents were surprisingly small.

The results of these tests are summarized in Table 23.1 above.

As the *t*-ratios indicate, the mean scores of the vulnerable incumbents in both houses were significantly higher than the mean scores of the nonvulnerable incumbents (at the 5 percent level for a one-tailed test).

A simple difference-of-means test of course, does not control for other conditions that may also explain whether a candidate is vulnerable. Senator Hutchinson, for example, lost his bid for reelection for personal reasons, not because he was a moderate. Most of the nonvulnerable incumbent Republican moderates were from the Northeast, and most of the nonvulnerable incumbent Democratic moderates were from the South. Controlling for these personal and regional conditions would almost surely strengthen the conclusion that the most vulnerable incumbents in the 2000 congressional elections were ideological moderates.

Moreover, the effects of this type of pattern appear to have accumulated over the past several decades. Each year, the *Congressional Quarterly* calculates and reports a "Party Unity" score on the basis of the roll call votes in which a majority of Republicans oppose the position of a majority of Democrats and the percent of votes that each member has voted with the party majority on these votes. As reported by Broder in the above-referenced column:

> When I averaged the year-by-year results for both chambers, I found the percentage of partisan-divide-roll calls has gone from 39 percent in the 1970s to 47 percent in the 1980s to 58 percent in the 1990s.
>
> Even more striking is the growth in cohesion—call it discipline or philosophical agreement—within both party caucuses. In the 1970s, on the partisan roll calls, the average member of Congress backed the party position 65 percent of the time. In the 1980s, the average degree of partisan loyalty rose to 73 percent; and in the 1990s, to 81 percent. In these past two years, it has been 87 percent.

Someone else could well use these Party Unity scores to confirm Broder's analysis of the increase in the polarization of Congress.

Implications for Voting Theory

The above results are strongly inconsistent with the standard median voter theory of public choice. One implicit assumption of the median voter theory is that the decision of *whether* to vote is independent of the issue positions of the candidates. Only in this case do candidates have an incentive to choose an issue position close to their perception of the preferences of the median voter because they do not risk the loss of votes from their party base. If the decision to vote, however, is endogenous, candidates have an incentive to choose an issue position closer to the median of their party base than to the median of the total electorate (in the relevant constituency). And if turning out two or more of your own probable voters is more efficient than attracting one swing vote, candidates will spend their time and campaign funds to energize their party base rather than to appeal to potential swing voters. This is consistent with the increasing relative attention of both parties to turnout efforts. In this case, the outcome of democratic elections will be increasingly determined by the relative size of the party base and the effectiveness of the party and the candidate in energizing that base.

The Republican victory in the 2002 congressional elections is broadly attributed to a greater effectiveness in energizing their party base; it is less clear whether the winning candidates represent the preferences of a majority of potential voters. Public choice scholars need to rebuild voting theory to incorporate the effects of a candidate's issue position on both the decision to vote and the choice among those who decide to vote.

Implications for the Ideological Distributions of Those Elected

Over time, this pattern of voting behavior will lead to an evolutionary reduction in the moderates in both parties and an increasing divergence of the ideological positions of the two major parties. On this issue, Broder was again an astute observer:

> Party caucuses on both sides of the Capitol have become more cohesive internally and further apart from each other philosophically. More and more issues divide on party lines. And the new leaders in the House and Senate, like the old ones, reflect that growing gulf between the parties.

This pattern was most apparent in the House of Representatives where Dick Armey was replaced as majority leader by Tom DeLay and Richard Gephardt was replaced as minority leader by Nancy Pelosi; I doubt whether DeLay and Pelosi agree on the time of day. This pattern is also consistent with the recent finding by political scientists Melissa Collie and John Mason that the variance of votes in Congress is more polarized than the variance of opinion in the electorate.[1]

Implications for the Potential to Govern

Finally, this pattern of voting behavior will make it more difficult for Congress to govern. More issues will be subject to partisan deadlock, more issues will be decided by near party-line votes, and a reduction of the number of moderates in both parties will make it much more difficult to achieve the bipartisan consensus that is necessary for a major reform to survive a change in the majority party. For different reasons, Congress is becoming more like the Italian parliament—more partisan, a reduced ability to address major reforms, and an increased centralization of political power in the executive. Not a happy thought.

References

Broder, D. (2003) "Don't Bet on Bipartisan Niceties." *Washington Post*, January 2.

Collie, M. P., and Mason, J. L. (2000) "The Electoral Connection between Party and Constituency Reconsidered: Evidence from the U.S. House of Representatives, 1962–94." In *Continuity and Change in House Elections*, ed. J. E. Cogan and M. P. Fiorina. Stanford, CA: Stanford University Press/Hoover Institution Press.

Niskanen, W. A. (2002) "Important Unnoticed Patterns in the Midterm Elections." *Investor's Business Daily*, November 20.

Note

1. I am grateful to John Samples, director of Cato's Center for Representative Government, for this reference.

24. Advice from a Friendly American on the Proposed Constitution for the European Union

Europeans are soon to address a proposed Constitution for the European Union.

What advice would a friendly American have to offer on this important advice? Why should a European pay any attention to this advice?

First, the United States is the oldest and largest surviving constitutional republic, a nation that has experienced a larger increase in area, population, and income—absorbing people of more diverse racial, ethnic, and language backgrounds—than any other contemporary nation.

So Europeans are well advised to understand and consider those characteristics of the U. S. Constitution that provided the political and legal framework for the American success story.

On the other hand, the United States was among the last major nations to eliminate slavery, in our case only at the cost of a massive civil war. Moreover, there has been a rapid expansion of the powers of the federal government, largely in my lifetime, without any formal amendment to the Constitution to authorize these expanded powers. So Europeans are also well advised to understand and consider those characteristics of the U.S. Constitution that allowed these conditions to develop.

Second, I have written extensively about the U.S. Constitution, reflecting my professional specialties in policy analysis and public choice. My exposure to the progressive drafts of the EU constitution,

This article was first published in *Coercive Power and Its Allocation in the Emergent Europe*, ed. Geoffrey Brennan (New York: Palgrave Macmillan, 2005). My thanks to Palgrave Macmillan for its permission to republish this article.

of course, is limited to those distributed through May 26, 2003, for deliberation by the convention.

Finally, and maybe most important, I am sympathetic with both of the conditions that are the primary cause of some tension in the final deliberations on the proposed EU constitution: the seemingly inconsistent desires to maintain some national identity and to form a more perfect European Union.

The Major Strengths of the U.S. Constitution

Several general characteristics of the U.S. Constitution have contributed to its relative success and survival as a body of foundation law:

1. The objectives of the Constitution are described in the brief, forceful, declaratory, and quite general prose of the preamble, which, by itself, provides no authority for any specific political decision. This avoids a wholly unproductive debate about the implications or relative importance of these objectives, because the necessary coalition to approve a specific measure often includes those who support the measure for quite different reasons.
2. The original structure of Congress, with the number of Representatives proportional to population and elected by popular vote and with two Senators from each state selected by the state legislatures, was a productive balance of popular and state government interests and enabled the Senate to resolve most constitutional disputes. This characteristic of Congress unfortunately ended in 1913 when the Seventeenth Amendment authorized the popular election of Senators.
3. The powers authorized to Congress and the executive and the powers denied to the federal government or the states are few, brief, and well defined. All residual powers are reserved to the states.
4. The Bill of Rights, with one exception, is a list of the rights of individuals "against" the state, not a list of claims by individuals on services to be provided by the state. The one exception is the right "to" a trial by jury. All residual rights are reserved to the people.
5. And all of this in a brief document that includes the preamble, the main text of the Constitution, and the 27 amendments to

date, and is in language that makes it possible for any citizen, in Madison's words, to interpret "the plain sense and intention of the instrument."

The Major Weaknesses of the U.S. Constitution

Several specific characteristics of the U.S. Constitution help explain some of our major political problems:

1. The Constitution does not define how constitutional disputes are to be resolved. Although without any specific authority, the Supreme Court, under Chief Justice John Marshall, first asserted this power in 1803. The result, at times, has been the politicization of this court and the implicit power to initiate or approve a change in the effective Constitution without any formal amendment.
2. There is no nullification authority; in other words, the state governments do not have the authority to act as "guardians of the charter," to nullify a specific action by the government on constitutional grounds. The Constitution of our "compound republic" is asymmetric; a vote by the legislatures of more than one-fourth of the states is sufficient to block a formal amendment, but there is no corresponding procedure for any number of states to force a formal constitutional test by enjoining a change in the effective constitution. Although Jefferson, Madison, Calhoun, and the State of Wisconsin asserted an authority of the state governments to nullify federal actions early in our political history, the conditions that led to these nullification attempts were resolved by political changes. The lack of a nullification authority was not very important prior to the Seventeenth Amendment because the Senate had the authority and incentive to serve this role. Since then, however, an agreement among Congress, the president, and the Supreme Court has been sufficient to increase the powers of the federal government without any formal amendment to authorize these powers. As a consequence, federal spending has increased from 2.6 percent of GDP in 1929, most of which was for the military and the deferred costs of prior wars, to 19.9 percent of GDP in 2002, most of which is for programs for which there is no constitutional authority.

3. There is no authority for one or more states to secede from the federal government. Our Constitution is also asymmetric on this issue, with clearly defined rules for admitting a new state but with no rules for approving a proposed secession. As a consequence, any attempt to secede has been regarded as an act of treason and was the specific condition that led to our massive Civil War.
4. Although the Constitution vests all legislative powers in Congress, Congress has chosen, with the acquiescence of the Supreme Court, to delegate most detailed rule making to regulatory agencies. There is now no procedure to require Congress to vote on a specific rule. As a consequence, the federal government now includes dozens of nonelected groups with the power to both make the rules and to enforce the rules within their general area of authority, and the cost of the federal regulation may now be as high as 5 percent of GDP.

The Major Strengths of the Proposed EU Constitution

Somewhat to my surprise, some of the major strengths of the proposed EU constitution are provisions concerning which the U.S. Constitution is weakest, and some of the major weaknesses of the proposed EU constitution are provisions concerning which the U.S. Constitution is strongest. Maybe we both have something to learn from each other.

The strongest provisions of the proposed EU constitution, I suggest, are the following:

1. The Council of Ministers is superbly designed to represent the interests of the national states, with one minister from each member state in each ministerial formation and a voting rule requiring a majority of the ministers, representing at least three-fifths of the population of the Union, for approval of any new legislation. In the absence of a nullification rule, the Council should be sufficient to assure that any legislation serves the interests of a broad majority of the Union population.
2. A "... delegated regulation may enter into force only if no objection has been expressed by the European Parliament or the Council within a period set by the law. . ." (Article 1-35, ss.2) *Bravo*! This should substantially reduce the abuse of delegated regulatory authority by the Commission.

3. The proposed EU constitution is at least less ambiguous than the U.S. Constitution about what body has the authority to rule on whether some action by the Union is consistent with the constitution. The problem is that the Court of Justice is only authorized to "... give *preliminary* (my emphasis) rulings, at the request of the member state courts, on the interpretation of Union law or the validity of acts adopted by the institutions" (Article I-28, ss.3). The question that remains is what body has the authority to make a final ruling on these issues.
4. The proposed EU constitution includes a provision for the voluntary withdrawal of a member state. This is a desirable difference from the U.S. Constitution but only half a step, because the conditions for withdrawal are not defined *ex ante* and any negotiated agreement must be approved by the Council and the Parliament.

The Major Weaknesses of the Proposed EU Constitution

1. The proposed constitution includes several pages on shared values, the objectives of the Union, and principles of democracy. This is wholly unnecessary and sure to provoke continued controversy. One sentence alone, for example, commits the Union to "work for a Europe of sustainable development based on balanced economic growth, with a social market economy aiming at full employment and social progress," a sentence that includes at least five undefined terms (Article I-3, ss.3).
2. The relation between the Union and the member states is not adequately defined. One sentence, for example, states that "Competences not conferred upon the Union in the constitution remain with the Member States" (Article I-11, ss.2). Fine. But the next sentence states that " ... in areas which do not fall within its exclusive competence the Union shall act only if ... the objectives of the intended action ... can rather, by reason of the scale or effects of the proposed action, be better achieved at the Union level" (Article I-11, ss.3). This sentence suggests that the Union might exercise some competence outside its exclusive authority if someone (who?) decides that the Union could do it better than a member state.
3. "Except where the Constitution provides otherwise, Union acts can be adopted only on the basis of a Commission proposal"

(Article I-25, ss. 2). This is a dreadful provision. The executive has no comparative advantage in recognizing the need for and formulating new legislation, and this provision gives the Commission a large first-mover advantage. Another provision also magnifies the role of the Commission: "In the discharge of their duties members of the Commission shall neither seek nor take instructions from any government or other body." (Article I-25, ss. 4) One wonders why anyone would want to serve in the European Parliament.

4. The most important difference between the U.S. and proposed EU Constitution involves the concept of rights. The U.S. Bill of Rights, as mentioned above, is a list of individual rights against the state. In contrast, the Charter of Fundamental Rights, which constitutes Part II of the proposed EU constitution, includes a list of rights to services provided by the state. The list, for example, includes rights to education, a free placement service, paid maternity leave, social security benefits and social services, housing assistance, preventive health care, services of general economic interest, and high levels of environmental and consumer protection (Articles II-14, ss.29, and 33 through 38).

   Such rights, in effect claims on the state, represent the most important potential tension in the European Union. On the one hand, the proposed EU constitution states that the "Free movement of persons, goods, services and capital, and freedom of establishment shall be guaranteed within and by the Union . . . [and] any discrimination on grounds of nationality shall be prohibited" (Article I-4, ss. 1 and, ss. 2). Fine. On the other hand, any citizen of the Union seems to have a claim on a wide range of social services wherever he or she chooses to live. This will either lead to either a massive movement of people to member states with a higher level of social services or the harmonization of these services among the member states. The only way to resolve the potential tension between the right of free movement and the rights to social services is to allow each member state to restrict access to social services, not on nationality, but on such personal conditions as the number of years of work in that state and the absence of a felony conviction. Unless member states are allowed to impose such requirements for access to social services, the European Union would become a massive harmonized welfare state, relegating the member states to only such roles as "... ensuring the territorial integrity of the State, and for maintaining law and order and safeguarding internal security" (Article I-5, ss. 1).

5. One issue that the United States has also not yet sorted out is the inherent conflict between nondiscrimination and affirmative action. The proposed EU constitution, for example, states that the "Equality between men and women must be assured in all areas, including employment, work and pay. [But this] ... shall not prevent the maintenance or adoption of measures providing for specific advantages in favour of the under-represented sex" (Article II-23). For the moment, in both the United States and the European Union, discrimination against people is usually illegal but discrimination in favor of some people is sometimes required. This minor madness, hopefully, will not last.
6. A final point of irritation, at least to an American: The text of the proposed EU constitution is pretentious. Many of the substantive provisions are described as if they were derived directly from some first principle, as if the formulation of a Constitution is some form of algebra rather than the result of political negotiation and agreement. Among the many such principles that are described as the basis for these provisions (I may have missed a few) are loyal cooperation, conferral, subsidiarity, proportionality, solidarity, democratic equality, representative democracy, participatory democracy, sound financial management, equality before the law, legality, and the proportionality of criminal offences and penalties. Broad agreement on the substantive provisions of a constitution is necessary to its effectiveness and survival; broad agreement on principles is not. An agreement on any one or more of these principles is neither sufficient nor necessary to assure broad agreement on any specific substantive provision. Not sufficient, since some other substantive provision may also be consistent with the principles. Not necessary, since the coalition necessary for an effective constitution may support any specific substantive provision for quite different reasons. On such issues, I suggest, Madison is a better guide to an effective constitution than is Descartes.

A Final Word

If I were a European, I would share some of the reasons to hope for a more perfect European Union. But be careful about any major political structure that is being presented for your approval. The early drafts that led to the proposal before you were described as a constitutional treaty, the final version as a proposed EU constitution. Do you really want a constitutional treaty among the member states? Or what looks to me more like a proposed constitution for a European government? Even if you favor the major provisions of the proposed constitution, be especially careful that the constitution limits the authority of the European Union to define its own powers, because all governments seek broader powers than first authorized. Over time, a demonstrably imperfect Europe of national states may be a better protection of your liberty than approving the proposed constitution in the hope for a more perfect European Union.

25. A Case for Divided Government

For those of you with a partisan bent, I have some bad news:

Our federal government may work better (less badly) when at least one house of Congress is controlled by a party other than the party of the president. The general reason for this is that each party has the opportunity to block the most divisive measures proposed by the other party. This opportunity, of course, may not be effective in every issue; control of the Senate by the Democrats in 2002, for example, was not sufficient to block the Iraq war resolution. Other conditions, of course, also affect political outcomes, but the following types of evidence for this hypothesis are too important to ignore:

1. The rate of increase of real (inflation-adjusted) per capita federal spending is usually lower when the government is divided. As Table 25.1 indicates, the average annual increase in real per capita federal expenditures under unified government was about three times that under divided government, and a statistical test indicates that this a significant difference. For comparison, the average annual increase in real per capita GDP during this period was 2.13 percent. The only two long periods of fiscal restraint were during the Eisenhower administration and the Clinton administration, during both of which the opposition party controlled Congress during the last six years of the administration. Conversely, each of the three periods of unusual fiscal expansion was during a period of unified government.
2. Much of the variance in real per capita federal spending is due to changes in defense spending. If most of the variance of defense spending is exogenous, it may be only a coincidence that the largest increases in real per capita federal spending

This article was first published in the *Washington Monthly*, October 2006, as part of a set of articles by disgruntled Republicans titled "It's Time for Us to Go." My thanks to the *Washington Monthly* for its permission to republish this article.

Table 25.1
ANNUAL PERCENT CHANGES IN REAL PER CAPITA FEDERAL EXPENDITURES

Years	Unified	Divided
1949–1954	9.79	
1955–1960		−0.40
1961–1968	5.39	
1969–1976		2.63
1977–1980	2.74	
1981–1992		2.65
1993–1994	−0.47	
1995–2002		1.03
2003–2005	3.05	
Average	5.26	1.73

are during a period of unified government. My judgment, however, is that a large part of the variance in real per capita defense spending has been a function of domestic political conditions. I find it hard to dismiss the implications of a nearly 200-year pattern in which American participation in *every* war involving more than a week of ground combat was initiated by a unified government. Each of the four major American wars during the 20th century, for example, was initiated by a Democratic president with the support of a Congress controlled by Democrats. The current war in Iraq, initiated by a Republican president with the support of a Republican Congress, is consistent with this pattern and has already proved to be the only use of military forces involving more than a week of ground combat that was initiated by a Republican president in over a century. Divided government may have a lower rate of increase of real per capita federal expenditures, in part, because it has been an important constraint on American participation in war.

3. The probability that a major reform will last is usually higher with a divided government because the necessity of bipartisan support on first passage is more likely to protect the reform against a subsequent change in the majority party.

The Reagan tax laws of 1981 and 1986, for example, were both approved by a House of Representatives controlled by the Democrats and have largely survived. The major potential reforms of agriculture, telecommunications, and welfare in 1996 were approved by Clinton and a Republican Congress, although only the welfare reform has survived subsequent legislative and regulatory changes. The primary exception to this pattern, of course, is the Great Society. My judgment, however, is that the prospect for the necessary future reforms of the federal tax code, Medicare, and Social Security will be dependent on more bipartisan support than now seems likely in a united Republican government. As a lifelong Republican and occasional federal official, I must acknowledge that I do not much care how a divided government is next realized.

American voters, in their unarticulated collective wisdom, have voted for a divided government for most of the past 50 years. Divided government is not the stuff of which political legends are made, but the separation of powers is probably a better protection of our liberties when the presidency and at least one house of Congress are controlled by different parties.

26. Alternative Political and Economic Futures for Europe

Defeat of the proposed constitution for the European Union by voters in France and in the Netherlands opens an opportunity to reflect on a broader range of alternative political and economic futures for Europe. It is important to reconsider the major current European political and economic institutions as well as alternative steps toward further European integration. For the major current institutions were created under different conditions, and the experience to date suggest that they may not best serve the peoples of Europe under current and expected future conditions. The major alternative political and economic futures for Europe are nationalism, selective functional integration, an association of European states, and a European state. My remarks today address the considerations that bear on the choice among these alternatives. Vaclav Klaus, the president of the Czech Republic, may have provided the best general guidance on how Europeans should make this choice:

> We must first make clear what kind of Europe we want. Using understandable language, we have to say what the future Europe should like and what costs and benefits such a solutions would have. It must not be about turning in on ourselves. It must not be about hindering spontaneous integration or globalization processes. No costly, freedom-constraining uniformity, harmonization, and centralization should be part of it, nor any obligatory "European" ideology (because the market for ideas must remain open for future political developments on the left-right spectrum of individual European countries)."[1]

This article was presented on December 8, 2005, in Bratislava and was first published (in English and Slovak) in *In Defense of the Free Market*, ed. Peter Gonda and Pavel Chalupnicek (Bratislava, Slovakia: Conservative Institute of M.R. Stefanik, 2007). My thanks to the Conservative Institute in Bratislava for its permission to republish this article.

Nationalism

For understandable reasons, Europeans have become wary of nationalism because, for too long, conflicts among national states made Europe a field of blood. And the first selective measures of European integration after World War II were primarily designed to reduce the prospect of another such holocaust. I will use the term "nationalism" merely to describe a system of independent national states. I need not remind you of the potential dangers that are inherent in such a system. At the same time, however, it is important to understand the reasons whey national states have been the basic building blocks of most political orders.

First, the political loyalty of most people is to the state of an area with a common language, culture, and history. One should not dismiss this condition based on wishful thinking, for example, that the creation of a European state would create a European political identity. Or, similarly, that the creation of a new Iraqi state would create an Iraqi political identity. The breakup of the Soviet Union is only one of many examples of the fragility of states without a common language, culture, and history.

Second, there are very few government services for which there are any significant economies of scale. There is no significant relation between per capita income and the area and population of state. The per capita incomes of Luxembourg, Singapore, and Switzerland, for example, are about the same as that in the United States and far higher than in the much larger states of China, India, and Russia. Specifically, there are no significant economies of scale in the provision of such major domestic government services as education, the courts and police, public health, and transportation.

Third, the only major government services for which there are significant economies of scale over some range are defense, environmental policy, trade policy, monetary policy, and scientific research. These economies, however, can usually be realized by voluntary alliances among national states without the problems of creating and maintaining a broader multinational state.

In summary, I suggest, Europeans should take nationalism—by which I mean a set of independent national states open to selective voluntary integration processes—as a serious alternative to the "costly, freedom-constraining uniformity" of a European state.

Selective Functional Integration

As mentioned above, there are only a few government services for which there are significant economies of scale over some range. Moreover, in each of these cases, there is already a specific institutional arrangement among most of the European states, although the list of member states differs somewhat among these arrangements. But some changes in these existing arrangements should also be considered as part of the process of choosing a political and economic future for Europe.

Agriculture

One common function of the European Union, however, serves no common purpose: the common agricultural policy. There is no reason to coordinate agricultural policies across governments and no economies of scale in providing this function. The Swiss government manages to do enough mischief with its own agricultural policy without being a member of the European Union. One other cost of this common agricultural policy is that it may destroy the prospect for success of the Doha Round of multilateral trade negotiations, since many of the poorer nations of the world have little reason to accept the exports and investments by the industrial countries if they cannot sell us their agricultural products. The common agricultural policy now costs about one-half of the European Union budget. The first step toward making the European Union a serious regional government would be to eliminate the common agricultural policy, maybe in exchange for increasing expenditures for those functions for which there are significant economies of scale.

Defense

The case for a traditional defense alliance is based on geometry: The cost of defense increases with the perimeter of the defended area. The number of people defended increases with the size of the defended area. And the ratio of the perimeter to the area declines with the size of the area (for a square, for example, the ratio of the perimeter to the area is equal to four divided by the length of each side). So the cost of defense per person declines with the number of people in the defended area.

In that sense, the North Atlantic Treaty Organization was a traditional alliance, organized to defend Western Europe against the Soviet-dominated Warsaw Pact. It is now much less clear how to describe NATO, following the breakup of the Soviet Union and the Warsaw Pact and the addition of eight other NATO member governments. The other major change is the increasing shared concern of member governments about military or terrorist threats against nonmember governments. For all of these changes, there has been no change in the NATO charter.

Article V obligates every member government to respond to an attack on any NATO country. This probably increases the risk of a NATO war with Russia, now that the three Baltic countries on the Russian border are now NATO members. Each of these countries includes a substantial number of ethnic Russians, and a dispute with Russia over their treatment or a minor border issue increases the risk of a major war with Russia over issues that are not of general concern to the other member governments; the three Baltic countries clearly add more liabilities than assets to NATO. That is probably also the case with respect to the Ukraine.

NATO has also long had a vague implicit "consensus" rule for approving out-of-area military operations. This has sometimes been interpreted as meaning that any member government—now including, for example, Slovakia—that is strongly opposed to an out-of-area NATO military operation may veto this operation, although this rule has generally been interpreted as meaning that the participation of any member government, in such military operations as in Afghanistan, is dependent only on the approval of that government.

The continuing viability of NATO under conditions that are now very different from those when NATO was established, I suggest, will be dependent on changing both Article V and the consensus rule. My suggestion is that approval of a NATO response to an attack on a member country or an out-of-area military operation be subject to the same dual supermajority rule: Approval of either type of NATO military response would require the approval of four of the six governments of the largest member countries and two-thirds of all other member governments. This would protect NATO against an obligation to defend any member country without the approval of most of the large and smaller member governments. This would also protect NATO from the ability of one or a few member governments to veto a NATO out-of-area military operation. In the absence of this or a similar change in the approval rules, I would personally endorse the withdrawal of the U.S. government from NATO and to let the Europeans choose the defense alliance that best serves their interests.

Environmental Policy

Many environmental effects, of course, have little respect for national borders. For that reason, some regional alliance or government should set common standards for all environmental conditions that have significant cross-border effects. In this case, a multifunction alliance or government would probably be better than a voluntary environmental alliance, because it is important to include upwind and upstream countries that may be not otherwise join a voluntary environmental alliance.

The European Union already has a complex system of environmental regulation of two forms: A regulation is binding on all parties and is directly applicable without any further action by the national governments. A directive, in contrast, is binding on the member state as to the result to be achieved but leaves them the choice of the form and method they adopt to realize the EU objectives within the framework of their internal legal order. This is an adequate framework for environmental regulation but presents two challenges: As much as possible, European environmental regulations should specify goals but not means. And, it is very important to limit such regulation to environmental conditions with significant cross-border effects, leaving such issues as drinking water standards, forest management rules, and so on, to the national governments.

Trade Policy

A larger area subject to common rules of trade generates economies of scale for a reason first recognized by Adam Smith: "the potential division of labor is dependent on the extent of the market." For this reason, the original and most valuable government service by the European Union has been to set the rules for a large regional customs union with no internal constraints on the movement of goods, services, labor, and capital; moreover, these rules have been extended to four nonmember countries.

For all of that, there are two major problems of the European Union trade area:

One problem is common to any bilateral or regional free trade agreement, relative to either a multilateral agreement or a unilateral reduction of trade barriers: they create a preference for the most efficient producer in the region relative to the most efficient producer in the world that is equal to the common external tariff, an effect first recognized by Jacob Viner in 1950.[2] For this reason, any bilateral or regional free trade agreement involves a trade-off between trade expansion and trade diversion, where the amount of trade expansion relative to trade diversion is dependent on the size of the external tariff and whether the most efficient producer in the world is included in the agreement. For this reason, the proliferation of bilateral free trade agreements by the United States government makes no economic sense because they are likely to create much more trade diversion than trade expansion.

The major problem specific to the European Union trade area, however, is that it is difficult for a government to join this area without bearing a proportion of the costs of all EU activities. The North American Free Trade Agreement, for example, has about the same aggregate GDP as the European Union, but it has operated smoothly with only a few dispute settlement committees—no budget, no bureaucracy, and no Brussels! Most of the governments that had been in the European Free Trade Association, however, chose to join the European Union—decisions, I suggest, that may not have been in their interests. If I were an official in a European government, one of my priorities would be to restore or maintain membership in a European-wide free trade area that does not require membership in the European Union.

Monetary Policy

The economies of scale from adding a country to a common currency area result from reducing the transactions costs on exchanges with that country. These economies of scale, however, are ultimately limited by the increasing probability of a major asymmetric shock, the costs of which are substantially higher without a flexible exchange rate. The primary problem of the European Monetary Union (EMU) is that it does not have any of the attributes of a well-functioning currency union:

- The economies and economic policies of the EMU countries are too heterogeneous not to be subject to a major asymmetric shock.
- There is very little labor mobility among the EMU countries.

- There is a very little fiscal redistribution among the EMU countries that is a function of changes in the relative unemployment rates.

This should not be surprising; the United States did not have a well-functioning common currency for 150 years—not until federal unemployment insurance was created in the 1930s and the demand for labor during World War II broke the barriers on the movement of labor from the South to the North.

The potential problems of the EMU are best illustrated by the breakdown of the European Exchange Rate Mechanism in September 1992. At that time, the major asymmetric shock was the reintegration of Germany, which redirected West Germany's net capital exports to the rebuilding of East Germany. As a consequence, the currencies of all of the perimeter countries of the EU from Finland around through Greece were devalued substantially against the deutsche mark, in some countries following the imposition of very high interest rates or a major commitment of reserves in a futile attempt to maintain their exchange rate. At that time, I forecast that the unemployment rates in those countries that devalued against the mark would decline relative to the rates in those countries that maintained their exchange rate with the mark, and that proved to be the case. Somewhat to my surprise, moreover, there was no significant increase in the relative inflation rates in those countries that devalued against the mark.

My own guess is that the European Monetary Union will not survive 10 more years. Britain, Denmark, and Sweden have continued to reject membership in the EMU. There is already grumbling among senior officials in some of the member governments about the EMU restrictions on monetary and fiscal policy. The major prospective asymmetric shock is the difference among the public pension and health care systems of the member governments. Governments that have promised generous pension and health care benefits in countries with a declining population will be the most vulnerable, and this will be increasingly apparent after the first post–World War II baby boomers begin to retire in the next few years; these governments will necessarily face some combination of tax increase and reductions in the promised pension and health care benefits. On the other hand, those governments with smaller or more completely funded benefits and a relatively young and growing population will have a much less severe problem during the next few decades. I do not understand how the EMU could survive this asymmetric shock.

For those governments that have recently joined the EU but have not yet joined the EMU, my advice would be to delay this decision as long as possible. Those governments that are already in the EMU should consider their alternatives in response to a major asymmetric shock. Those governments that have not yet developed the expertise, institutions, and reputation for a responsible independent monetary policy are best advised to create a currency union with the best currency among the country's major trading partners. Most countries, in summary, are best served by a responsible independent monetary policy and a flexible exchange rate.

Scientific Research

The economies of scale from scientific research are a result of inherent limits on both private and public institutions that prevent them from capturing all of the benefits of research. In that sense, much research is a worldwide public good and would be undersupplied by any person, company, or government that bore the full cost.

The European Union's main instrument for the funding of research and development in science, engineering, and technology has been the Framework Programme. Since its inception in 1984, this program has grown considerably in scale and scope. Any legal entity within the member states and certain other countries may apply and receive support. For the four years ending in 2006, the EU budget for this program was 19 billion euros. The budget for the subsequent four years has not yet been determined, but the European Commission has proposed a doubling of the current budget. I have not had the opportunity to evaluate the record of this program, but it is surely more valuable, for example, than the outrageous and much larger EU subsidies to agriculture.

A Concluding Comment

The membership of a European national government in any one of these five forms of selective functional integration may or may not be valuable to its own population. Moreover, there is no reason to believe that the value of membership in most of these forms is dependent on membership in one or more of the other forms: in other words, there are few obvious economies of cross-functional integration. For that reason, there should be no expectation or requirement that participation in any of the functions should be dependent on participation in other of these functions. The one exception to this conclusion is that environmental policy should be addressed by the broadest regional association or government, probably that which sets the trade rules, in order to include all those countries in the region that may be net exporters of environmental problems.

An Association of European National States

The next step toward regional integration would be a multifunctional association of European national states, what Vaclav Klaus proposed to name the Organization of European States. The members of this association would be the individual national states, and the association would be governed by representatives selected by these states. There would be no common citizenship in the association or direct popular election of those who govern the association. The basis for representation could be equal among the member governments or, more realistically, by population. The association would have no direct power to tax, and the grants from the member governments would be proportional to their representation. The initial powers of the association would be limited to those defined in the treaty establishing the association, and any addition to these powers or to the member governments would be subject to the approval of all of the then-current member governments. Finally, any government needs some check on the abuse of its enumerated powers. This would be best achieved by two measures:

- Any majority of the member governments should have the authority to nullify any action of the association, regardless of the balance of support of this action by the representatives. In effect, every action by the association would have to be approved by both a majority of the representatives and a majority of the member states.
- Any member government should have the authority to secede from the association by an authorized procedure that does not require the approval of the other member governments.

The first of these measures would prevent the association from being dominated by its largest member states. The second measure would protect every member government against measures that would eliminate the net benefits of membership in the association.

The major steps to move from the current structure and powers of the European Union to this form of limited association would be to repeal the several treaties since the Single European Act, change the basis of representation in the Council of the European Union from equal representation by member state to representation in proportion to population, allow the Council to initiate legislation, and abolish the European Parliament.

A European State

The proposed constitution for the European Union would be a major step toward a European state. I do not understand the case for a European state, but that is for Europeans, not a friendly American, to decide. The primary condition that might lead to a European state would be international developments that lead to a shared European concern for a unified foreign and defense policy that is independent of the United States. In that case, the primary intellectual challenge would be to design a constitution for a compound European republic, in which the European state protects the constitution from an abuse of powers by the member states and the member states protect the constitution from an abuse of powers by the European state.[3] The latter objective should be adequately protected by the Council of the European Union, with equal representation among the member states and its double majority rule, but several major changes to the proposed constitution for the European Union should be considered before it is again submitted for ratification:[4]

1. The relation between the Union and the member states is not adequately defined. One article, for example, states that "Competences not conferred upon the union in the Constitution remain with the Member States" (Article I-11-2). Fine. But the next sentence states that ". . . in areas which do not fall within its exclusive competence the Union shall act only if . . . the objectives of the proposed action . . . can rather, by reason of the scale or effects of the proposed action, be better than a member state. This is an open invitation to an increase in the powers of the Union.
2. The Commission is much too powerful. One article states that "Except where the Constitution provides otherwise, Union acts

can be adopted only on the basis of a Commission proposal" (Article I-26-2). This is a dreadful provision. The executive has no comparative advantage in recognizing the need for and formulating new legislation, and this provision gives the Commission a large first-mover advantage. Another article also magnifies the role of the Commission: "In the discharge of their duties members of the Commission shall neither see nor take instructions from any government or other body" (Article I-26-7). One wonders why anyone would want to serve in the European Parliament.

3. And the entire Charter of Fundamental Rights should be replaced by a list of political and economic rights against the state, a list more like the U.S. Bill of Rights. The Charter is a detailed list of claims on the state for such services as education, a free placement service, paid maternity leave, social security benefits and social services, housing assistance, preventative health care, services of general economic interest, and high levels of environmental and consumer protection. Unless the member states have the independent authority to determine the composition of welfare services and the requirements for access to these services, the European Union would become a massive harmonized welfare state, relegating the member states to such limited roles as ". . . ensuring the territorial integrity of the State, and for maintaining law and order and safeguarding internal security" (Article I-5-1).

Conclusion

As I have written elsewhere, if I were a European, I would share some of the reasons to hope for a more perfect union. But be careful about any major political structure that is being presented for your approval. Do you really want a constitutional treaty among the member states? Or what looks to me more like a proposed constitution for a European government? Even if you favor the major provisions of the proposed constitution, be especially careful that the constitution limits the authority of the European Union to define its own powers, because all governments seek broader powers than first authorized. Over time, a demonstrably imperfect Europe of national states may be a better protection of your liberty than approving the proposed constitution in the hope for a more perfect European Union.

Notes

1. Václav Klaus, "Why Europe Must Reject Centralization," *Financial Times*, August 30, 2005.

2. Jacob Viner, *The Customs Union Issue*, 1950.

3. William A. Niskanen, "On the Constitution of a Compound Republic," *Constitutional Political Economy* 10 (2), 1999.

4. William A. Niskanen, "Advice by a Friendly American on the Proposed Constitution for the European Union," *Revista di Politica Economica* (July–August 2004).

27. On Wisconsin: Some Friendly Constitutional Advice

On reading the Constitution of the State of Wisconsin, I am reminded that one's understanding of a constitution is very dependent on a detailed understanding of the history of the political community for which it is presumably the higher law. In retrospect, when I wrote an article on the proposed constitution for the European Union,[1] I had a much better understanding of the relevant European history than my current understanding of the relevant Wisconsin history. So any number of provisions of the Wisconsin Constitution seem odd or puzzling to me, and I ask you to forgive a friendly stranger for my innocent mistakes. I am especially intrigued to understand why the longest section of the constitution is a detailed set of rules about gambling.[2] And why several sections describe the authority of state officials to repel an invasion[3] or to charge someone with treason,[4] not being aware that Wisconsin was ever threatened by invasion or subversion.

The State of Wisconsin

As an economist, I am first inclined to survey the economy and government of a state before passing judgment about whether some change in the constitution is likely to be valuable. The data summarized in the following tables, most of which are in the Statistical Abstract of the United States for 2006,[5] proved to be the most accessible and helpful.

For the most part, general economic conditions in Wisconsin are quite favorable. The increases in real gross state product and real personal income per capita from 1990 through 2004 were higher than

---

This article was presented on October 6, 2006, at Marquette University in Milwaukee and was first published in the *Marquette Law Review* 90, no. 3 (2007). My thanks to the *Marquette Law Review* for its permission to republish this article.

Table 27.1
GENERAL ECONOMIC CONDITIONS

Annual percentage change 1990–2004	Nation	Wisconsin
Real gross state product[6]	3.2 percent	3.6 percent
Population[7]	1.2 percent	0.9 percent
Real personal income per capita[8]	1.7 percent	2.0 percent
Recent economic conditions		
Personal income per capita (2004)[9]	$32,937	$32,157
Average annual salary (2003)[10]	$37,765	$33,425
Employment rate (2004)[11]	62.3 percent	68.1 percent
Unemployment rate (2004)[12]	5.5 percent	5.0 percent
Poverty rate (2003)[13]	12.7 percent	10.5 percent

the national average.[14] The rate of population growth was somewhat lower than the national average, although higher than in any other state in the Great Lakes region.[15] The Wisconsin economy appears to have adjusted better to the decline in manufacturing employment than any other state in this region, probably due to the higher diversity of manufacturing employment by industry.[16] Recent economic conditions in Wisconsin are also quite favorable. Personal income per capita in Wisconsin is about the same as the national average despite a significantly lower average salary, primarily because of an unusually high employment rate.[17] The primary economic policy challenge suggested by these data is to increase the average salary of Wisconsin workers; the most effective way to achieve this objective, according to Terry Ludeman, may be to provide incentives to reduce the substantial outmigration of Wisconsin college graduates.[18] The general economic conditions in Wisconsin, however, are not sufficient to make the case for a significant change in the Wisconsin Constitution.

Expenditures, taxes, and borrowing per capita by the Wisconsin state and local governments are each somewhat higher than the national average.[19] As in most states, the balance of general revenues and expenditures in Wisconsin was negative in 2002 but increased to a surplus by 2004; even in 2002, however, the outstanding state and local debt per Wisconsin resident was about 5 percent lower than the national average.[20] Somewhat surprising, the relatively high

Table 27.2
STATE AND LOCAL GOVERNMENT CONDITIONS

	Nation	Wisconsin
Expenditures per capita (2002)[21]	$6,026	$6,251
Tax revenue per capita[22]	$3,143	$3,421
Top personal tax rate (2006)[23]	5.5 percent	6.8 percent
Top corporate tax rate (2006)[24]	6.9 percent	7.9 percent
Budget balance per capita (2002)[25]	−$160	−$267
Employees per 100 residents (2003)[26]	5.42	5.26
Average annual salary[27]	$43,056	$44,298

government expenditures per capita in Wisconsin are *not* due to an unusually high number of government employees: the number of full-time equivalent state and local government employees per capita is 3 percent lower than the national average, offset by an average salary that is about 3 percent higher.[28] The average salary of state and local employees in Wisconsin, however, is about one-third higher than the average salary of all employees in the state, whereas the national average salary of state and local employees is 14 percent higher than the average salary of all employees;[29] this raises the question whether some change in the structure of government in Wisconsin would make it possible to hire qualified employees at a lower salary to provide some tax-financed services.

A more important question is whether the residents of Wisconsin value the level and quality of government services in the state by enough to offset their higher taxes. For the moment, that seems to be the case; Wisconsin is the *only* state in the Great Lakes region to experience a net internal immigration from 2000 through 2004.[30] State and local government conditions in Wisconsin are also not sufficient to make a case for significant change in the Wisconsin Constitution.

But good enough for government work is not good enough. The citizens of Wisconsin should consider changes to the Constitution of Wisconsin that would make their economic and political conditions demonstrably *superior* to those in other states.

The Fiscal Constitution

Professor McChrystal asked me to address the constitutional rules bearing on spending and taxes and I agreed, subject to the opportunity to address one other topic as well. I have been thinking about state fiscal constitutions for about 30 years, first serving on the committee that drafted Proposition 1 in California[31] (along with Anthony Kennedy, now a Justice of the Supreme Court), as chairman of the committee that drafted the Headlee Amendment in Michigan,[32] and as a friend of several people that have recently been promoting TABOR-like amendments[33] in other states.

The Wisconsin Fiscal Constitution

My reading of the written Constitution of the State of Wisconsin, however, provided very little guidance about the effective fiscal constitution. For routine budget decisions, according to article VIII, section 5, the legislature is instructed to limit estimated expenditures to estimated revenues for each year with any actual deficit to be repaid in the following year.[34] The quorum for such decisions, according to section 8, is three-fifths of the members of each house.[35]

For extraordinary expenditures, according to section 6, the legislature is allowed to contract debt with such debt to be retired within five years, "but such debts shall never in the aggregate exceed one hundred thousand dollars."[36] (A reality check: the outstanding debt of the State of Wisconsin was nearly $15 billion in 2002.)[37] Such debts must be approved by a majority of all members elected to each house.[38] And one wonders what might constitute an extraordinary expenditure, for section 10 states that "the state may never contract . . . debt for . . . internal improvement."[39]

The long and complicated section 7 appears to override any of the above fiscal constraints but provides no clear guidance about what is the effective fiscal constitution.[40] I have not studied the implicit fiscal rules of the Wisconsin legislature, but I doubt that they are consistent with any of these provisions of the written fiscal constitution.

Changes to Consider

What, if any, changes in the Wisconsin fiscal constitution should be considered?

First, I do *not* support a TABOR-like amendment for several reasons: such amendments limit the rate of growth of state spending to the inflation rate plus the rate of growth of the population, but they have not proven to be stable. As far as I know, all such amendments at the state level have been subject to suspension or the exemption of some major types of spending or revenues. Second, any temporary increase in spending has a ratchet effect on future spending. More important, such amendments make state spending independent of real per capita income, and thus, do not give those who provide or most value state services a stake in economic growth. In some cases, of course, a general reduction in state spending and tax revenues may increase economic growth, but many other state policies also influence economic growth. For example, the composition of state spending, the level of marginal tax rates, the details of regulation and commercial law, and so on, also affect economic growth but are not addressed by a general limit on state spending and tax revenues. A fiscal rule that permits some increase in state spending in response to an increase in real per capita income is necessary to encourage those who especially benefit from state spending to pay attention to these other policies that also affect economic growth.

Again, what, if any changes in the fiscal constitution should be considered?

Let's start with the several objectives that you may, or maybe should, be trying to accomplish by an amendment to the constitution:

- Stabilize the state government spending and tax revenue share of personal income, *unless changed by a broadly supported political decision.*
- Stabilize the level of state government spending relative to temporary changes in state economic conditions.
- Improve the incentives of those who make the state's fiscal decisions.
- Reduce the dependence of the budget process on estimates.
- Express the fiscal rules in clear, concise constitutional language.

The following fiscal rules, I suggest, are consistent with each of these objectives:

Suggested Fiscal Rules

1. State general expenditures in any fiscal year may not exceed 110 percent of the state general revenues in the second prior fiscal year without the approval of a majority of those elected to each house of the legislature.
2. The rate or base of no state tax may be increased without the approval by a majority of those voting in the next election for members of the legislature.

3. The state must compensate local governments for the estimated incremental cost of any new state mandate on those governments.

Rule 1 establishes a limit on state general expenditures that is a fixed multiple of the known level of state general revenues in the second prior fiscal year. The specific percent in this rule should be based on the average two-year increase in some aggregate nominal measure of the state economy over an extended prior period. Over the period 1990 through 2004, for example, nominal personal income in Wisconsin increased at an average two-year rate of 10.4 percent.[41] Since the Wisconsin tax structure is slightly progressive, a spending limit that is 110 percent of the revenues in the second prior fiscal year would maintain the spending share of personal income over any extended period.

The two-year lag between revenues and expenditures serves several objectives. Expenditures would be stabilized relative to short-run changes in the state economy; expenditures during the weak economy of 2002, for example, would be based on the revenues in the strong economy of 2000. The fiscal incentives of both voters and legislators would be better when any increase in tax rates must be approved by the voters two years before the legislature may approve a spending increase. In addition, as mentioned before, this type of spending rule increases the incentive to promote measures that increase economic growth, increasing tax revenues for any given tax rates. And the two-year lag greatly reduces the role of estimates in the budget process. There may be occasions when it is appropriate to increase the spending limit for a specific year; this decision can be left to the legislature because it has no ratchet effect on subsequent spending. The suggested quorum for this vote is that specified for extraordinary expenditures in the constitution.[42]

Rule 2 establishes the level of state expenditures and tax revenues relative to the size of the state economy, a decision that should be made only by the voters. This rule also stabilizes the details of the tax code.

Rule 3 is necessary to constrain the state government from the incentive to shift some of the fiscal burden of its agenda to local governments. Any estimate of the incremental cost of a new state mandate, of course, should be expected to provoke some controversy. The experience in other states, however, also suggests that

Table 27.3
PUBLIC EDUCATION IN WISCONSIN

	Nation	Wisconsin
Costs and inputs		
Annual cost per student (2004)[43]	$8,237	$9,472
Teachers per 100 students[44]	6.3	6.8
Annual teacher salary[45]	$46,800	$42,900
Outputs		
High school graduation rate (2002–2003)[46]	73.9%	85.8%
College board SAT (2005)[47]	1,028	1,191

this rule would increase the popular support for approving a general fiscal limit in the state constitution.

The Supply of Tax-Financed Services

There is broad support in Wisconsin for a number of tax-financed services. No *general* interest, however, is served by an explicit or implicit constitutional rule that any such service be supplied only by a government organization and government employees. There is no reason to expect better service from a government monopoly than from a private monopoly.

Education

The most important of these services, of course, is education. In a 1998 ruling on the amended Milwaukee Parental Choice Program, the Supreme Court of Wisconsin observed that "[e]ducation ranks at the apex of a state's function."[48] So it is important to evaluate the status of public education in Wisconsin and any changes in the constitution that would improve this status.

The record of public education in Wisconsin is impressive *relative* to the national average. The annual cost per student is 15 percent higher than the national average, despite a somewhat lower average teacher salary.[49] But both the percent of ninth-grade students that graduate from high school and the SAT scores are among the several highest in the nation.[50] Again, as with the general economic and state government records in Wisconsin, the record of public education is not sufficient to make a case for a significant change in the Wisconsin Constitution.

The problem, however, is that the current national average grossly underestimates the potential performance of American students. The difference between the relative and absolute performance of a school system is illustrated by the new Cato Index of Education Market Performance;[51] Wisconsin has the highest score of any state on this index but with an absolute score of 26 on a 100-point scale.[52] Professor Caroline Hoxby of Harvard has estimated that the average productivity of American schools *declined* by around 55 percent (based on math tests for 9-year-olds) or 73 percent (based on math tests for 9-year-olds) or 73 percent (based on reading tests for 17-year-olds) between the 1970–1971 and 1998–1999 school years.[53] The average 17-year-old in the 1970–1971 school year had a score that fewer than 5 percent of American 17-year-olds now attain.[54] Wisconsin, in its own interests, has the opportunity to demonstrate to the nation that the academic performance of Wisconsin students could be dramatically increased. As Allan Odden has emphasized, "Wisconsin needs to move a 'good' education system to a 'great' education system."[55]

The education article in the Wisconsin Constitution, however, describes a quite bureaucratic system of public education that would be substantially regulated and financed by the state, without a hint of any role for tax-financed private suppliers. There is an intriguing opening in the initial Declaration of Rights, however, which states that "Nothing in this constitution shall prohibit the legislature from providing for the safety and welfare of children by providing for the transportation of children to and from any parochial or private school or institution of learning."[56] So some amount and type of tax-financed support for students attending private schools has been authorized for 40 years. More important, several decisions by the Supreme Court of Wisconsin have affirmed the constitutionality of the Milwaukee Parental Choice Program on the basis of the "public purpose doctrine,"[57] although this doctrine has no basis in any specific provision of the state constitution.

The MPCP has been one of the most successful policy experiments in many years. State-financed vouchers were first available to students from poor families in Milwaukee in 1990. The Wisconsin legislature has since expanded the number of voucher-eligible students from 1 percent of the Milwaukee public school enrollment to 15 percent, removed the restriction that participating private schools must be nonsectarian, and reduced the state regulations to which these schools are subject.[58] The most arbitrary of the remaining regulations is that the participating private schools may not charge a tuition higher than the state aid per student in the public schools, an amount about 60 percent of the total expenditures per student enrolled in the public schools; this regulation severely limits the number and types of private schools participating in the voucher program. As the Supreme Court of Wisconsin observed correctly, "the schools participating in the amended MPCP are also subject to the additional checks inherent in the notion of school choice."[59] The value of the voucher is the lesser of state aid per student ($5,734 in 2004) or the private school tuition, and state aid to the public schools is reduced by one-half the voucher amount. So each student that attends a private school with a voucher increases both the state and local revenue per student remaining in the public schools.

A careful paper by several scholars found that the academic performance of the voucher students exceeded those voucher-eligible students who stayed in the Milwaukee public schools by their third or fourth year in a private school.[60] More interesting, Professor Hoxby's innovative study demonstrated that the productivity growth in those Milwaukee public schools most threatened by a potential loss of students to voucher schools was significantly higher than in Wisconsin schools with a similar mix of students that were not eligible for vouchers.[61] Increased competition had a powerful effect, and almost every student was a winner. Moreover, private schools participating in the Milwaukee voucher program are much less segregated than the Milwaukee metropolitan area public schools, a finding consistent with the conclusion of similar studies of the Cleveland and Washington, D.C., schools.[62] The only significant remaining opposition to this program has been that by public school administrators and teachers.

Based on this record, the Wisconsin legislature should now consider the MPCP as a model for a statewide voucher program. Some language such as the following should be considered as an amendment to the education article of the Wisconsin constitution:

Suggested Education Rules

1. Any student eligible to attend a public primary or secondary school is also eligible for a voucher to attend a private school,

the value of the voucher equal to the lesser of the state aid per student in that school district and the tuition of the private school attended.

2. State aid to local school districts would be reduced by the amount of the vouchers to students in that district.
3. Local school districts are authorized but not required to increase the value of the vouchers to some local students from other revenues.

Rule 1 would extend the MPCP rule to all students in the state, regardless of location or the income of the parents. Rule 2 would modify the MPCP rule by reducing the state aid to a local school district by the full amount of vouchers to students in that district; this would substantially increase the incentives of the public schools to avoid losing voucher students to private schools. Even in this case, a voucher student would increase the average local revenue per student remaining in a public school. Rule 3 would authorize a school district to augment the voucher from local revenues to meet the special expenses of some students or to close a public school with few enrolled students.

This suggested amendment would maintain a substantial role of the state in financing and monitoring primary and secondary education in Wisconsin. But it would dramatically change the supply of tax-financed education. Local school districts would have a much stronger incentive to meet the educational demands of local voters. Parents would have a much stronger incentive to monitor the costs and performance of the schools that their children might attend. Innovative school administrators and teachers would have more opportunity to experiment. And there is every reason to expect that the performance of Wisconsin students and the productivity of Wisconsin tax-financed education would dramatically increase.

Other Services

In conclusion, I would like to leave you with one other suggested constitutional amendment that would apply to *all* state services. Consider the following language, probably as an amendment to the Declaration of Rights:

Suggested Rule for All State Financed Services

1. Nothing in this constitution should be interpreted to imply that any service financed by the state must necessarily be supplied by a state or local government organization.

The primary value of this suggested rule is to avoid the type of lawsuits that significantly delayed the implementation of the Milwaukee voucher plan and, for the moment, have voided the Florida voucher plan.

On Wisconsin!

Notes

1. William A. Niskanen, "Advice from a Friendly American on the Proposed Constitution for the European Union," in this volume.
2. See WIS. CONST. art. IV, § 24.
3. See WIS. CONST. art. VIII, § 7(1).
4. See Wisconsin Constitution art. I, section 10.
5. U.S. Census Bureau, Statistical Abstract of the United States 2006, http://www.census.gov/compenia/statab/2006/2006edition.html.
6. Id. at 446 tbl.654.
7. Id. at 21 tbl.17.
8. Id. at 452 tbl.662.
9. Id.
10. Id. at 427 tbl.630.
11. Id. at 390 tbl.581.
12. Id.
13. Id. at 471 tbl.692.
14. Id. at 446 tbl.654, 452 tbl.662.
15. Id. at 21 tbl.17.
16. Id. at 390 tbl. 581.
17. Id. at 452 tbl.662, 427 tbl.630, 390 tbl.581.
18. Terry Ludeman, former Chief Economist for Wis. Dep't. of Workforce Dev., Address at Wisconsin Constitution Conference—Is the Wisconsin Constitution Obsolete?, (Oct. 6, 2006), audio available at http://law.marquette.edu/webcasts/events/wi/06-TerryLudeman.mp3.
19. See supra text accompanying notes 19–23.
20. U.S. CENSUS BUREAU, supra note 5, at 287 tbl.432.
21. U.S. CENSUS BUREAU, *supra* note 5, at 285 tbl.431.
22. Id. at 287 tbl.432.
23. FED'N OF TAX ADM'RS, STATE INDIVIDUAL INCOME TAX RATES TABLE (2006), available at http://www.taxadmin.org/fta/rate/ind_inc.pdf.
24. FED'N OF TAX ADM'RS, STATE CORPORATE INCOME TAX RATES TABLE (2006), available at http://www.taxadmin.org/fta/rate/corp_inc.pdf.
25. U.S. CENSUS BUREAU, *supra* note 5, at 287 tbl.432.
26. Id. at 311 tbl.456.
27. Id.
28. See supra tax accompanying notes 24–25.

29. See supra tax accompanying notes 10, 25.
30. U.S. CENSUS BUREAU, *supra* note 5, at 24 tbl.20.
31. Proposition 1 provided for tax and expenditure limitations on state government to be included in the California state constitution. See Lewis K. Uhler, *Setting Limits: Constitutional Control of Government* 175–177 (1989); see also California Ballot Proposition 1 (1973), available at http://library.uchastings.edu/ballot_pdf/1973s.pdf.
32. Michigan Constitution art.IX, sections 25–34.
33. See, e.g., Assemb.J.Res.55, 96th Leg., Reg. Sess. (Wis. 2003).
34. Wisconsin Constitution.art. VIII, C5.
35. Id. art. VIII, § 8.
36. Id. art. VIII, § 6.
37. U.S. Census Bureau, supra note 5, at 296 tbl.440.
38. Wisconsin Constitution art. VIII, section 6.
39. Id. art. VIII, § 10.
40. Id. art. VIII, § 7.
41. U.S. CENSUS BUREAU, supra not 5, at 451 tbl.661.
42. See Wisconsin Constitution art. VIII, section 8.
43. U.S. Census Bureau, supra note 5, at 156 tbl.230, 164 tbl.243.
44. Id. at 156 tbl.230, 161 tbl.238.
45. Id. at 161 tbl.238.
46. Marilyn Seastrom et al., National Center for Education Statistics, U.S. Department of Education, public No. NCES 2006-601, The Averaged Freshman Graduation Rate for Public High Schools from the Common Core of Data: School Years 2001–02 and 2002–03, at 5 tbl.1, 2005, available at http://nces.ed.gov/pubs2006/20060601.pdf.
47. College Board, Table 3: Mean SAT Reasoning Test Verbal and Math Scores by State, with Changes for Selected Years, 2005, available at http://www.collegeboard.com/prod_downloads/about/news_info/cbsenior/yr2005/table3-mean-SAT-reasoning-test.pdf.
48. *Jackson v. Benson*, 218 Wis. 2d 835, 287, 578 N.W.2d 602, 629 (1998).
49. See supra text accompanying notes 44, 46.
50. See supra text accompanying notes 47–48.
51. Andrew J. Coulson, Cato Institute, Policy Analysis No. 585, the Cato Education Market Index (2006), available at http://www.cato.org/pubs/pas/pa585.pedf.
52. Id. at 13, 14 tbl.2.
53. Caroline M. Hoxby, "School Choice and School Productivity: Could School Choice be a Tide that Lifts All Boats?" in *The Economics of School Choice*, ed. Caroline M. Hoxby, 287, 289 (Chicago: University of Chicago Press, 2003).
54. Id.
55. Allan R. Odden, professor, Department of Education Leadership & Policy Analysis, University of Wisconsin-Madison, address at Wisconsin Constitution Conference—"Is the Wisconsin Constitution Obsolete," October 6, 2006, http://law.marquette.edu/webcastsevents/wi/06-AllenOdden.mp3.
56. Wisconsin Constitution art. I, section 23.
57. *Vincent v. Voight*, 2000 WI 93, § 41, 236 Wis. 2d 588, § 41, 614 N.W.2d 388, § 41 ("[T]he purpose of [a] tax must be one which pertains to the public purpose of the district within which the tax is to be levied and raised." (quoting *Buse v. Smith*, 74 Wis. 2d 550, 577, 247 N.W.2d 141, 153 (1976)); *Jackson v. Benson*, 218 Wis. 2d 835, 900, 578 N.W.23d 602, 630 (1998) ("[T]he amended MPCP does not violate the public purpose doctrine because it fulfills a valid public purpose, and it contains sufficient and reasonable controls to attain its public purpose."); *Davis v. Grover*, 166 Wis. 2d 501, 513, 480 N.W.2d 460, 463 (1992) ("[T]he MPCP does not violate the public purpose doctrine.").

58. Jay P. Greene et al., "Effectiveness of School Choice: The Milwaukee Experiment," *Journal of Education and Urban Society* 31 (1999): 190, 194.
59. Jackson, 218 Wis. 2d at 899, 578 N.W.2d 602, 630.
60. Greene, supra note 58, at 200.
61. Hoxby, supra note 53, at 323.
62. Greg Forster, Segregation Levels in Milwaukee Public Schools and the Milwaukee Voucher Program (Milton and Rose D. Friedman Foundation, August 2006, http://www.Friedmanfoundation.org/Milwaukee.pdf.

28. A Reformulation of Voting Theory

Our standard theory of voting behavior—the core of public choice—is a mess! The theory of voter behavior is asymmetric with the theory of candidate behavior. And more important, the theory does not explain some of the more important changes in the outcomes of American elections. This is not a new observation. Samuel Huntington in 1950, Morris Fiorina in 1974, Richard Fenno in 1977 and Sam Peltzman in 1984 were among the most vocal critics of the median voter theorem, arguing that divergent platforms are needed to adequately explain political behavior. But none of these distinguished scholars offered a coherent competing theory of voting behavior. This chapter summarizes a major problem of the standard theory of voting behavior, develops an alternative theory based on a joint determination of voter and candidate behavior, and presents some evidence from recent elections that is more consistent with the alternative theory.

A Major Problem with the Standard Theory of Voting Behavior

The standard theory of voter behavior is dramatically asymmetric with the theory of candidate behavior. (For a good recent summary of the standard theory, see Munger, 2001.) Voters are assumed to make a *joint* determination of *whether* to vote and *for whom* to vote, based on their understanding of the issue positions of the alternative candidates. Candidates, in contrast, are represented as assuming that voters have made a decision whether to vote that is invariant to the issue positions of the candidates but that their decision for whom to vote is still open and is dependent on these issue positions. The assumptions about the sequence with which the candidates'

This article was presented at a conference at the University of San Pablo in Madrid in December 2005 and was first published in *Public Choice and the Challenges of Democracy*, ed. Jose Casas Pardo and Pedro Schwarz (Cheltenham, U.K.: Edward Elgar, 2007). My thanks to Edward Elgar for its permission to republish this article.

issue positions are revealed are also asymmetric: voters are assumed to know the issue positions of the candidates when they make a decision whether to vote, whereas candidates are assumed to know the preference distribution of those who vote before they choose and announce their issue positions. When the decision *whether* to vote is invariant to the issue positions of the candidates, a candidate does not risk losing votes from his (or her) party base, and there is a strong incentive to choose issue positions close to that of the alternative candidate, gaining two net votes for every swing voter that he attracts. Only in this case (plus the usual assumptions that voter preferences are single peaked on all issues and that there are only two candidates) do both candidates have an incentive to choose issue positions close to the median preferences of those who vote. An encouraging result, perhaps, suggesting that the variance of the issue positions among our elected representatives is lower than the variance of voter preferences, reducing the bargaining costs of the compromises necessary to govern. The problem is that this result does not seem consistent with the evidence.

An Alternative Theory Of Voter And Candidate Behavior

In a prior article on these issues (Niskanen, 2004), I concluded that "Public choice scholars need to rebuild voting theory to incorporate the effects of a candidate's issue position on both the decision to vote and the choice among those who decide to vote." That is what I try to do in this section.

We shall start with the following two equations describing the conditions that determine the number of votes for the candidate of the left and of the right, respectively,

$$V_L = a - b(L - L_M)^2 - c(L - R)^2, \quad (1)$$

and

$$V_R = d - e(R - R_M)^2 - f(R - L)^2, \quad (2)$$

where

V_L = total votes for the candidate of the left
L = position in issue space of the candidate of the left,
L_M = position in issue space of the median potential voter on the left,
R = position in issue space of the candidate of the right,

V_R = total votes for the candidate of the right, and
R_M = position in issue space of the median potential voter on the right.

The issue space is represented by a scale from 0 through 100, with 0 representing the position of the extreme left and 100 the extreme right. The first squared term in each equation represents the votes that a candidate loses, primarily by potential voters choosing not to vote, by choosing a position in issue space different from the party base. The second squared term in each equation represents the votes that a candidate loses, primarily to the other candidate, by choosing a position in issue space different from the other candidate. The challenge for each candidate is to choose a position in issue space such that the marginal votes gained by attracting swing voters is equal to the marginal votes lost by members of his own party choosing not to vote.

The following two equations describe the conditions that determine the vote-maximizing position in issue space for each of the two candidates:

(3) $$L = (bL_M + cR)/(b + c),$$

and

(4) $$R = (eR_M + fL)/(e + f).$$

The candidate of the left, for example, is pulled toward his party base by the ratio $b/(b + c)$ and to the issue position of the candidate of the right by the ratio $c/(b + c)$. If either candidate is confident that he knows the issue position of the other candidate, his own equation is sufficient to determine his own vote-maximizing position in issue space. More generally, however, both candidates choose a vote-maximizing position in issue space on the assumption that the other candidate does also, in which case their positions are jointly determined. In this case, Equations 3 and 4 must be solved jointly to determine both L and R. This leads, for example, to the following equation for L that does not include the specific issue position of the candidate of the right:

(5) $$L = [b(e + f)L_M + ceR_M]/[(b + c)(e + f) - cf],$$

and the level of L from this equation can then be inserted into Equation 4 to determine the level of R.

Table 28.1
EFFECTS OF VARYING VOTER RESPONSES TO DIFFERENCES IN A CANDIDATE'S ISSUE POSITION FROM THE PARTY BASE AND THE OTHER CANDIDATE

Variables	0.5	1.0	1.5
b			
L	50.0	46.67	45.00
R	55.0	53.33	52.50
V_L	125	111.11	106.25
V_R	150	111.11	87.50
c			
L	44	46.67	48.57
R	52	53.33	54.29
V_L	152	111.11	87.50
V_R	72	111.11	134.69

The primary lessons from this model of the behavior of voters and candidates may best be illustrated by a quantitative example. For the example presented in Table 28.1, the coefficients *a* and *d* (the magnitude of the respective party bases) are both set equal to 200, L_M (the issue position of the median potential voter on the left) at 40, and R_M (the issue position of the median potential voter on the right) at 60. Table 28.1 then presents the effects of separately varying the coefficients *b* and *c* from 0.5 to 1.5, leaving all other coefficients set at 1. The effects of varying the coefficients *e* and *f* are symmetric with those illustrated.

This table illustrates the following major patterns from this model, in each case given the assumed values of the coefficients *a*, *d*, L_M, and R_M:

- When the coefficients *b*, *c*, *e* and *f* are all equal to 1, the vote-maximizing positions of both candidates are a symmetric *difference* from the median position in issue space, the votes for each candidate are equal, and the voter participation rate (given these coefficients) is 55.6 percent.
- An increase in the votes lost by choosing an issue position different from the median of the party base (such as the illustrated increase in the coefficient *b* relative to the coefficients *c*, *e* and *f*) pulls the issue positions of *both* candidates (in this case)

toward the left, reduces the voter participation rate of both parties, and increases the *relative* vote (in this case) for the candidate of the left.

- An increase in the votes lost by choosing an issue position different from that of the other candidate (such as the illustrated increase in the coefficient c relative to the coefficients b, e and f) pulls the issue position of *both* candidates (in this case) toward the right, and increases the *relative* vote (in this case) for the candidate of the right.

Another pattern of the model (not illustrated by Table 28.1) is the effect of a shift in the median issue position of the party base. A change in L_M in the direction of R_M for example (a move to the right), shifts the issue position of *both* candidates to the right, increases the vote for both candidates, *but does not change the relative votes for the two candidates*. Again, increasing the coefficients e and f, or reducing R_M would have just the opposite effects.

Some Relevant Empirical Tests

The primary condition that seems inconsistent with the standard theory of voter behavior is the increased polarization of Congress. David Broder, a leading political commentator, summarized this condition in a January 2, 2003, column in the *Washington Post*, observing:

> Party caucuses on both sides of the Capitol have become more cohesive internally and further apart from each other philosophically . . . with almost every session, [there are] fewer moderates or progressives on the Republican side and fewer conservatives among the Democrats—especially when it comes to fundamental economic and social questions and the role of government in American life.

Broder based this observation on an analysis of the "Party Unity" scores calculated and reported each year by the *Congressional Quarterly*. These scores are the percentage of roll-call votes in which a majority of Republicans oppose the position of a majority of Democrats and the percentage of votes that each member has voted with the party majority on these votes.

In the same column, Broder reported:

> When I averaged the year-by-year results for both chambers, I found the percentage of partisan-divide-roll calls has gone from 39 percent in the 1970s to 47 percent in the 1980s to 58 percent in the 1990s.
>
> Even more striking is the growth in cohesion—call it discipline or philosophical agreement—within both party caucuses. In the 1970s, on partisan roll calls, the average member of Congress backed the party position 65 percent of the time. In the1980s, the average degree of partisan loyalty rose to 73 percent; and in the 1990s, to 81 percent. In the past two years, it has been 87 percent.

Since Broder wrote this column, the Party Unity scores increased to the highest level in five decades in 2003, only to decline slightly in 2004 (Poole, 2004).

My own contribution to empirical tests of this issue has been an analysis of the votes for Congress in 2002 and 2004, my study of the 2002 election concluding: "U.S. elections are increasingly biased against *moderates*," (Niskanen, 2004, original emphasis). My null hypothesis, again, is that the most vulnerable incumbents in these two congressional elections were moderates. My measure of the moderation of Republican incumbents is their Americans for Democratic Action rating. Similarly, my measure of the moderation of Democratic incumbents is their Americans Conservative Union rating for the same period. Very few incumbents were defeated in either election, so I defined the vulnerable incumbents as those who won less than 55 percent of the major party popular vote in their states or districts. Even by this measure, the samples of vulnerable incumbents were surprisingly small. The samples of nonvulnerable incumbents exclude those that had no major party opposition candidate. I test this hypothesis for both the Senate and the House for both 2002 and 2004 by a difference-of-means test. The results of these tests are summarized in Table 28.2.

In the congressional election of 2002, the vulnerable incumbents in both the Senate and the House had significantly higher scores (ratings by the standards of the other party) than the nonvulnerable incumbents. In the congressional election of 2004, the scores of the vulnerable and nonvulnerable Senate incumbents were not significantly different, but the vulnerable House incumbents again had a significantly higher score than the nonvulnerable incumbents.

Table 28.2
WERE THE VULNERABLE INCUMBENTS MORE MODERATE THAN OTHER INCUMBENTS?

			Score			
	Year	Sample	Median	Mean	S.D.	*t*-ratio
Senate	2002					
Vulnerable		6	30	24.00	13.13	
Nonvulnerable		21	10	12.19	9.90	
Difference		20	11.81	5.78	2.04	
Senate	2004					
Vulnerable		3	16	17.00	2.65	
Nonvulnerable		22	17.5	17.27	11.16	
Difference			−1.5	−0.27	2.83	−0.10
House	2002					
Vulnerable		18	12	22.06	23.16	
Nonvulnerable		368	5	11.34	14.59	
Difference			7	10.72	5.51	1.94
House	2004					
Vulnerable		15	20	23.00	20.40	
Nonvulnerable		318	5	11.51	13.28	
Difference			15	11.49	5.32	2.16

For the congressional election of 2004, I also carried out one other test to determine whether there was a significant relation between the ratio of the vote for the incumbent to the vote for the candidate of the major opposition party and the "moderation score" of the incumbent, again excluding those incumbents who had no major party opposition candidate. Consistent with the findings presented in Table 28.2, there was no such relation for Senate incumbents but a highly significant negative relation for House incumbents.

Most of these tests, in summary, indicate that a favorable ranking by the standards of the other party makes an incumbent more vulnerable by reducing the ratio of their popular votes relative to that for the candidate of the major opposition party. At the same time, there seems to be little risk for most incumbents to be considered a moderate, because the average incumbent in the 2004 congressional election received around twice as many popular votes as their major party opposition candidate. For most incumbents, their first election to Congress is close to a lifetime appointment.

All in all, I suggest, my alternative model of voter and candidate behavior is a better explanation of the major recent changes in American elections than the standard model. One major change is the increased polarization of Congress, as summarized above. Another major change has been the increased attention of Republican candidates to energize their party base, rather than to reach out to a broader range of uncommitted voters. For example, the focus of the 2004 Bush campaign, as described by political scientist Morris Fiorina, was:

> [to get out] the votes of a few million Republican-leaning evangelicals who did not vote in 2000, rather than by attracting some modest proportion of 95 million other non-voting Americans, not to mention moderate Democratic voters who could have been persuaded to back a genuinely compassionate conservative.

There will still be those who claim that the median voter theorem is a sufficient explanation of voter and candidate behavior within each constituency and that the increased polarization of Congress reflects an increased polarization of policy preferences among states and congressional districts. That may be true, but I doubt it. A study by political scientists Melissa Collie and John Mason found that the variance of votes in Congress is more polarized than the variance of opinion in the electorate. A major recent book by Fiorina (Fiorina et al., 2004) concludes that it is the political activists who are polarized, not the public. He asserts that

> political elites do not take extreme positions because voters make them. Rather, by presenting them with polarizing alternatives, elites make voters appear polarized, but the reality shows through clearly when voters have a choice of more moderate alternatives. . .

An analysis of county-level data from the 2004 election by political scientists Philip A. Klinkner and Ann Hapanowicz (2005) shows only slight increases in geographic and political segregation, with no evidence that strongly partisan counties became more so between 2000 and 2004. And an analysis of panel data from U.S. states over the 1963–2002 period by economist Andrew Leigh (2005) found that there are surprisingly few differences in policy settings, social outcomes and economic outcomes under Democrats and Republicans.

Conclusion

My reading of this evidence is that the behavior of American voters and political candidates leads to a larger polarization of American politics than is consistent with the median voter theorem. The evolutionary biologists, interestingly, describe this type of pattern—where two regional subspecies develop contrary characteristics when they compete for resources—as "character displacement." Over time, this pattern of behavior will lead to an evolutionary reduction in the moderates in both parties and an increasing divergence of the issue positions of the two major parties. This pattern will also make it more difficult for Congress to govern.

References

Broder, David. (2003) "Don't Count on Bipartisan Niceties." *Washington Post*, January 2.

Collie, Melissa P., and John L. Mason. (2000) "The Electoral Connection between Party and Constituency Reconsidered: Evidence from the U.S. House of Representatives, 1962–94." In *Continuity and Change in House Elections*, ed. David W. Brady, John E. Cogan, and Morris P. Fiorina. Stanford, CA: Stanford University Press/Hoover Institution Press.

Fenno, Richard F. (1977) *Home Style*, Boston, MA: Little, Brown.

Fiorina, Morris P. (1974) *Representatives, Roll Calls, and Constituencies.* Lexington, MA: Lexington Books.

______. (2004) "What Culture Wars?" *Wall Street Journal*, July 14.

Fiorina, Morris P., Samuel J. Abrams, and Jeremy C. Pope. (2004) *Culture War? The Myth of a Polarized America.* New York: Pearson Longman.

Huntington, Samuel. (1950) "A Revised Theory of American Party Politics." *American Political Science Review* 44 (3): 669–77.

Klinkner, Philip A., and Ann Hapanowicz. (2005) "Red and Blue Déjà Vu: Measuring Polarization in the 2004 Election." *The Forum* 3 (2): Article 2.

Leigh, Andrew. (2005) "What's the Difference between a Donkey and an Elephant? Using Panel Data from U.S. States to Estimate the Impact of Partisanship on Policy Settings and Economic Growth." Draft Working Paper. Canberra: Australian National University.

Munger, Michael C. (2001) "Voting." In *The Elgar Companion to Public Choice*, ed. William F. Shughart II and Laura Razzolini, pp. 197–239. Cheltenham, UK, and Northampton, MA: Edward Elgar.

Niskanen, William A. (2004) "U.S. Elections Are Increasingly Biased against *Moderates*." *Cato Journal* 23 (3): 463–67.

Peltzman, Sam. (1984) "Constituent Interest and Congressional Voting." *Journal of Law and Economics* 27: 181–210.

Poole, Isaiah J. (2004) "Party Unity Vote Study: Votes Echo Electoral Themes." *Congressional Quarterly*, distributed by the office of the House Democratic whip Steny Hoyer.

Part III

Book Reviews

29. *Pop Internationalism*, by Paul Krugman (Cambridge, MA: MIT Press, 1996), 214 pp.

Competitiveness! The word has a somewhat vague macho connotation—a favorite theme of many business writers and some economists. Paul Krugman, however, makes a case that competitiveness is almost always a bad guide to international economic policy, more often a cover for subsidy or protection of some industry. This is also the experience and judgment of this reviewer; for years, my standard lecture to business groups has been on "Competitiveness vs. Productivity."

This book includes 13 articles written by Krugman for various audiences, all but one of which were previously published. The one exception is a generally favorable review Krugman had prepared on *Who's Bashing Whom?* by Laura Tyson. The editor of the *New York Review of Books* rejected the review on the basis that "you're criticizing some very prestigious people." (So much for open political debate on the left.)

As with any collection of articles, this set is somewhat redundant, but there are four primary themes: (1) competitiveness is a mindless and dangerous obsession; (2) the decline in manufacturing employment and the real wages of production workers is primarily a consequence of domestic conditions, not increased international trade; (3) NAFTA will have minimal economic effects; and (4) the high growth rates of the "Asian tigers" are primarily due to a rapid increase in inputs and cannot be sustained.

In treating the competitiveness theme, Krugman directs special criticism at his MIT colleague Lester Thurow, whose book, *Head to Head: The Coming Battle Among Japan, Europe, and America*, conveys the false perception that international trade is a zero-sum game.

This review first appeared in the *Cato Journal* 16, no. 1 (Spring/Summer 1996). My thanks to the *Cato Journal* for its permission to republish this article.

Authors of several other books with a similar geostrategic theme include Jeffrey Garten, Ira Magaziner, and Robert Reich, each of whom was appointed to a senior position in the Clinton administration. Krugman takes these and other authors to task for both confused theory and careless arithmetic.

With regard to the second theme, one should note that the decline in manufacturing employment is a result of relatively high productivity growth in manufacturing, both in the United States and other countries. The decline in agricultural employment, of course, has been a consequence of the same condition.

The slow growth in average real wages, in contrast, is primarily due to a slow growth of average productivity (plus the increase in nonwage compensation). There remains a serious debate among economists about whether increased international trade has contributed to the decline in real wages (or the increased unemployment) of low-skilled workers in the high-wage countries, because increased trade is expected to lead to an equalization of factor prices. The case for a trade explanation, interestingly, is usually made by labor economists and the opposing case by trade economists. This debate is not yet settled, but the best evidence against the trade explanation is that the relative employment of low-skilled labor appears to have declined in both the sectors most affected by trade and those least affected. It is less clear what has caused the increased variance of wages, and Krugman and other trade economists may be too quick to attribute this condition to changes in technology.

Regarding NAFTA, one can argue that it is probably worthwhile, but both the advocates and critics of NAFTA overstated their case. Krugman makes an effective case that NAFTA will have no effect on the number of jobs, will have only a small positive effect on average real income and a small negative effect on the real wages of low-skilled U.S. workers, will not hurt and may help the environment and, for the United States, is primarily a foreign policy issue. With wisdom beyond his years, Krugman is both a general skeptic of regional trade agreements and a supporter of NAFTA.

"The Myth of Asia's Miracle" may be the most interesting and important article in this volume. Krugman summarizes the evidence that most growth of output in the Asian tigers has been due to a rapid increase in labor force participation, increased education, and a high saving rate, rather than to a high rate of productivity growth.

This was also characteristic of the Soviet Union during its period of rapid growth. "If there is a secret to Asian growth," Krugman concludes, "it is simply deferred gratification, the willingness to sacrifice current satisfaction for future gain."

For too long, there seemed to be a negative relation between an economist's writing ability and the quality of his analysis. Galbraith, Heilbroner, and Thurow, for example, are more widely read than most Nobel laureates. Krugman is one of the few exceptions to this pattern, a creative writer and a brilliant analyst. He is not always right (see my review of his *Peddling Prosperity* in the *Cato Journal*, vol. 14, no. 2), and he can be as arrogant when he is wrong as when he is right. The only hesitant note in this book is a concern that other people may have taken Krugman's own exposition of strategic trade theory too seriously. For the issues addressed in this book, however, Krugman is right where all too many others, including some economists, are wrong.

30. *Everything for Sale: The Virtues and Limits of Markets*, by Robert Kuttner (New York: Alfred A. Knopf, 1997), 410 pp.

Robert Kuttner may be the most thoughtful, best informed writer about economics on the American left. He is also profoundly wrong about many issues. Those who would argue with him, however, need a much better understanding of the economy than is characteristic of new Ph.D.s in economics. Kuttner is correct to observe that, "In sharp contrast to Adam Smith, many advanced students of economics in this century have been startlingly innocent of the actual institutions of commercial life; they were simply virtuosos at the math."

Like others who share his political views, Kuttner has several concerns about market economies. Those concerns involve the "moral limitations" of markets, the occasional failure to equilibrate aggregate demand and supply, and the inequality of income. This book, however, is about the more broadly accepted role of the market: the organization of production and the allocation of goods and services. Kuttner acknowledges that many markets work quite well when the government plays no role beyond providing and enforcing the general legal framework—except, by his judgment, the markets for labor, health care, finance, innovations, telecommunications, air travel, electricity, safety, and the environment. In each case, Kuttner claims that specific and detailed government regulations, or other interventions, are necessary to achieve allocative efficiency in those markets. And he proposes his own *dirigiste* policy agenda for each market. No single review of Kuttner's book could respond to each of his market analyses, but I encourage students and specialists in each market to evaluate Kuttner's analysis and proposed policies to

---

This review first appeared in *Regulation* 20, no. 4 (Fall 1997). My thanks to *Regulation* for its permission to republish this article.

test their own understanding and policy perspective. You will surely learn something though, by my guess, you will not be convinced.

From the beginning, Kuttner states that "this is not a book about economic theory or one primarily for the professional economist." His statement is a bit deceptive, because Kuttner's broader targets are mainstream microeconomic theory and economists who base their policy advice on that theory. The special villains of his story are the Chicago school, benefit-cost analysis, public choice, law and economics, and libertarianism. As a graduate of Chicago, an occasional contributor to each of the suspect subfields, and the chairman of the Cato Institute, I do not recognize any of the straw men that Kuttner describes. But he is no more forgiving of economists such as Arthur Okun, Charles Schultze, and Alfred Kahn who served as appointees under Democratic presidents.

His argumentative technique is to identify the simplifying assumptions that are characteristic of economic theory, correctly point out that those assumptions are seldom realistic, and then dismiss any policy position based on the theory. His technique is either naive or deceptive, because it misrepresents the role of assumptions in economic theory. Such assumptions are the beginning, not the conclusion, of economic analysis, and are not meant to be directly tested. Kuttner correctly observes that many participants in the market are not fully informed or rational, and more narrowly self-interested. He also correctly observes that many markets have some transaction costs and are not perfectly competitive. But that is irrelevant. The test of economic theory is whether the behavioral hypotheses developed from the analysis are broadly consistent with the available evidence, not whether the assumptions are realistic. On occasion, in fact, economists are all too quick to modify their assumptions when the preliminary empirical tests are not satisfactory. Occam's razor, which Kuttner dismisses as "the most overrated tool in the scholarly medicine cabinet," is an essential characteristic of any successful broad-based theory. A proposed policy, in turn, must meet a double standard: whether the effects of the policy change are likely to be consistent with those claimed and whether those effects are consistent with the values of the policymakers.

On net, although I would like to believe otherwise, Kuttner has overstated the influence of the free market, limited government advocates; maybe to energize his own coalition. He claims, for example, that marketization, of late, has swamped the polity. The dynamics are cumulative. Government has less popular legitimacy and fewer resources with which to treat escalating problems. A more accurate perception is that the left has made some rhetorical concessions to secure their policy base. In fact, the left maintains a near monopoly of the policy debate in the academy and the national media. Few spending programs have been reduced and fewer have been terminated. The regulation of health, safety, and the environment has nearly broken any restraints based on scientific evidence and net benefits. American government has never commanded more resources, even in wartime. But the end of the Cold War, a broadly healthy economy, and a temporary lull in the dependency rate make it difficult to convince the broad American public that we face escalating problems.

In a comment in the *Washington Post*, Suzanne Garment writes: "To understand the economic policy debate that will take place in the next few years, you can't do better than to read Kuttner's spirited book." She is half-right in her judgment. This book should give ample warning of the next round of assaults on personal liberty, a market economy, and constitutional government. Read it and weep. Better yet, read it and prepare.

31. *Perspectives on Public Choice: A Handbook*, ed. Dennis C. Mueller (New York: Cambridge University Press, 1997), 685 pp.

Public choice has now been a cumulative intellectual discipline for only about 25 years. For the most part, the modern founders of public choice made their original contributions without knowledge of their scattered intellectual predecessors. Kenneth Arrow, Duncan Black, James Buchanan, Anthony Downs, Mancur Olson, and Gordon Tullock created the foundation of public choice almost by themselves, even though Buchanan was strongly influenced by chance exposure to the 1896 treatise by Knut Wicksell and Downs built on the spatial economics developed by Harold Hotelling in 1929.

Dennis Mueller's new *Handbook* is a collection of 25 new articles by and about those who have built on this foundation. As with any book with many authors, the style is somewhat uneven, but this handbook is likely to be the standard reference on public choice for some years. Any review of this handbook, thus, is inherently a review of the current state of public choice. Following a valuable introductory perspective by Mueller, the handbook surveys the state of public choice in five major sections:

Part I addresses the structure of several types of collective institutions. Russell Hardin first summarizes the economic theories of the state, a literature this reviewer regards as a romantic mishmash. A state exists because some group has an effective monopoly of the instruments of force, not because of the demands for order and other public goods; how state powers are used depends on the incentives of the controlling group and the options available to its subjects. (Presumably by editorial oversight, Hardin's name and brief bio are not included in the list of contributors.) Elinor Ostrom and James

This review first appeared in *Public Choice* 97, no. 4 (December 1998). My thanks to *Public Choice* for its permission to republish this article.

Walker contribute a valuable summary of the conditions that lead people to organize institutions between the market and the state plus a summary of the experimental evidence that bears or these issues. The article by Robert Inman and Daniel Rubinfeld is a conventional summary of the political economy of federalism with no discussion, unfortunately, of the "flypaper effect" or the problems that arise when there is not a clear division of roles between the national and regional governments. The article by Bruno Frey summarizes the studies of international organizations, many of which are by his Swiss and other European colleagues; American scholars would benefit by more attention to this literature before endorsing an international resolution of the issues of the day. The article by Dennis Mueller summarizes the developing field of constitutional public choice but without an adequate discussion of the conditions that maintain a constitution.

Part II addresses the formal analysis of voting and preference aggregation. The article by James Enelow focuses on the conditions for which majority rule leads to cycling without providing any insight why cycling, in fact, is quite rare. Douglas Rae and Eric Schickler summarize the more general effects of majority rule, concluding with a somewhat casual dismissal of the case for protecting some rights by a supermajority rule. The article by H. Peyton Young summarizes the recent analysis of the relation of group choice and individual judgments, based on the original contributions by Borda and Condorcet; Young concludes by making the case for a maximum likelihood ranking voting rule. Prasanta Pattanaik summarizes the "very large and diverse class of negative results" from the formal analysis of preference aggregation. And Nicolaus Tideman summarizes the modern development of "demand revealing" rules for voting on public activities. A reader of this review may correctly surmise that I do not understand this literature very well and may thus underestimate its value.

Part III addresses the broader set of public choice studies of elections. Peter Ordeshook provides a valuable summary of the four decades of spatial analysis building on the major original contribution by Downs with special attention to both the strengths and limits of this type of analysis. The article by Norman Schofield is a fine analysis of proportional representation and multiparty politics with interesting examples from Europe and Israel. David Austen-Smith summarizes the too-formal literature on the role of interest groups, concluding that "we cannot say much . . . about the extent to which interest groups influence policy, and we can say even less about the normative properties of any such influence." The article by Thomas Stratmann is a good summary of the literature on logrolling, concluding correctly that we still lack a good understanding of the institutional conditions that contribute to the stability of logrolling coalitions. Martin Paldam summarizes the literature on political business cycles, a research topic that should now be quietly interred; economic conditions clearly affect voting behavior, but there is no evidence that the strict periodicity of U.S. elections has led to any regular periodicity of U.S. economic fluctuations.

Part IV addresses the relation between individual behavior and group outcomes. The article by John Aldrich asks the question, which apparently goes back at least to Hegel, about why anyone votes in an election with a large number of potential voters. The default answer is that voting is an expressive act, not an instrumental act; once in the voting booth, however, the common assumption is that the choice of candidate or issue position is based on instrumental considerations. This whole issue must still be regarded as a puzzle. Morris Fiorina summarizes the large body of more conventional political science literature on voting behavior; the value of this literature to public choice analysis is that the macrovoting patterns appear more consistent (rational?) than individual voting behavior. The chapter by Elizabeth Hoffman is a good summary of the experimental literature on alternative voting rules, including the design of markets for the allocation of network commodities.

Part V summarizes the public choice analysis of several applied topics. Ronald Wintrobe and Terry Moe each contribute a fine chapter on bureaucracy; in retrospect, my own contribution to this literature seems to have been to suggest a framework for an increasing number of other scholars to prove that I was wrong. A chapter by Walter Hettich and Stanley Winer addresses the political economy of taxation, a literature that is generally pessimistic about the prospects for conventional tax reform; the authors should have added a section comparing the normative public choice model and the normative public finance model of the tax structure, that is, a comparison of the perspectives of Buchanan and Musgrave. Robert Tollison contributes a fine chapter on the rapidly developing literature on rent-seeking (and rent protecting). I am skeptical, however, of the estimated magnitude of rent-seeking costs; the primary remaining puzzle is the large difference between the magnitude of the potential rents and the small documented expenditures for lobbying, campaign contributions, etc. The chapter by Stephen Magee summarizes his perspective on endogenous policy with special attention to trade protection. This is a very discouraging perspective to someone who has spent most of his career as a policy analyst, but I suspect that Magee has overstated his case; his model, for example, leads to a very wide variance of economic policies across countries depending on their initial factor endowment. The final chapter by Cheryl Holsey and Thomas Borcherding summarizes the confused literature on the relative growth of government. The empirical evidence is similar for most countries: a long period of stability in the relative size of government (in peacetime), followed by a progressive increase in the relative size of government beginning sometime in this century; Borcherding's own analysis concludes that the demand for government services explains less than half the relative growth of government in the United States. Public choice does not contribute much to understanding the most important general political event of our lifetime.

The handbook concludes with a comprehensive reference list, a name index, and a good subject index.

All in all, the handbook is a very good summary of the current state of public choice analysis. Readers should make their own judgments about the most promising directions of future analysis and about the accumulating collection of analytical and empirical dead ends.

32. *Power and Prosperity: Outgrowing Communist and Capitalist Dictatorships*, by Mancur Olson (New York: Basic Books, 2000), 199 pp.

Shortly before his untimely death in 1998, Mancur Olson had nearly completed a manuscript that he first titled "Capitalism, Socialism, and Dictatorship," a title reflecting the inspiration of Joseph Schumpeter's classic 1942 book on *Capitalism, Socialism, and Democracy*. Far better than any other economist since Schumpeter, Olson addressed the most important issues of political economy and explained them in language accessible to a broader audience. In effect, the book just published is Olson's elegant but unfinished last symphony—his not-quite-completed manuscript plus a foreword by his Maryland colleague Charles Cadwell and a new title.

As the new title suggests, the book addresses two loosely related themes. In Chapters 1 through 5, Olson summarizes his general theory of the relation between "power and prosperity"—between the structure of the political system and economic outcomes—based on his own prior analyses and the other major contributions of modern public choice. The most important new insights in those chapters build on his 1991 article on "Autocracy, Democracy, and Prosperity" and a 1996 article (with Martin McGuire) on "The Economics of Autocracy and Majority Rule: The Invisible Hand and the Use of Force." Other sources of material for those chapters include his 1982 book on *The Rise and Decline of Nations* and his delightful put-down of the Panglossian political economy of some Chicago economists in a 1996 article on "Big Bills Left on the Sidewalk: Why Some Countries are Rich and Others Poor." These chapters reflect

This review first appeared in the *Cato Journal* 20, no. 1 (Spring/Summer 2000). My thanks to the *Cato Journal* for its permission to republish this article.

Olson's special ability to explain and illustrate subtle analytic concepts in lively English and with historical examples.

The power and scope of the insights from this perspective are impressive. Government is fundamentally the exchange of tribute for protection—against both local and foreign predators. And the primary and continuing political challenge has been to design institutions that prevent a government that is effective in its protective role from itself becoming the most oppressive local predator. During the long prehistory of hunter-gatherer bands there was almost no government, primarily because there was little property to protect or to steal. Government first became an important institution to protect and support agriculture and other time-dependent and site-specific forms of production.

Olson attributes the origin of autocratic government to the acts by a roving predator to become the dominant local predator in a specific area. This autocrat has a purely self-interested incentive to set a revenue-maximizing tax rate and use part of the tax receipts to provide a level of government services for which the value of the last unit is equal to the inverse of that tax rate. The local population is better served by an autocrat than by competitive predators in the same area, primarily because a monopoly predator has a more "encompassing interest" than one of several predators. Moreover, the population is better served by an autocrat with a long horizon and has ample reason to wish that "long live the king" if the only alternative is another autocrat with a shorter horizon.

Autocrats appear powerful but are often vulnerable. Their power and wealth attract attempted coups and foreign aggressors. And the death of the autocrat often provokes a succession crisis. Olson attributes the origin of democracy to accidents of history that lead to four conditions: a broadly equal dispersion of power among those groups that overthrow the autocrat so that no one leader can declare himself the new autocrat; no group is sufficiently strong in some region to create a miniautocracy; the number of groups is small enough to permit voluntary collective decisions; and the area over which the new democracy is established is spared conquest by some foreign aggressor. The same conditions that lead to a democracy also lead to checks on the power of the executive. Olson expects a democracy to have both a lower tax rate and a higher level of government services than an autocracy because the controlling group in a democracy has a stake in the level of the general economy as well as the benefits of government that accrue only to that group.

Over time, Olson expects democracies to be subject to two contrary tendencies: On the one hand, Olson finds that property and contract rights are more secure the longer the span of democratic systems or the tenure of individual autocrats. On the other hand, Olson expects democracies to become increasingly controlled by coalitions of special interests over time. That leads him to conclude that some "hard" autocracies that suppress special interest groups and have a long horizon may have higher economic growth than older democracies, at least for a generation or two. That is an awkward conclusion because he does not explain why only a few such autocracies adopt good economic policies.

Olson introduces his second theme with a brief transition chapter on "The Sources of Law Enforcement and Corruption." What Olson finds is that the most influential private interests support market-augmenting government policies, such as the enforcement of property rights and contracts. On the other hand, the most directly affected private parties have an incentive to evade market-contrary policies, such as price controls. That simple lesson deserves repetition.

Chapters 7 through 9 summarize Olson's special theory of Soviet-type autocracies and some conjectures about why the post-Soviet Russian economy, to date, has contracted. This material is largely based on research by the Center on Institutional Reform and the Informal Sector that Olson founded at the University of Maryland. Olson offers a unique and convincing explanation of why the Soviet economy generated a much higher output for the state during the Stalin period than is suggested by his general theory of autocratic governments: the combination of forced saving and declining marginal tax rates. His explanation of why the post-Soviet Russian economy has contracted is plausible but less convincing. In contrast with Germany and Japan after World War II and China after the Cultural Revolution, Olson contends, Russia did not go through enough of a crisis to strip away the layers of special interests accumulated during the Stalin period. In that case, the prospects for a successful transition to a market economy and liberal democracy seem quite pessimistic in the absence of another crisis or a new autocrat.

The final chapter, appropriately, summarizes Olson's normative and positive perspectives on political economy. He favored laissez-faire economic policies that permit individual firms to make extraordinary profits without government interference or to fail without subsidy or protection. On the other hand, he favored social insurance for individuals because many fortunes are due to luck. His economic judgment led him to observe that, to be successful, a market system requires two essential conditions: (1) "Secure and well-defined individual rights" and (2) "the absence of predation of any kind." And his political judgment led him to conclude that "These two conditions are most likely to be satisfied, I think, in secure, rights-respecting democracies where the institutions are structured in ways that give authoritative decisionmaking as much as possible to encompassing interests."

Mancur Olson was a friend, we shared a similar research agenda, and we argued about many, mostly little, issues. I will miss his important insights, his humor, and his humanity.

33. *In Defense of Free Capital Markets: The Case Against a New International Financial Architecture*, by David F. DeRosa, (Princeton: Bloomberg Press, 2001), 201 pp.

Foreign exchange crises convulsed much of Europe in 1992 and 1993, Mexico in 1994, much of Asia in 1997, and Russia and Brazil in 1998. Long-Term Capital Management, a major U.S. investment firm, the general partners of which included two financial economists who are Nobel laureates, collapsed in 1998. And Japan's economy has now been in the doldrums for more than a decade.

Those financial crises, in turn, led to numerous proposals for "a new international financial architecture" including proposals for controls on international capital flows, a worldwide tax on foreign exchange transactions, target bands on exchange rates, a requirement that private lenders participate financially in the restructuring of any new sovereign debt owed to them, and a new tax-financed international credit insurance corporation.

Fortunately, we now have a readable book describing those financial crises, the lessons we should have learned from them, and an evaluation of the major proposals for a new international financial architecture. David DeRosa has the right credentials for this task—a professional foreign exchange trader, an adjunct professor of finance at the Yale School of Management, and a regular columnist for Bloomberg News. Most important, for those who are mystified by financial issues, DeRosa is a disciplined analyst and a fine writer.

The general thesis of this book is that ". . . the concept of financial contagion . . . is dubious at best as a cause of financial turmoil. [As a rule, a financial crisis] . . . can be explained by looking at the

---

This review first appeared in the *Cato Journal* 21, no. 2 (Fall 2001). My thanks to the *Cato Journal* for its permission to republish this article.

domestic policies that ministries of finance and central banks have laid out for their own countries." This is a valuable perspective because it focuses attention on the conditions that were common to the countries that experienced a financial crisis. Most important among those conditions, all of the countries that experienced a foreign exchange crisis were trying to maintain a pegged exchange rate. In addition, beginning with the Mexican crisis, the other common conditions were a large volume of short-term debt denominated in some reserve currency (such as the U.S. dollar) and a substantial government role in the allocation of credit.

Although other analysts have also identified those same conditions, DeRosa's distinctive contribution is to describe the important role of the *carry trade* in triggering an exchange rate crisis and overwhelming the official efforts to avoid a devaluation. This involves a number of trading strategies that go long the domestic currency and short the reserve currency, solely to capture the interest rate differential between the two currencies; in effect, those trades are a bet that the pegged exchange rate will be maintained. Although that differential is usually small, the potential profits are huge if these investments are hedged and the exchange rate is maintained. The potential losses, of course, are also huge if the exchange rate is devalued. That is what leads traders to herd behavior in the attempt to be the first ones to liquidate their positions if there are any signals that the exchange rate will be devalued.

In the end, however, DeRosa's effort to counter the contagion perspective is not wholly successful, in part because the sequence of crises in Europe in 1992 and in Asia in 1997 do not appear to be random events, in part because losses to the carry trade in one country probably increase concern about similar losses in other vulnerable countries. That is unfortunate, because the debate on the role of the International Monetary Fund is primarily about the relative importance of the contagion effect and the moral hazard effect, with defenders of the IMF emphasizing the contagion effect and critics of the IMF emphasizing the moral hazard effect. One might hope that, 17 years after the Mexican crisis, we would have more than anecdotes and perspectives on the relative magnitude of those two effects.

This book also has a good summary of the reasons for the continued stalemate in Japan. This chapter, however, does not quite fit the rest of the book, because the yen has long been a floating currency and Japan is a big net exporter of capital. DeRosa's special insight in this chapter is that the near-zero interest rate in Japan is not sufficient evidence of a "liquidity trap," and he concludes, as do most western observers, that Japan would now be well served by Bank of Japan purchases of government debt to increase the money supply.

On two developments in the 1980s, I have a somewhat different interpretation than that by DeRosa: My judgment is that the substantial increase in the foreign exchange value of the dollar in the early 1980s was primarily due to the investment provisions of the 1981 U.S. tax legislation, not, as is the conventional explanation, the result of the combination of a loose fiscal policy and a tight monetary policy. And the end of the 1980s boom in both Japan and the United States, I contend, was primarily due to the tighter bank capital standards required by the Basel Accord.

DeRosa concludes, I believe correctly, by rejecting all of the proposals for a new international financial architecture. He recognizes that countries have many economic problems other than a faulty exchange rate system, but the primary lesson of this book is that "The '90s, far from being an indictment of the international financial system, are a striking reminder of how potentially destructive fixed exchange rate regimes can be. Equally striking is the fact that once broken fixed exchange rate systems are replaced with floating regimes, no further disruptions occurred."

For a broad audience, this book is the best introduction to this history and these issues, although probably not the final word.

34. *Virginia Political Economy: The Selected Works of Gordon Tullock*, Volume 1, ed. Charles K. Rowley (Indianapolis: Liberty Fund, 2004), 642 pp.

Virginia Political Economy is the first volume in a 10-volume series of the scholarly articles and monographs by Gordon Tullock from 1954 through 2002. The complete series has been edited by Charles K. Rowley, who has also written a separate introduction for each volume. This first volume, in effect, is an introduction to the whole series by including selected early articles in each subject area to which Tullock has made a major contribution. This first volume also includes a brief biographical note and a table of contents for the whole series. Each of the subsequent volumes includes one or more of the most important contributions by Tullock to a specific subject area.

The most impressive characteristic of the first volume is a reminder of the range of subjects to which Tullock has made an important contribution. The major sections of this first volume address the following issues:

- the imperialism of economics, especially with respect to political science;
- the problems of majority voting;
- the demand-revealing process;
- rent seeking;
- redistributive politics;
- the problem of social cost;
- law and economics;
- bioeconomics; and
- the limited relevance of the public interest theory.

This review first appeared in the *Cato Journal* 24, no. 3 (Fall 2004). My thanks to the *Cato Journal* for its permission to republish this article.

Tullock has maintained a roughly constant utilitarian perspective on each of these issues over the past 50 years, even when it leads him, as in law and economics, to a position that is quite different from most other scholars working on these issues. But he does not insist that utilitarianism explains all human behavior, only that part which is explainable without knowing the distinctive personalities and biographies of those involved. In addition to his coauthorship of *The Calculus of Consent* (with James Buchanan), the major individual contributions for which Tullock still deserves the Nobel Prize are his proofs that democracy usually works rather better than suggested by the theories of Kenneth Arrow and Duncan Black and that the social costs of inefficient policies are substantially larger than suggested by Arnold Harberger. But there should also be some reward, wherever economists spend their afterlife, for making valuable contributions to so many subjects, for good writing, and for relatively little use of mathematics.

One of Tullock's major early articles, in 1959, explains the effects of vote-trading (logrolling) in a legislature, pointing out that this process permits expression of the intensity of preferences and explains both the protection of intense minorities and special interest legislation. An important 1967 article demonstrates that the misallocation caused by political favors such as tariffs or legal monopolies includes the costs of both acquiring and defending the favors, a process that would later be described as rent seeking. (A similar article explains why it is so difficult to get rid of blue laws, limits on taxicab licenses, etc.) A 1969 article explains the conditions that determine the optimal degree of centralization in a federal system, pointing out that decentralization may increase the share of voters that favor the outcomes of the political process. A series of articles published in the 1970s explores such topics as anarchy, bribery, corruption, and revolution. Tullock brings his utilitarian perspective and training as a lawyer to articles on crime, juries, trials, and judicial errors. And starting in the 1970s, Tullock was one of the first economists since Malthus to recognize the similarity of biological and economic reasoning, leading him to write interesting articles on "The Coal Tit as a Careful Shopper" and on "The Economics of (Very) Primitive Societies" and to be a founder of the modern field of bioeconomics.

All of us have been Tullock's students, even those, as in my case, who have never taken one of his courses. In the summer of 1967, he worked at the Institute for Defense Analyses where I was the director of the economics division. In lunchtime conversations, he recognized that I had been thinking about bureaucratic behavior for some years but that I had not yet formulated a general theory about such behavior; these conversations and his encouragement led me to write my 1968 article ("The Peculiar Economics of Bureaucracy") and my 1971 book (*Bureaucracy and Representative Government*) on this issue. Subsequent discussions about most any subject have made it clear that Tullock reads a great deal more history than I do; I don't know how he finds the time. One way or another, we are all in his debt.

The quality of any series of edited volumes, of course, also depends on both the editor and publisher. Judging by the first volume, Charles Rowley has done a first-rate job of editing these volumes, with special care in selecting those Tullock articles and monographs that are most likely to make a lasting contribution; the first volume reflects special care in choosing articles that are an effective introduction to the whole range of subjects to which Tullock contributed. The Liberty Fund also merits special thanks for investing in these volumes. The paperbacks are handsome and are priced at only $12! All in all, one of the most impressive academic collections in some time.

35. *Pay Without Performance: The Unfulfilled Promise of Executive Compensation*, by Lucian Bebchuk and Jesse Fried (Cambridge, Mass: Harvard University Press, 2004), 304 pp.

Lucian Bebchuk and Jesse Fried's book *Pay without Performance* is based on a simple premise:

> Managers use their power to secure rents. . . . Because managers and directors might have to bear market penalties and social costs if they adopt pay arrangements that are perceived as egregious, "outrage" costs and constraints place some limits on deviations from arms-length contracting. To avoid outrage, compensation designers attempt to hide, obscure, and justify . . . the amount and form of executive pay.

In other words, corporate managers, with the approval of compliant boards, effectively choose the amount and form of their own compensation, subject only to the limit that the compensation not provoke "outrage." As this book may become the standard reference for the law professors, sociologists, and journalists who share this managerial power perspective, it is important to evaluate the authors' reasoning and the empirical conditions that they claim as evidence for this perspective.

Bebchuk and Fried weave together a story with elements that are neither implausible nor new: CEOs who seek to increase their personal wealth even at the expense of the shareholders; directors who support the CEO out of loyalty, collegiality, and a desire for reappointment and who have neither the time, information, nor financial incentive to challenge him; and shareholders who have a

This review first appeared in *Regulation* 28, no. 1 (Spring 2005). My thanks to *Regulation* for its permission to republish this article.

very limited power to intervene. (The only internal error in this story is that the financial incentives of a director are a function of the total value of the shares that he owns, not his fraction of the total shares.)

The implications of this perspective for the level and form of executive compensation, however, cannot be directly tested, because there are no objective measures of the degree of board compliance and the limits on compensation that would not provoke outrage. But the authors claim that other types of evidence support their managerial power perspective. First, they make a prior personal judgment about the types of executive compensation that they believe are performance enhancing and those that are not. Second, they find that their favorite type of compensation is rare and that other types of compensation that they have judged to be ineffective are rather common.

But Bebchuk and Fried are wrong in their judgments about the types of compensation that are more or less performance enhancing. They assert, for example, that an option indexed to some broader industry or general stock index is much superior to an unindexed option because it does not reward or punish the executive for conditions common to the industry or the general stock market. But they apparently do not recognize that an executive would have to be offered many more indexed options or a higher salary to compensate him for the much lower expected return of an indexed option.

In contrast, Bebchuk and Fried judge that executive loans are not performance enhancing. A study by Lawrence Cunningham of the Boston College Law School, however, concludes,

> Loans are often tailored bonus schemes, forgiven or modified if executives achieve certain results. In that sense they resemble the incentive features of stock options, except that they are better. One reason loans are better than stock options is they have a downside if targets aren't met [the borrower must pay], whereas options expiring worthless pose no penalty.

In its infinite wisdom, of course, Congress has banned company loans to executives in the recent Sarbanes-Oxley Act. Other types of evidence are also strongly inconsistent with the managerial power perspective on executive compensation. In contrast to Bebchuk and Fried's assertion that CEO compensation is only weakly related to firm performance, a 2000 paper by Brian Hall and Jeffery Liebman reported their estimate that a 10 percent increase in a firm's market value, which would add billions to the value of shareholders' wealth, would add $1.25 million to the value of a median CEO's accumulated stocks and options. In contrast to Bebchuk and Fried's assertion that corporations "camouflage" the amount and form of executive pay, a 2001 paper by Venky Nagar, Dhananjay Nanda, and Peter Wysocki found that the level of disclosure "is positively related to the proportion of CEO compensation based on stock price." In a 2002 paper, Kevin Murphy reports that the average first-year compensation of CEOs hired from outside the firm (and thus who have little power over the existing board) is nearly twice that of CEOs promoted from within. In another 2002 paper, Michelle Hanlon, Shivaram Rajgopal, and Terry Shivlin report that "the future operating income associated with a dollar of Black-Scholes value of an ESO (executive stock option) grant is $3.82" and conclude that there is "little evidence in support of rent extraction" by top managers.

A 1994 summary of studies of executive compensation for the National Bureau of Economic Research by Nancy Rose concluded, "We find no evidence for the popular view that boards typically fail to penalize CEOs for poor financial performance or reward them disproportionately well for good performance." A similar 2003 survey for the Federal Reserve Bank of New York by John Core, Wayne Guay, and David Larcker concluded that "in contrast to the allegation of many media pundits . . . who assert that incentive levels are random, arbitrary, or out of equilibrium, empirical evidence suggests that, on average, firms base their equity incentives on systematic and theoretically sensible factors."

Other evidence that Bebchuk and Fried offer in support of their managerial power perspective is that less than 1 percent of all CEOs resigned or were forced out each year because of poor performance in the years from 1993 through 1999; the authors do not mention that the stock market increased nearly 20 percent a year during that period. This situation, however, changed dramatically after the stock market peaked in early 2000. By 2002, Margarethe Wiersema would observe, "The firings of CEOs when performance nosedives has become commonplace in U.S. business."

Executive compensation differs substantially among firms and has changed dramatically over time. Bebchuk and Fried provide no explanation of those differences or changes. They tell a plausible story that corporate executives have some managerial power, but they make no case that the differences in executive compensation are explained by the unmeasured differences in board compliance and the limits on compensation that would not provoke outrage, either among firms or over time. In summary, there is no reliable body of evidence that is consistent with substantial managerial power over their own compensation, and the managerial power perspective provides no explanation of the substantial differences in executive compensation among firms or over time.

36. *The Market for Virtue: The Potential and Limits of Corporate Social Responsibility*, by David Vogel (Washington, D.C.: Brookings Institution Press, 2005), 173 pp.

David Vogel, a political scientist and professor of business ethics at the University of California, Berkeley, has written a valuable analysis and summary of the massive literature on "corporate social responsibility" (CSR). His new book summarizes the evidence that bears on whether there is a business case for CSR; describes the demand for CSR by consumers, employees, and investors; describes the effects of CSR on working conditions in poor countries, on the environment, and on human rights; and concludes by making a case for an increased political role of corporations in promoting the goals of CSR.

The Business Case

Many corporate executives, apparently, want to be perceived as being socially responsible by the contemporary standards of their community. So they have made a case that CSR is essential to the business objectives of their corporations. For instance, Jeffrey Hollander, the CEO of household products maker Seventh Generation, claims that CSR is "the future of business. It's what . . . companies have to do to survive and prosper in a world where more and more of their behavior is under a microscope."

A 2002 survey by PricewaterhouseCoopers reported that "70 percent of global chief executives believe that CSR is vital to their companies' profitability." Another survey reported that 91 percent of CEOs believe that CSR management creates shareholder value.

This review first appeared in *Regulation* 28, no. 4 (Winter 2005–2006). My thanks to *Regulation* for its permission to republish this article.

Vogel is quite dismissive of this apparent perception of business executives. He observes,

> Unfortunately, there is no evidence that behaving more virtuously make firms more profitable. This finding is important because, unless there is a clear business case for CSR, firms will have fewer incentives to act more responsibly. . . . An extensive body of academic research examines the relationship between corporate responsibility and profitability. . . . Its central conclusion can be easily summarized: at best, it is inconclusive.

The reasons why those studies are so inconclusive are also apparent. In one survey of 95 empirical studies, for example, financial performance is measured in 70 different ways and corporate social performance in 27 different ways. The most widely used measure of CSR is a subjective ranking of five measures of corporate performance—two of which, employee relations and product safety and quality, are not indicators of social responsibility.

There is no general pattern, however, that the profits of corporations are negatively related to CSR activities. This leads Vogel to conclude,

> It is possible for a firm to commit resources to CSR without becoming less competitive. In brief, there is a place in the business system for responsible firms, but the market for virtue is not sufficiently important to make it in the interest of all firms to behave more responsibly. . . . Of the myriad factors that affect corporate earnings, CSR remains, for most firms most of the time, of marginal importance.

Demand for CSR

The demand for CSR arises primarily from customers, employees, and investors. However, there is a large difference between expressed preferences and behavior.

In two surveys, more than 75 percent of American consumers report that they would avoid purchasing products made under poor working conditions and 65 percent state that they would pay more for products that protect the environment. One analyst, however, estimates that only 10 percent of American consumers are willing to pay more for green products. A 2004 European survey found that while 75 percent of consumers indicated that they would change their purchases based on social or environmental criteria, only 3 percent had actually done so.

In a 2004 survey of more than 800 MBAs, 97 percent stated that they would be willing to forgo an average of 14 percent of their expected income in order to "work with an organization with a better reputation for corporate social responsibility and ethics." In another 2004 survey of MBAs, however, the 10 companies for which they would most like to work had little correspondence with those with a high CSR rating.

There are now about 800 "socially responsible investment" (SRI) funds that make it possible for investors to make a wide variety of investment preferences. According to Vogel, however,

> The consensus of more that 100 studies of social investment funds and their strategies is that the risk-adjusted returns of a carefully constructed, socially screened portfolio is zero. In other words, share returns are neither harmed nor helped by including social criteria in stock selection.

One reason for this finding is that the SRI funds appear to be too inclusive. One survey of 600 SRI funds found that more than 90 percent of the Fortune 500 companies were included in at least one SRI portfolio. A high CSR rating, in addition, has been no protection against some other dimension of business performance that is not in the interest of shareholders. The oil company BP, for example, recently increased their "beyond petroleum" advertising about the time that it was revealed that the firm's largest U.S. refinery was unusually unsafe. Enron was a favorite of the SRI funds, but—well, you know the rest of that story.

Achievements

Any summary of the aggregate effects of CSR on corporate performance may lead one to be skeptical or cynical about the whole idea. One should recognize, however, the selective achievements of CSR. Vogel dedicates three chapters to describing some of those achievements and the conditions that produced them.

Vogel highlights the following major examples of CSR achievements since the beginning of the 1990s:

- Nike monitors working conditions in its supplier factories in poor countries.
- Ikea requires its rug supplier in India to prohibit the employment of children and provides families with financial assistance to help keep their children out of the labor market.
- Starbucks guarantees coffee producers an above-world market price for their products.
- Home Depot no longer sells products harvested from old-growth or endangered forests.
- BP has significantly reduced its greenhouse gas emissions.
- Shell has adopted policies to address human rights and environmental abuses associated with its investments in poor countries.
- Citibank has developed criteria for assessing the environmental impact of its lending decisions in poor countries.
- PepsiCo has withdrawn its investments from Burma because of human rights concerns.
- McDonalds has adopted the European Union restrictions on the use of growth-promoting antibiotics for its suppliers of beef and chicken in the United States.
- Chiquita has implemented stringent environmental practices for its suppliers of bananas in Central America.
- Timberland allows its employees to take one week off with pay each year to work with local charities.

Many companies have followed the lead of the above companies to amplify the effects of most of these actions. Vogel tells an interesting story about each of the actions, but there are no obvious common conditions that explain the performance of the specific corporations.

What I Missed

The primary issue that I hoped Vogel would address concerns the basic concept of corporate social responsibility. Why is a corporation regarded as socially responsible or virtuous if it spends funds owned by the shareholders for actions that do not increase shareholder value? In that case, why not distribute the funds to the shareholders and let them decide how to hand out the money? Who appointed corporations to act as the agent of shareholders' political preferences? Why is it considered virtuous not to invest in South Africa, Burma, Israel, or whatever other country with government policies someone does not approve, when the investment would increase the well-being of local employees and residents? The basic language with which Vogel addresses the issue begs those questions.

The other issue about which I would have valued Vogel's analysis is the supply of corporate social responsibility. What explains why some firms have a high CSR rating and other firms do not? Vogel drops some hints about this issue, but without pulling them together to identify the most likely explanations. My own guess is that the list of conditions associated with a high CSR rating would include the following:

- firms that sell retail products in North America and Europe with suppliers from poor countries,
- firms in which most of the management and staff are relatively young college graduates,
- firms in which the ownership is closely held, such that the management owns or controls most of the shares, and
- firms in which there is substantial managerial discretion.

My hope is that a second edition of this book would have a chapter entitled, "The Supply of Corporate Social Responsibility."

A Final Beef

Vogel concludes, unfortunately, on a jarring note. He wants virtuous firms to petition the government to force other firms to be similarly virtuous. Vogel asserts,

> The definition of corporate social responsibility needs to be redefined to include the responsibilities of business to strengthen civil society and the capacity of governments to require that all firms act more responsibly. . . . Simply providing a good example is not enough. Responsible firms also need to support public policies that establish minimum standards for their less virtuous competitors—not just to create a level playing field, but because such requirements are frequently necessary to accomplish the goals of CSR. . . . A firm that supports the establishment of minimum regulatory standards—but that has not reduced its own emissions—is arguably more virtuous than one that has voluntarily cut back greenhouse gas emissions but opposes additional regulatory requirements.

I have not read a more misguided policy proposal in some years. Virtue is an attribute of choice, not of ends; coerced virtue is an inherent contradiction. I dread the prospect of a swarm of lobbyists, wearing the mantle of virtuous corporations, descending on Washington to petition the administration and Congress to require their competitors to meet their own self-chosen standards. I expect the church of which I am a member to promote individual virtue but not to represent itself as an agent of the diffuse political preferences of the members of the church or denomination. Similarly, I expect the corporations in which I have invested to maximize the return to their shareholders, consistent with the relevant laws, but not to represent themselves as an agent of the diffuse political preferences of their shareholders.

Neither churches nor corporations have a comparative advantage in politics. Both sacrifice some of their net social value by succumbing to the temptation to be political agents.

37. *Why I, Too, Am Not a Conservative: The Normative Vision of Classical Liberalism*, by James M. Buchanan (Cheltenham, UK: Edward Elgar, 2005), 106 pp.

The main title of this book, of course, expresses James Buchanan's personal agreement with the famous 1960 essay by F. A. Hayek on "Why I Am Not a Conservative." Most of this small book, however, is better described by the subtitle. For this book is the only summary of Buchanan's important contribution to the philosophy of ethics.

Only the first and last of the 12 chapters were written specifically for this book, primarily to summarize the development of Buchanan's personal perspective on the book's two titles. The other 10 chapters are revisions of lectures that Buchanan has presented over the past decade. This small, dense book merits careful reading and reflection, chapter by chapter rather than at one sitting.

Buchanan, like Hayek, has long tried to distinguish his views as a classical liberal from those of a conservative—views that are often confused because classical liberals and conservatives have often been tactical allies. He differentiates these views primarily on the following four dimensions:

1. Classical liberals are open to consensual change; conservatives more generally support the stability of the social order.
2. Classical liberals assume a natural equality of humans; conservatives assume a natural hierarchy.
3. Classical liberals assume that individual responsibility is a necessary corollary of individual freedom; conservatives are more inclined to paternalism.

This review first appeared in the *Cato Journal* 26, no. 3 (Fall 2006). My thanks to the *Cato Journal* for its permission to republish this article.

4. For classical liberals, value is subjective; conservatives are more likely to assume that there is an objective order of values.

For this reviewer, Buchanan's classical liberal seems more like an ideal type and his conservative more like someone we might meet in the real world.

Most of the remainder of this book makes the case for realistic utopias based on the ethic of reciprocity. Buchanan starts by rejecting the possibility of "a viable socio-economic-political-legal order in which the legal incentives are such that persons behave as Kantians quite independent of whether or not they feel ethically constrained."

Like Adam Smith, Buchanan emphasizes the importance of attitudes and rules of conduct in addition to the law—individual responsibility, manners, and a mutual commitment to the ethics of reciprocity. In that sense, the institutions of a liberal society are dependent on conservative individual values. And he concludes,

> There is surely a minimal level of voluntary adherence to the whole set of norms implied by the Kantian precept—a level that must be reached by a substantial number of persons in the relevant social nexus.

On this issue, he acknowledges a major difference with Gary Becker, George Stigler, and Gordon Tullock. Buchanan next builds the case that "for either effective political democracy or a market economy to function well, persons must confront interactions with each other under some presumption of reciprocity". The relations of people in these institutions need not involve caring, but only that strangers, those beyond tribal limits, be treated with norms of mutual respect:

> In a sense, this shift reflects the limits of man's moral capacities. To treat other persons outside the tribe in accordance with norms of reciprocation—this was within the possible; to universalize the idealized tribal ethics of love—this was not.

For some readers, Buchanan's comments about some other contemporary writers will be a surprise. Buchanan has high praise for John Rawls and his development of the concept of "justice as fairness" as the basis for the ethical rules among natural equals. On the other hand, he is moderately critical of the later writings of Hayek, along with those by George Stigler and Donald Wittman, for their

Panglossian conclusions that the institutions that have survived a cultural evolution cannot be improved.

My major reservation about the philosophy summarized by Buchanan is his concept of the natural sociopolitical equality of all humans. Are we obligated to extend the franchise in all interpersonal relations to all humans on the assumption that they are capable and willing to follow the ethics of reciprocity? What about children? What about the mentally handicapped? What about those from a nonliberal society with no experience with the rule of reciprocity in institutions larger than the family? What about those who have demonstrated by their own behavior that they are not committed to the rule of reciprocity and would most likely take advantage of those who are? How is the effective franchise of a liberal society determined, by whom and by what criteria? Buchanan makes little contribution to understanding these important issues.

My own judgment is that the case for a liberal society cannot be based on an assumption of the natural sociopolitical equality of all humans. Every person in a liberal society should be treated as having equal rights, not because he or she was born equal, but because that is what defines a liberal society. In that sense, the equality of all persons in a liberal society is a created equality, not a natural equality. Also in that sense, a liberal society is a created society—created by limits on the effective franchise, some social reinforcement of the rule of reciprocity, and some tolerance for those who do not follow this rule—and one for which a natural equality of all humans is neither necessary nor sufficient.

Buchanan has made a major contribution to understanding the necessary conditions for a liberal society and an important challenge to those who would advance an understanding of the sufficient conditions. In the end, he leaves us with a sermon:

> The "system of natural liberty" is worth getting exited about . . . and it can be realized only if we treat it as potentially attainable. We lose our focus if we stay too closely with the scientific cocoon of observed reality. It is the imagined reality that might be which pulls us forward.
>
> We must hold fast to the faith that human animals are uniquely capable of organizing themselves within social structures that make liberty, peace and prosperity simultaneously achievable. We must refrain from crude polemics, while continuing to teach, and to preach, the simple verities.

38. *The Age of Turbulence: Adventures in a New World*, by Alan Greenspan (New York: The Penguin Press, 2007), 505 pp.

Alan Greenspan, for an $8 million advance, has written two books in one. The first 11 chapters are a personal memoir from his earliest childhood memories through the end of 2006. The final 14 chapters are a series of lectures about the major recent changes in the United States and the world economy. The book is written in clear English, not Greenspan's occasional "Fedspeak," and is a pleasure to read—the result of a productive collaboration with Peter Petre, who taught him to write in the first person as a participant rather than only as an observer of the many important events in the past several decades. This is important because Greenspan has a lot to say about the people and policies of six administrations from that of Richard Nixon to that of George W. Bush. And it is important for both economists and others to understand the major lessons from this period.

For economists, it is important to understand Greenspan's preparation for his several public roles. Most of his broad economic education seems to have been self-taught, derivative of his long experience as an economic consultant. His only course in macroeconomics was from Arthur Burns, a distinguished academic specialist in business cycles and later a chairman of the Federal Reserve. Like most economists of his age, Greenspan's own macroeconomics may best be described as casual Keynesianism. Like his mentor Burns, Greenspan believed that most major trends in the inflation rate were the result of *nonmonetary* forces—Burns, as an explanation (or rationalization) of the rapid increase in inflation on his watch, and Greenspan, as an explanation of the broad reduction of inflation and long-term interest rates on his watch. And, again like Burns, Greenspan

---

This review first appeared in the *Cato Journal* 27, no. 3 (Fall 2007). My thanks to the *Cato Journal* for its permission to republish this article.

believed that the most important general cause of inflation was excess government spending. Greenspan never had an academic appointment or a record of articles in peer-reviewed professional journals, which seems like a very strange background for someone who would become the most important central banker in the world.

The memoir section of this book is long on commentary about the people with whom he dealt but short on reflections about his experience as chairman of the Fed.

Among issues that I had hoped to read about are the following.

The book does not mention what might have been Greenspan's reflections about the lessons to be learned from the experience of his predecessor. Paul Volcker inherited an inflation rate (of the consumer price index) of 13.7 percent in 1979 and immediately implemented a tight monetary policy, leaving a healthy economy and a 4.4 percent inflation rate to Greenspan in 1987. I wonder what nonmonetary condition Greenspan considers may have explained this substantial reduction of inflation.

The book describes in some detail the decisions by the Federal Reserve in response to the sharp reduction in stock prices in October 1987 and the series of financial crises in 1997 through 1999. But it does not recognize that the Fed may have overreacted to these financial crises or say anything about the postcrisis effects of the Fed intervention. One might hope that the Fed intervention in response to a financial crisis would be sufficient to prevent a decline in aggregate nominal demand relative to some target path, but in each case the intervention led to a postcrisis bubble. The monetary tightness necessary to eliminate the bubble following the 1987 crisis led to the mild 1991 recession and a slow early recovery. Similarly, the monetary tightness necessary to eliminate the second bubble led to the mild 2001 recession and a slow early recovery. A third demand bubble developed during the last three years of Greenspan's watch, leaving the reduction of demand growth to the target path to his successor, Ben Bernanke.

The book does not mention the Basel Accord of 1988. This accord, to which Greenspan agreed, established an international standard on commercial bank portfolios with the goal of reducing the risk of bank failures and a bank run. Implementation of this standard increased the shares of government securities and mortgages in bank portfolios at the expense of a lower share for commercial and industrial loans. In the United States, this standard constrained any increase in commercial and industrial loans from 1989 through 1994, contributing to the mild 1991 recession and the slow early recovery.

On the other hand, the book records that Greenspan was increasingly strident about the increasing federal budget deficits during both the first and second Bush administrations, warning that "history suggests that an abandonment of fiscal discipline will eventually push up interest rates, crowd our capital spending, lower productivity growth, and force harder choices upon us in the future." Such public comments significantly weakened the relations between Greenspan and the two Bush administrations. Greenspan was correct to make a case against the prospective deficits, although the Federal Reserve has no responsibility for fiscal policy, but his simple Keynesian argument was wrong. In fact, there have been no significant effects of the budget deficit on inflation and interest rates in the United States and other major countries. Deficits *do* matter, however, but for different reasons. First, a tolerance for deficits leads to *increased* government spending, an outcome quite contrary to the "starve the beast" hypothesis favored among Republican politicians. Second, deficits represent an involuntary transfer from future taxpayers, many of whom are not yet born, to current voters. In this sense, deficits are *immoral* unless they lead to significant future benefits.

(One minor irritation: in this book by a former chairman of the Council of Economic Advisers, the word "advisers" is consistently misspelled as "advisors.")

The later chapters address a wide range of topics. The chapters on economic growth, the modes of capitalism, China and the other Asian tigers, Russia, and Latin American are informative and wise without being especially controversial. The chapter on the U.S. current account deficit makes the case for his view that this is a rather benign condition. I hope he is right, but I am not confident. The chapter on globalization and regulation makes the case for accepting most of the changes resulting from globalization without overregulation. He attributes the unusually low long-term interest rates of the past 15 years to the global capital market and increased global saving, not to monetary policy. Greenspan directs his strongest policy criticism to the poor performance of our public schools and to the huge unfunded promises for future Social Security and Medicare benefits.

Somewhat to my surprise, he endorses expensing stock options and autocratic CEOs in his chapter on corporate governance.

I was flabbergasted, however, that Greenspan believes that "the Iraq war is largely about oil." Even in desperation for trying to find a credible rationale for the Iraq war, the Bush administration never used the oil rationale. Greenspan concludes his chapter on energy by stating, "Until industrial economies disengage themselves from, as President George W. Bush put it, 'our addiction to oil,' the stability of the industrial economies and hence the global economy will remain at risk." But somehow, the real dollar price of oil has tripled over the past five years without a serious risk to either the U.S. or world economy. This is the least well reasoned chapter in his book. Unfortunately, Greenspan's views on energy are shared by other people who ought to know better.

In the final chapter, Greenspan returns to his professional specialty as an economic forecaster. He discusses the conditions that will affect America's economic future and then makes a forecast of U.S. economic conditions in 2030. On one issue, I am concerned that Greenspan may be too optimistic. He writes, "Since knowledge is never lost, productivity will always rise." But knowledge about the conditions that contribute to economic growth has often been forgotten or dismissed in the pursuit of other values. On another issue, I hope that Greenspan will prove to be too pessimistic. He anticipates substantial increases in the average inflation rate and the interest rate on 10-year bonds, outcomes that he regards as the normal condition since the end of the gold standard and the growth of the welfare state. The book ends on an awkward note that the conditions that led to a substantial reduction in the inflation and interest rates in the past three decades were an accident and are not likely to be repeated. How sad.

Part IV

Personal Reflections

39. A Reflection on the Major Developments in the World, 1951–2000

We made it! We are the lucky ones. We beat the odds. When we were born, our expected life span was about 62 years for baby boys and about 65 years for baby girls. And most of us now have reason to expect another 10 to 20 years for those important activities for which we have not previously had the time, money, or inclination. So let us be thankful for the blessings of life, liberty, and—with an assist from modern medicine—the pursuit of happiness.

I am honored that you have asked me to reflect on the most important developments in America and the world over the past 50 years—subject only to the constraint that I be mercifully brief. There were many important developments in this period, of course, and my selection and interpretation of the most important of these developments almost surely reflects my own background and experience; I doubt whether someone who grew up in Berlin or Beijing or who graduated in 1940 or 1960 would have the same perspective on this issue as someone, say, who graduated in Bend in 1950. Some of you may even have a different perspective, and that can be the basis for an interesting conversation. In any case, my remarks summarize my perspective on politics, science, the economy, the arts, and popular culture; and my focus is on those developments during the past 50 years that are likely to be considered to be most important over the next 50 years.

Politics

The most dramatic and important political developments of this period were the collapse of the Soviet Empire and the end of the

---

This was my speech in June 2005 to a reunion of my high school class on the 50th anniversary of our graduation from Bend High School in Bend, Oregon.

Cold War; this directly freed about 400 million people from Soviet tyranny and greatly reduced the threat of nuclear war to much of the rest of the world. We should remember and honor those political leaders who initiated or sustained the measures that made it possible for the West to prevail in the Cold War: Truman and Reagan, Churchill and Thatcher, Adenauer and Kohl.

Some of the other major political developments were related to the Cold War and the way it ended. One is the dog that didn't bark—the fact that there was no world "hot" war during this period, in contrast to the two devastating world wars in the first half of the 20th century. A second is that communism is no longer considered an ideal political and economic system, except in some of the sheltered groves of academe—a consequence of a broader recognition of the terror on which it was based and of its shabby economic record. A third is that much of the world's population, for the first time, now lives under some form of democracy.

Some other major political developments, from my cranky perspective, are not so favorable. The idea of a constitution as a body of laws that even a democratic government cannot change has almost died; as a consequence, the relative size of government has increased substantially in almost every democracy, primarily to finance the growth of the welfare state. The promises already made for future retirement and health benefits, in turn, will require another large increase in taxes when the baby boom retires. And democratic governments have progressively substituted law for other types of social rules, mandating or banning behavior that is regarded as desirable or undesirable, weakening the important institutions between the individual and the state, and restricting the scope of individual liberty. A democracy without an effective constitution provides little protection against a tyranny by some majority.

Science and Technology

Our adult lifetime has been witness to the creation and initial development of two extraordinarily important technologies: digital technology and biotechnology. In some dimensions, moreover, these two technologies will merge, both in rhetoric and reality: System-wide computer problems, for example, are already described as viruses, and tiny implanted computers will soon augment or substitute for human organs.

The first personal computer was marketed in the late 1970s, and it is already clear that the potential effect of digital technology and the Internet is a virtual revolution in the way we work, how we shop, where we live, our health care, our entertainment, our cultural attitudes, and even our politics. This technology became important only toward the end of our working careers but will have a much broader effect on the next several generations.

The first products produced by genetic engineering were also marketed about 20 years ago. In addition to a continued increase in agricultural yields, biotechnology promises a substantial increase in how well and how long we humans live, maybe even in our own lifetime. Only recently, for example, gene therapy restored the immune systems of two boys who would otherwise have had to spend their lives in plastic bubbles, and an experiment with therapeutic cloning offers the promise of cures for Alzheimer's, Parkinson's, and other diseases characteristic of old age. A bright student graduating from high school this year would be well advised to specialize in genetics, probably the most exciting scientific field of the next 50 years.

Some of the major technologies of the past 50 years proved to be disappointing. In the 1950s, nuclear energy promised to be too cheap to meter; it is now too expensive to maintain, at least until there is a large increase in the price of fossil fuels. The moon landing was the dramatic conclusion of the race to space between the United States and the Soviet Union but had little broader effect; for the next 50 years or so, space exploration will be conducted primarily by satellites and robots. One of the important lessons from the past 50 years is that science is likely to be much more creative when it bubbles up from the labs rather than being directed from Washington.

The Economy

The past 50 years was a period of extraordinary economic improvement in much of the world. In the United States, output per employee is now about 2.3 times the level 50 years ago; moreover, since employment increased substantially relative to the population, our average purchasing power is now nearly 3 times the level at that time. The U.S. economy has become much less vulnerable to boom and bust; both the frequency and severity of recessions were much lower than in the first half of the 20th century. And this economic record was combined with an improvement in almost all dimensions of environmental quality.

Changes in the composition of output and employment during the past 50 years were also important. Agricultural employment declined from about 10 percent of total employment to less than 3 percent. Employment in the goods-producing industries, transportation, and public utilities declined from about 50 percent to about 25 percent. Union membership declined from about 35 percent of private employment to about 10 percent. The number of women in the paid labor force increased from about 29 percent of total employment to nearly half. And the international trade share of U.S. output has roughly tripled. The change in the composition of employment, in turn, is both a cause and a consequence of the rapid increase in the employment opportunities for women and the decline in union membership. Although the variance of wages by skills increased, the variance of wages by sex and race declined; in that sense, the American wage structure has become more meritocratic, more a function of acquired skills and less a function of conditions at one's birth. Many countries, moreover, experienced similar trends during this period. Economic growth was higher in Germany until the 1980s and in Japan until the 1990s, and other East Asian countries have had the highest economic growth for the past several decades. Economic growth was lower in Latin America, Africa, the Middle East, Central Asia, and, during the 1990s, the countries that had been part of the former Soviet Empire. The most important lesson from this experience is that the strongest correlates of economic growth among countries have been monetary stability, the security of property rights, and economic freedom.

As an aside, my own profession of economics has not made much of a contribution to this record, with too many of our brightest students opting to be second-rate mathematicians rather than first-rate economists. We have spent the past 25 years trying to unlearn the macroeconomics that we learned in the prior 25 years. We are just beginning to relearn the institutional conditions that constitute the necessary "soft infrastructure" of a market economy. Although our understanding of the economy has not improved much, my profession has been quite imperialistic—with major incursions into the poorly defended provinces of sociology, political science, and the law. Again, this is a personal aside; contemporary economics was *not* one of the most important developments of the past 50 years.

The Arts

My remarks about the arts are blunt and brief: The arts have been a vast wasteland over the past 50 years. Modern art, music, and literature may have produced *nothing* that will be valued as a classic in another 50 years. Although my profession is not in the arts, my perceptions about the arts may be grumpy but are not uninformed: We have fine art in our home, my musical tastes run from Bach to bluegrass, I sing in a fine concert choir, and I read widely. And I realize that some of the arts that we now value as classic were not recognized as such during the lives of their creators. But modern art seems designed more to perplex or offend than to appreciate; the only modern art that seems likely to survive is the graphic art that has already become subliminal in advertising and design. Modern music is a cacophony of which only the Broadway musical seems likely to survive. Among contemporary American writers, Saul Bellow may be the best novelist and my college classmate John Updike the best literary stylist, but neither has produced a novel that seems likely to have an enduring appeal. Only Alexander Solzhenitsyn has produced a body of profound literature, but his writing seems too Russian and too gloomy to have broad appeal. And the art, music, and literature created in other countries during this period seems equally empty of enduring value. Maybe I am just a grumpy old man about the arts; if I am correct, however, someone else will have to explain why the arts have been unusually uncreative over the past 50 years. My suspicion is that too many artists, musicians, and writers now produce to impress each other, sheltered from the market by academic tenure or a government grant; the combination of art and engineering in architecture may be the only major exception to this pattern.

Popular Culture

Several developments in American popular culture during the past 50 years will cast a very long shadow on the next 50 years—some for the worse, some for the better. I am not sufficiently well informed to judge whether the popular cultures in other countries have developed in the same direction or degree.

Maybe the most disturbing development was the massive erosion of the family as the primary social institution to raise children and establish values. About 25 percent of white babies and 70 percent of black babies are now born to single mothers—a condition that will contribute to low school performance, employment problems, and a high crime rate for many years. Since the early 1950s, for example, the employment rate for young black males declined from 53 percent, then about the same as the rate for young white males, to 27 percent. On visiting the new high school in Bend some years ago, I was most dismayed that my young escort pointed with pride to the separate wing for young mothers and their babies.

Another disturbing development was the dismal performance of the American public school system. Although real spending per student increased over 30 percent a decade since 1950, the average composite SAT score declined substantially from 1965 to 1980 and has since increased only slightly. At the 12th grade, American students score among the lowest in the world on international math, science, and reading tests, although their self-perception is that they do better. On entering college, 22 percent of freshmen in public four-year colleges and 41 percent in public two-year colleges are required to take one or more remedial courses on topics they should have mastered in junior high school.

A third development that offends me but may not have serious adverse consequences is television, which seems to have become a sort of electronic Prozac for the young, the old, and the feeble minded. For too many people, reality is defined by what they see on television, without recognizing how easy it is to manipulate visual images. I bless that fact that I grew up before television was ubiquitous, and I worry about those for whom television is an important part of their lives. Again, this may be only the perception of a grumpy old man, not a serious problem, and I am not sure whether I want to hear your answer.

All is not lost. Several developments in modern popular culture have enriched my life and that of many others. I value the increased diversity of goods, services, and opportunities that economic growth and new technology has made possible. I value the increased confidence and contributions of women in the paid labor force, making new opportunities for them and life more interesting for the rest of us. I especially value that Americans have become more meritocratic, more willing to judge people by their individual character and contribution rather than as part of some family, race, or class into which they were born.

In the past, Americans bore the burden of problems created by slavery and oppression, both at home and abroad. In the future, we face the prospect of problems created by those who pass up the opportunities to get an education, get a job, and get married—the characteristic portals to the American dream.

That is an improvement, but we can do even better. Most of the remaining conditions that many of us regard as undesirable are problems that can be resolved or reduced. The major challenge of the next 50 years will be how Americans sort out these problems.

40. Policy Proposals from the Libertarian Right

A half-century ago, the comfortable ideologues of the left concluded (quoting Charles Kesler from the *Claremont Review of Books*) that "American conservatism was inarticulate—'bookless,' John Kenneth Galbraith once remarked acidulously—because it had nothing to say either about or to America. With his usual acuity, Galbraith's pronouncement came in the midst of the century's greatest outpouring of conservative books."

And after a decade or so of gestation, almost all of the major economic policy proposals during the past 30 years have originated on the libertarian right—many of which were first proposed by one man, Milton Friedman, in one book, *Capitalism and Freedom* published in 1962. The list is an impressive record of the power of ideas when guided by principle, preparedness, and patience:

- Military conscription ended in 1973.
- Economic deregulation started in the late 1970s.
- Spending and tax limit amendments have been approved in more than one-half of the states, beginning in 1978.
- The supply-side perspective reoriented fiscal policy to focus on increasing long-term economic growth by reducing marginal tax rates, beginning with the reduction of the tax rate on capital gains in 1978 and the general reduction of tax rates in 1981.
- Monetary policy became the primary policy to reduce inflation and stabilize the growth of aggregate demand, first implemented by Paul Volcker in 1979 and reinforced by the Reagan administration in 1981.

This was my speech to the University of Maryland's School of Public Policy's Tuesday Forum, May 2, 2006.

- The first broad-based tax reform was approved in 1986.
- Marketable emission rights were first approved in the Clean Air Act of 1990.
- The North American Free Trade Agreement was approved in 1993.
- The combination of welfare reform and an increase in the earned income tax credit was approved in 1996, reorienting welfare from a payment for not working to a subsidy of the earnings of low-wage workers.
- Limited school choice programs have been approved in several states, and in 2002 the Supreme Court approved the right of voucher students to attend schools run by religious organizations.
- In several cases, the Supreme Court ruled in favor of restrictions on the legal taking of property until the disastrous 2005 ruling in the *Kelo* case.
- In several cases, the Supreme Court ruled in favor of restrictions on the reach of the commerce clause until the disastrous 2005 ruling in the *Raich* case.
- The Bush administration is reorienting foreign aid to poor countries in which the government is enforcing property rights, reducing corruption, and so on.
- Health savings accounts were approved in the Medicare legislation of 2003.
- All national class action suits were moved to federal courts by 2005 legislation.

Most of these measures required the support of a Democratic president or substantial Democratic support in Congress and, once approved, are unlikely to be reversed by a change in the majority party.

Similar policy proposals that have been broadly considered but not yet approved include the following:

- Social Security choice was the major domestic policy initiative by President Bush in 2005. No legislation has yet been proposed, and a major debate on the issue has now been indefinitely deferred.

- Immigration reform has been endorsed by an odd couple of cosponsors, John McCain and Ted Kennedy, but this issue strongly divides both parties for different reasons and is likely to be deferred.
- A major reduction of agricultural subsidies is being considered to increase the prospect of success for the Doha Round of multilateral trade negotiations, and
- A reduction of corporate welfare is a most likely target of any bipartisan effort to reduce federal spending.

All of the above policy proposals were either first proposed or were brokered by libertarian-right policy institutes. In addition, these institutes have been instrumental in helping stop or defer such major proposals from the left as the following:

- U.S. approval of the Law of the Sea Treaty,
- the BTU tax,
- national health insurance,
- U.S. approval of the Land Mine Treaty,
- U.S. membership in the International Criminal Court, and
- an increase in the minimum wage.

Among the very few major policy proposals originating on the left that have been approved in the past 30 years include the following:

- the Americans with Disabilities Act,
- the tax *increase* legislation of 1991 and 1993,
- the child-care tax credit,
- the McCain-Feingold campaign finance regulation,
- the Sarbanes-Oxley regulation of corporate governance, and
- prescription drug coverage by Medicare.

"So who's bookless now? (again quoting Kesler) "The publisher of the *New Republic*, no less, admitted recently: 'it is liberalism that is now bookless and dying. Who is a truly influential liberal mind in our culture?' Martin Peretz asked. 'Whose ideas challenge and whose ideals inspire? . . . There's no one, really. What's left is the laundry list: the catalogue of programs . . . that Republicans aren't funding, and the blogs, with their daily panic dose about how the Bush administration is ruining the country.'"

The Democrats, moreover, are sharply divided about whether ideas matter.

Jonathan Chait, a senior editor of the *New Republic*, recently wrote that winning elections is important, but that new policy ideas are not necessary to win elections. The favorite guru of the Democratic leadership is Professor George Lakoff, a linguist from Berkeley who argues that it is only how ideas are "framed" that is important. On the other hand, the new Democracy Alliance has received financial commitments of at least $80 million over the next five years "to promote consistently and coherently a set of ideas, policies, and messages" by funding left-leaning policy institutes and training centers.

As a libertarian with no enduring commitment to either major party, I welcome a new competition of ideas from the left. The Bush administration and too many Republicans have embraced a form of big government conservatism that does not address the major problems of either foreign or domestic conditions. New policy ideas from any source can be valuable. And substantial support from both major parties is usually necessary to approve and sustain most major policy reforms. I welcome the new policy institutes. When they are ready, I look forward to a discussion of their new policy proposals.

41. A Personal Reflection on the Trinity

Good morning. Today is Trinity Sunday, the sermon for which many rectors assign to a seminarian. For the church has never been very clear about the doctrine of the trinity, and a seminarian would at least remember the orthodox version.

My brief remarks this morning summarize how this one lay Christian has come to terms with the Nicene Creed. I must acknowledge that I have repeated the Creed almost every Sunday for years but with little more understanding or conviction than when I *sang* the Creed twice last weekend—in *Church Slavonic*! As a lay Christian, I do not have the education of a seminarian or the disciplined reflections of an ordained minister. As a consequence, I recognize that my understanding of the several sources of Christian authority on this issue is only "as through a glass darkly."

As a former Baptist, I am first inclined to look to the authority of the Scriptures. As it turns out, the Scriptures do not provide very clear guidance on the doctrine of the trinity. The word "trinity" is not included in the New Testament. The most explicit description of the trinity is a passage in the First Epistle of John that "There are three that bear witness in heaven: the Father, the Word, and the Spirit, and these three are one."

The problem is that there is *no* record of this passage in the early Greek manuscripts; this passage is almost surely an insertion by Jerome or some later Latin scholar. And the doctrine of the trinity may also reflect a misleading translation. Both the Greek and Latin words that have been translated as "persons," as in "One God in Three Persons," would be more accurately translated as "masks," as in "One God in Three Masks."

This lay sermon was presented on Trinity Sunday in June 2006 to Christ Church, Washington Parish in Washington, D.C.

Second, my reading of the several traditions of the early Christian church leads me to conclude that the doctrine of the trinity was a second- and third-century historical development, the by-product of an attempt to resolve major differences among these traditions on the nature of Jesus. One group believed that Jesus was human but not divine, another group believed that Jesus was divine but not human, and a third group believed that Jesus was born and died a human but was also divine from his baptism to his crucifixion. The Roman church claimed that they had resolved these differences by going beyond *any* of these positions, asserting that Jesus was both divine and human, as he always was and always will be. This then left the awkward problem of the nature of the Spirit, to which there are numerous references in the Scriptures. So the Roman church also escalated the Spirit to a co-equal and co-eternal status with the Father and the Son. And, *voilà*, the doctrine of the trinity was born—later to be affirmed by two major fourth-century church councils.

So where does this lead to the role of reason, the third source of Christian authority, in understanding the doctrine of the trinity? For the most part, this doctrine is beyond reason. The editor of *The Concise Oxford Dictionary of the Christian Church* writes that the doctrine of the trinity ". . . is a mystery in the strict sense, in that it can neither be known by reason apart from revelation, nor demonstrated by reason after it has been revealed . . ."

All of which leaves this lay Christian very uneasy. I am not averse to living with mystery; all sorts of conditions that I value are a mystery to me. But it does lead me to question whether there is some perspective on the trinity that is both better rooted in the Scriptures and more coherent. I suggest that there is. In the late second-century, two Latin theologians who contributed to the developing orthodoxy about the nature of Jesus described God as three in expression though one in essence. As Hippolytus of Rome describes the trinity, "With respect to the power, God is one; but with respect to how this power expresses itself, the manifestation is triple." Tertullian of Carthage, the first Latin theologian to use the word "trinity," describes God as three in degree, not condition; in form, not substance, in aspect, not power.

The most important later development of this perspective, I suggest, was by a third-century Roman churchman named Sabellius, who taught that God is one but is revealed to us through three distinct masks or manifestations. Sabellius believed that as Creator, God is Father; as Redeemer, God is Son; and as Sanctifier, God is Spirit. These three are not separate entities but the same entity that is revealed to us in three different manifestations. Sabellius likened his doctrine to the three-part division of human nature into body, soul, and spirit, all of which constitute one person. In one way or another, the substantial community of Sabellians all believed that Father, Son, and Spirit be taken as names for *different ways in which one God is revealed to us*. At this point, I must acknowledge that Sabellius was later declared to be a heretic.

My own suggested modification of the Sabellian perspective is that God is revealed to us in three ways: a transcendent manifestation, an incarnate manifestation, and an intimate manifestation.

The transcendent manifestation is the *order* that God created—the order of the physical universe that led Einstein to wonder how any intelligent person could be an atheist, the *evolutionary* order of the biological universe that too many of our fellow Christians deny, and the order reflected by those social institutions that make it possible to live peacefully and productively with many people and joyfully and lovingly with some. Several weeks ago at Christ Church, in one verse of a favorite hymn, we sang in witness to this transcendent manifestation:

> O wide-embracing wondrous love, we read thee in the sky above.
> We read thee in the earth below, in seas that swell and streams that flow.

The incarnate manifestation, of course, is the life and teachings of an itinerant rabbi named Jesus, who revealed God to us in human form in Galilee around 2,000 years ago. As Christians, this manifestation is what most inspires us and most distinguishes our religious beliefs from those of other religions. In the next verse of that favorite hymn, we sang in witness to the incarnate manifestation:

> We read thee *best* in him who came to bear for us the cross of shame.
> Sent by the Father from on high, our life to live, our death to die.

The nature of the Holy Spirit has been a puzzle to many Christians. The Latin word that has been variously translated as Spirit or Ghost, however, means breath—a condition that is no less real because it is neither visible nor touchable. Jesus used similar words to describe the Spirit in his goodbye conversation with his disciples, saying (from the Gospel of John) that ". . . the Father . . . will give you another Counselor, to be with you for ever, even the Spirit of truth, whom the world cannot receive, because it neither sees him nor knows him. You know him for he dwells with you, and will be in you." I suggest that it is only a little stretch to describe this intimate manifestation of God to each of us as that still small voice that comforts us when we are grieving, counsels us when we are uncertain, chastens us for something we have done, and reminds us of something we have left undone. Last Sunday, in a lovely hymn about the Holy Spirit, we sang

> Like the murmur of the dove's song, like the challenge of her flight,
> Like the vigor of the wind's rush, like the new flame's eager might:
> Come, Holy Spirit, come.

On occasion, that still small voice speaks to me so *clearly* that I am surprised that others in my presence do not also hear it. Like, right now, when it tells me that "Time's up. Episcopalians prefer short sermons."

This morning, my fondest hope is that my brief remarks lead each of you to think about what *you* mean when, together, we stand to say that "We believe in One God."

Amen.

Index

About the Author

William A. Niskanen has been chairman of the Cato Institute since 1985. He has served as a member and the acting chairman of President Reagan's Council of Economic Advisers, chief economist for the Ford Motor Company, professor at the University of California at Berkeley and Los Angeles, and defense analyst for the RAND Corporation. Author of the landmark 1971 book *Bureaucracy and Representative Government*, his other books include *Policy Analysis and Public Choice*; *Autocratic, Democratic, and Optimal Government*; and *After Enron: the Lessons for Public Policy*. Niskanen has contributed to a wide variety of policy research areas, including national defense, corporate governance, Social Security, budget policy, and trade. He has a B.A. from Harvard University and a Ph.D. in economics from the University of Chicago.

Cato Institute

Founded in 1977, the Cato Institute is a public policy research foundation dedicated to broadening the parameters of policy debate to allow consideration of more options that are consistent with the traditional American principles of limited government, individual liberty, and peace. To that end, the Institute strives to achieve greater involvement of the intelligent, concerned lay public in questions of policy and the proper role of government.

The Institute is named for *Cato's Letters*, libertarian pamphlets that were widely read in the American Colonies in the early 18th century and played a major role in laying the philosophical foundation for the American Revolution.

Despite the achievement of the nation's Founders, today virtually no aspect of life is free from government encroachment. A pervasive intolerance for individual rights is shown by government's arbitrary intrusions into private economic transactions and its disregard for civil liberties.

To counter that trend, the Cato Institute undertakes an extensive publications program that addresses the complete spectrum of policy issues. Books, monographs, and shorter studies are commissioned to examine the federal budget, Social Security, regulation, military spending, international trade, and myriad other issues. Major policy conferences are held throughout the year, from which papers are published thrice yearly in the *Cato Journal*. The Institute also publishes the quarterly magazine *Regulation*.

In order to maintain its independence, the Cato Institute accepts no government funding. Contributions are received from foundations, corporations, and individuals, and other revenue is generated from the sale of publications. The Institute is a nonprofit, tax-exempt, educational foundation under Section 501(c)3 of the Internal Revenue Code.

Cato Institute
1000 Massachusetts Ave., N.W.
Washington, D.C. 20001
www.cato.org